a voice in the tide

a voice
in the tide

*How I Spoke My Truth
in the Undertow of Denial
and Self-Blame*

A Memoir by Nancy Shappell

A VOICE IN THE TIDE

First Printing, 2015

ISBN # 978-0-9965421-0-4

Printed in the United States of America
Book Design: Susan Hood Design
Photo Credit: Joshua Greenblatt and Lisa DuFault
Credit: Jagger Creative Agency

Many names in this book have been changed. The author's
intent of this book is to offer it as a healing tool in the area of
fear.

Library of Congress Cataloging-in-Publication Data:
Shappell, Nancy. A voice in the tide: how I spoke my truth in
the undertow of denial and self-blame / Nancy Shappell
1. Nancy Shappell 2. Child Sexual Abuse 3. Incest
4. Trauma 5. Post Traumatic Stress Disorder 6. Memoir
7. Mothers and Daughters

Contents

Contents

Contents

Contents

You can't wake a person who is pretending to be asleep.

—*Navajo proverb*

a voice in the tide

Trapped

ONE SMALL HOLE at the end of the porch latticework beckons me to safety through its weathered wooden slats. My seven-year-old self climbs in. My hands are cold in the darkness of wet dirt and broken glass. Sharp rocks poke deeply at the sides of both kneecaps. The back of my shirt, only inches from the porch flooring above, catches on the splintered crossbeams. I can smell decaying rats and last night's road-kill skunk. The stench stings my eyes. At the far end of the porch a light shines through a hole in the broken, lattice boards. I must crawl toward that light for freedom. It is too far to go. I can't do it. My breath is hot and fast. I push at the entrance with the crown of my head, but my body, now grown to adult size, will not fit through. There is no way out. I am trapped in the tightness of fear, watching for my mother's shoes to walk by. For her to bend down and say, "There you are, my sweet girl. Let me take you out and love you up."

But that will never happen.

FOR decades that dream haunted my sleep.

Each time I woke from it, sweat-drenched and terrified, my prayer remained the same. That my mother would someday love me enough to hear my voice and save me from the shadows of something I had no conscious word to define until I was thirty-four years of age.

Incest.

As infants, my brother and I were adopted into a house of lies, where calculated secret grooming kept us locked in fear.

Fragmented memories of my father and me hid deep in all areas of my body. Each cell encoded a crippling historical truth I fought to ignore. For fifty years shame grew inside me like a cancer. Its source based on my parents' toxic words that I was nothing more than my birth mother's punishment for sinful premarital sex. "There must be somethin wrong with you for God sake," my adopted mother said again and again. That part was true. Everything was wrong. But people in our small town admired my parents for bringing two forsaken children into such a blessed life, and they praised my father for his religious and community leadership. And somewhere in my fear, even as a small child, I knew if I told what happened in our house, I would risk belonging. And who would love me then?

By age fifteen, I was dissociating from life. In my twenties, even though the love of my own two sons kept me alive, it wasn't enough to convince me I was deserving of it. Prescription drugs, alcohol, and debilitating spells of anxiety and flashbacks grew more fear. In my thirties, I stopped eating. I spent weeks in residential detox and psychiatric facilities. At age forty-seven, after a near-death experience with Oxycontin, I began to understand it had been the fear that kept me sick all along. The fear of knowing the truth about why I chose to anesthetize myself in the first place, and the fear of "making Mumma mad."

I hated that I loved her. She abandoned me the worst possible way a mother could, and yet even as a grown woman, all I wanted was for her to love me. I wanted to be validated by the one person who could have turned the tide in my history, but chose to look the other way.

I wished for my mother to be someone she was not strong enough to be, and I finally came to understand that maybe underneath it all she was not so different from me. We both spent our lives looking away from things too painful to acknowledge. I knew that as long as I lived in the shame and blame of our experiences, I remained the injured child. It was time to detox all that fear, heal my real truth, and ask myself, at my soul level, who I honestly believed myself to be.

Now, worn from crawling, I had reached the other side of that weathered porch, stood up in the light, and let go of the anger. It was my own voice that saved me in the end. All those years, I thought it would be her voice that would release me into healing. Of all the lies I told myself, that was the most unconscious one of all.

water

1

Tar and Ether

IT WAS THE kind of hot summer day we only have a few of in Maine. The kind that melts road tar into thick black oatmeal and swallows a bicycle kickstand in a slow-motion minute. The north end of Washington Street was being paved that day, but before the trucks came up through our neighborhood, we kids had to decide which side of the street we would be trapped on, the home side or the other.

After the tar in front of our house had been sealed and the road was still wet, my mother loaded my brother and me into our brand-new 1962 yellow Cadillac convertible and drove it down over the hill to Park Street. By the time we pulled into a space in front of the Bath Memorial Hospital, the under-carriage and door panels of Mumma's nice car were spattered with sticky blackness. Mumma got so mad when she stood beside it, she stamped one foot to the ground and yelled out loud, "I'll never be rid of this mess." Then she flumped back into the front seat, turned off the engine, and let out a long snort of disgust. For a few minutes Mumma, Tommy, and I sat in silence. I wished for my grandmother to hurry and finish her work inside. It was always better when Nanny was around.

Mumma pointed out her open window. "You see that brown house over across the street? That's where I grew up," she said, then pulled her hand back into the car and waved it across her chest in the other direction toward the hospital. I watched her amethyst ring, the one Nanny gave her on her sixteenth birthday, spin itself around on her finger and disappear into her clenched hand. "And that window right in front of us, that used to be the delivery room. I always knew when a baby was bein born, because I could hear the woman screamin and I could smell that sicky sweet ether comin right out towards me." She shook her head. "God." Then she turned fast to the backseat, hardened her eyes, and leaned close to my face. A shiver went down my arms. She looked me right in the eyes when she said it. "It's better to be unconscious. That way, you don't feel the pain."

Mumma kept talking until Nanny came out to the car, but I don't remember what she said. The coolness of the silver cigarette lighter was between my fingers. I pushed it into the outlet of the ashtray and waited for it to pop back up. I'm not sure why I did it, but for those moments it was good to be away. The coil was a beautiful fire red. With every pulse of heat I watched it turn a bit darker. With my thumb pressed hard to it, the hot pain felt icy numb. When I took my thumb away there were perfect rings of bubbled white flesh. In that moment I was free of me. Lost in the circle of the sting.

When my mother saw it, she got mad. "Nancy, why would you do that? For God sake, there must be somethin wrong with you."

I think it scared Mumma to hear those birth screams coming out the hospital windows. Maybe it scared her so badly, that's why she could never have children of her own. It was another woman who gave birth to me. I wonder if before the doctor put my first mother to sleep, she screamed like the women Mumma heard. I wonder if when my mother was unconscious, the doctor had to fight to yank me out of her. But most of all, I wonder if anyone smiled at my mother and me on the day I was born.

I'm not sure if I was carried to the nursery in shameful silence or if the nurses wished me to be loved and said I was beautiful. Maybe my mother cried tears that streamed down her flushed cheeks, dropping small salty puddles onto my pink skin. I wonder if she studied my hands as they lay tiny in hers, or if she memorized the shape of my lips. All I know for sure is after I was taken from her arms she signed legal papers and promised she would never see me again. That's what Mumma told me. It made me feel kind of sad for that woman.

2

Sometimes Things Happen

IT WAS THE year prior to my adoption when the orphanage people began making visits to Bath to review my parents' qualifications. In our front living room, from the glass-topped Duncan Phyfe table, Mumma served them tea out of English bone-china cups. Downtown on Centre Street, Daddy toured them through his plumbing and heating business. Then both my parents took those lady social workers to the Methodist church to show them where they worship and socialize. I guess after that the agency deemed them respectable churchgoing business-people.

It was May 1955 when I was taken from the Lying-In Hospital in Boston, Massachusetts and brought by train to The New England Home for Little Wanderers in Waterville, Maine. From there I was placed in a foster home in wait for someone to want me. It was two months after my birth, when Jim and Doris came to get me, leaving my short life history behind like a half-empty pop bottle on the side of the road. They named me Nancy and my new life as their adopted daughter began.

My brother, Tommy, came along a year later. He was four months old. Mumma told me he was born with bumps on his head and that was why no one wanted him. Decades would pass before our next-door neighbor, who I called Uncle Ike, told me she didn't want Tommy either but my father insisted.

On the outside my family will appear normal. Half a lifetime will pass before I remember the details of why we were not.

⌒

IT is nap time, midafternoon. Mumma is sitting at the top of the staircase with her head in her hands. Long sighs of frustration are streaming through fingers pressed hard to her eyebrows. She takes them from her face and yells as I squeeze my three-year-old body past her. "The doctor says your brother should be takin a nap for God sake. I'd like to see her come up here and make him stay in bed." Then she shakes her head and drops it back into her hands. In Tommy's bedroom, Mumma has spread rope netting across the top of his crib and tied it to the sides in big white knots. He screams from underneath it, drool stringing out of his mouth and soaking a blue-and-white crocheted bib beneath his double chin. I lay my forehead against the wooden slats, reach in and pat his tummy. His wet fingers grab for the barrette Mumma is taming my wild hair with. I stay at Tommy's side, shushing and singing until he goes to sleep and Mumma stops sighing.

When nap time is over, Mumma takes us into her bedroom. She leans Tommy into the pillows. I sit between her and my brother. From the bottom shelf of her nightstand, again, today my mother reaches for the set of gray adoption books, one a guide for adoptive parents and the other a children's storybook. *The Family That Grew* is printed bold over a dark pink border. As Mumma opens the book, the binding makes a loud, dry, cracking noise. On the first page is a colorless drawing of a couple dressed in business suits, holding a new, blanketed baby. Mumma reads the words at the bottom. "You are the chosen one." Her fingers turn the page. "Everyone wants to care for their babies."

I lean one shoulder into her feather pillow as Tommy wiggles beside me. "Why didn't my real mother want me, Mumma?"

She pauses, leaving her eyes on the sparseness of the paper. "Sometimes things happen," she begins. "Sometimes mothers and fathers can't take care of their children, so they give them away to people who can do a better job." Then she looks down at me. "Your father and I chose you special. Not all children are as lucky as you and Tommy."

As months go by, and it becomes more difficult for my brother to sit still, she never reads those books to us again. For fifty years they will remain on the bottom shelf of my mother's nightstand. And on that day I will sit on the worn carpet of my parents' bedroom, slide them off that dusty shelf, and remember her chosen words. "Sometimes things happen."

She was right.

3

Adopted Illusion

THE KITCHEN SMELLS of Sunday-morning bacon and eggs. I am listening to the electrical cord from Mumma's iron slap at the side of the stove where it is plugged in next to the board. Mumma slides the tip of the iron around each button of Daddy's white church shirt. Without turning her head, she speaks to Tommy behind her. "Hurry up, we're gonna be late." Tommy watches ketchup glob out of the bottle and plop next to his fried potatoes. He doesn't look at her. From the other side of the kitchen table I pick up a piece of yesterday's mail.

"'The New England Home for Little Wanderers,'" I read out loud. "That's where you got us from, isn't it, Mumma?" She doesn't answer. The back of her head is the color of gray storm clouds. Her apron is tied so tightly around her waist, fat droops over the starched cotton band. "What do they say, Mumma? Why did they write to you?"

Steam hisses from her iron. "They didn't write to me, Nancy. Your father sends them money, that's all."

"You mean you still have to pay for me, Mumma?"

She snatches Daddy's shirt off the ironing board, then lays it back down, hard stamping the collar and pressing left to right.

"Mumma? Do you know what my real mother was like? What was my real name?"

She slams the iron flat to the back of the shirt and turns fast at me. The overhead light reflects sharp streaks off her pale blue, metal-framed cat-eye glasses. "Just forget about it, Nancy. Just forget that you were adopted. I don't know why you persist in askin me."

I press my eyes shut tight. My lips quiver. I wish I hadn't said it. Again, I have made Mumma mad.

For all my life, having Mumma love me will be my greatest desire. Understanding why she couldn't, my greatest challenge.

Sitting in our family pew of the Methodist church, I watch Nanny tear the paper back on a roll of Cryst-O-Mint Life Savers and hold it out to me. She gives me a wink as I take one. The candy feels smooth and cool in my mouth. I twist the pearl buttons on my tiny white gloves. Mumma scolds me with her eyes as I swing my black patent leather shoes close to the pew in front of us, shoes that strap like straitjackets on feet created to run free. After the service, my father stands at the front door of the church and shakes hands with the minister. Three men gather around Daddy and ask questions about a men's committee meeting he is in charge of. Mumma, Tommy, and I are standing at the foot of the sanctuary staircase next to the rope that rings the steeple bell. Mumma says people depend on my father and that's why he is gone so much. I feel her grip one of my gloved hands and the pearl button pushes tight against my tiny wrist veins. "Oh for God sake, come on, Jimmy," she says, just loud enough for me to hear. Then she slides her mouth to one side of her face and squints her eyes at my father across the crowd.

When we get home from church and open the front door, the savory smell of roasting pork welcomes us. Daddy loves a big meal after church. Again, this Sunday when we have finished, he leans back in his chair, picks at his fake front tooth with a fingernail, and tells Tommy and me to thank Mumma for making such a good Lord's Day meal. Then he gets up, stands behind Mumma, still sitting in her chair next to the stove, bends over her head, and plunges his hand down the front of her dress like he is grabbing for a fish in a bucket. Tommy and I concentrate on spooning every last bit of chocolate pudding from the fancy Sunday dessert bowls and tune out the sounds of Mumma's bra straps snapping and Daddy's grateful moaning.

4

Satin Ribbons

TODAY IS MEMORIAL Day. Just like every year, we are going to stand in front of Daddy's shop holding on to balloons and watch the bands march down over Centre Street hill and right up to City Hall. At home, I am sitting on the rock wall next to where Daddy parks his car, waiting for Mumma to call me in to get ready. My redheaded doll is almost as tall as I am. I have bent her long, hard-plastic legs so she can sit next to me. They make a wide *V*, pointing off in different directions. Her eyes are green like mine, and her short hair is ratted from too many brushings. Some hair is not meant to be touched. I have dressed her in my favorite outgrown dress, the one with silky flowers across the front and a pink satin ribbon I have wound twice around her waist.

When I go inside, Daddy is sitting in his spot at the end of the living room couch dressed in clothes that smell of furnace soot and oil burners. He picks up a glass from the low bookcase that divides the living room from the kitchen. He swirls and clinks the ice, then takes a long drink from it. Then he smacks his lips, calls out for my brother, and laughs as he does it. "Time to get you dressed for the parade, Tom the gom."

I see Daddy's fingers go full around Tommy's little arm, then pull his blue seersucker shorts to the floor. My heart vibrates my chest, like when the drums in the parade march by. I watch my father pull my brother's matching seersucker shirt up over his head, then undress my redheaded doll. Daddy laughs as the pink flowered dress goes down over my brother's crew cut and Tommy's arms slide out through the puffed sleeves. My voice shakes as I call for Mumma to come out of the bathroom. She stands in front of them with a rattail comb in one hand and the other hand on her hip. "For God sake, Jimmy, you've had too much to drink. You think I want the whole city of Bath seein you like this? I guess we had betta just forget the whole damn thing and stay home."

Daddy ties a big satin bow at Tommy's back and shakes him a bit like he is proud of what he did. I stand in silence, watching Tommy's face, waiting for him to cry, waiting for Mumma to tell Daddy to stop. But she doesn't. She makes a disgusted snort, turns her back to us, slams the comb on top of the television set, and stomps downstairs to the laundry room.

My father's slitty eyes look at me. His thin lips smile crooked over dark, dying teeth that smell like burnt cherry pipe tobacco. "Well, I guess your mother didn't like that, did she?" Then with both hands firmly on Tommy's waist, he turns my brother to face me. "I think he looks pretty sweet in your dress, don't you, Nancy?"

My knees feel floppy and my throat is thick as the words squeeze out. "No, Daddy."

Tommy's eyes are on mine as Daddy grabs at the hem of the dress, and without undoing the buttons, he yanks it up over my brother's head. Tommy rubs at his nose from where the neckline caught under it. Daddy stands up, clears his throat, and spits from the side of his mouth into a red bandana. Then, stuffing the rag back into a greasy, finger-print pocket, he hauls up on the waist of his green work pants and pours himself another drink.

We all missed the Memorial Day parade that year.

5

Don't Make Mumma Mad

MUMMA SAYS TOMMY can't throw a ball to save his life. I don't know if that is true, but one thing I do know is that my brother is the best underwater swimmer of all the elementary school kids in town. He can dive into the YMCA pool and skim the bottom almost all the way to the other end without coming up for air. This morning I watched him get a special award for it. I clapped my hands so hard, they turned as red as the whites of Tommy's chlorine-washed eyes. I made so much noise, Mumma shushed me up and told me to lower my voice because people were looking at us. But I think some of those people were almost as happy as I was. They congratulated my brother all the way up through the locker room and back out to where we left our car in the library parking lot.

Back at home, Saturday-morning cartoons are over for the day and there is a black-and-white western playing on our living room television set. Tommy turns the volume up louder and drops down into the blue chair next to the bathroom door. He hugs a jar of mayonnaise tight to his chest and shovels a soup spoon into it. My redheaded doll and I settle onto the couch across from him and watch as big mounded white globs find their way to his mouth again and again.

"You're a fat pig for God sake. What the hell ails you?" Mumma walks up next to Tommy wringing her hands on a frayed terry-cloth dish towel, then slaps it against her thigh. It makes a whipping noise as she does it. "We never should have adopted you kids. God never meant for us to have children. When they saw us comin, those people at the adoption agency said, 'Now there's a couple of suckers.' Suckers.

Yup, that's what was written all over us. Now it's our lot in life to be stuck with you till the day we die." She makes a snort and goes back to her dishes in the kitchen.

Tommy's face looks numb of emotion as he leans over and sets the jar on the floor. Mumma's words make a knot in my stomach, but they are nothing that my brother and I haven't heard before. I watch Tommy get up, walk to the kitchen drawer next to the stove, rip a piece of aluminum foil off the roll, wad it up, and pop it into his mouth. From my spot on the couch I see him chew it flat between his back teeth. Mumma doesn't turn around from where she stands at the sink. Pots bang. Tommy chews.

I press my doll tight to my body before I say it, wishing her arms would bend and hug me back. "Mumma, do you love me even though I'm not your real daughter?"

Mumma slams the kitchen drawer shut on her way to the table, and Tommy goes back to the blue chair. "Your father wanted a daughter, Nancy, so we adopted you." She pulls a chair out from the table and sits down, crossing one leg over the other and scratching at her elbow rash.

"What about Tommy? Do you love him?"

One foot taps midair. "Well, the adoption agency called us one day, and what the hell were we supposed to say?"

Looking back, I think Tommy must have loved the freedom of that deep pool. I think it must have been his own beautiful, private world, because he was really good at holding his breath.

In my room at night, things tease and poke at me. Low, hot, smelly voices breathe dark words of disease in my ear, words that hide inside the growing parts of my body.

Tonight Mumma bends over me and slides her hands around the edge of the blankets and under my mattress.

"Tuck them in tight, Mumma, so they won't come undone."

"Nancy, you're bein foolish. Why the heck do you need all these quilts?" From my closet shelf, she takes another and throws it over the double width of my bed. I grip a handful of it, tuck it under my chin, and lay my head on the pillow. "Don't leave me, Mumma. Please don't leave me. I need you to talk to me." But she walks away shaking her head and calling back, "I don't know why you always choose bedtime for that, Nancy."

Sometimes late at night, after my parents are in their bed, I sneak down the hall to their room. In the dark, they lie like matching mounds of dirt on a newly dug grave. On my mother's side, white nylon underpants dangle from the bedpost. I push at her arm.

"Mumma, I'm scared. Please come sit with me."

Her head lifts slightly off a pink satin pillowcase. "Oh for God sake, Nancy, there's nothin to be afraid of. Now go back to bed and leave me alone. You can't stay here."

From the other side of the bed, my father coughs and rumbles phlegm in his throat. The room smells of Vicks VapoRub. A blackened pot boils camphor on a hot plate. "Can I please sleep on the floor beside you, Mumma?"

"No, Nancy. Go to bed."

In my bed I wait. I hold my breath. If I pretend to be asleep, maybe tonight will be different. My nightgown hem is pulled through my legs and clenched tight in one hand. The other is locked on the covers under my chin. With my knees drawn up to my chest, I lie very still. My dolls are lined up like guards on either side of me. I am waiting. Listening. Reaching beyond what I cannot see. I hear floorboards make a slow, deep groan in the hallway outside my door. In panic, beads of sweat flush across me. Pins and needles poke at my underarms. Every nerve is live-wired. I pull the covers over my mouth. My shallow breath dampens the sheet. I watch a dark outline move across the foot of my bed. A toxic mist of soot and Old Spice drifts thick to my nose. My father's throat-clearing vibrates each cell of my body.

"Mumma, come in here. Please, Mumma. I need you."

Her quick, hard voice, "Nancy, for God sake go to sleep." Now I hear only Daddy's anxious breathing, then the grind of bedsprings.

In my frozen fear, before I leave my body, I watch the wallpaper flowers morph into monster faces and smell decaying rats between the walls. Details of my father and me break and scatter into secret pockets of my body.

Things happen in my house I have no words to describe.

TOMMY and I have been sold into a sort of slavery. Purchased, ensnared, attacked. We are taught to remain silent. "Don't tell Mumma. You'll make her mad," our father says day after day. Tommy and I will be unable to save each other. Our memories shatter into pieces and burrow into hidden places in our effort to survive. As the years go by, it will feel like we have been in a horrific plane crash together, which I will finally get up and walk away from, leaving my brother alone in the flames.

Tommy will say he hates me. I won't blame. I will hate me too.

6

Low Tide

WE LIVE AT the north end of Bath on the Kennebec River, the dead end of the city, where the road is narrow and traffic is slow. Across the street from our house, through the field, up the hill, and just beyond it, is the city dump. On hot summer days, when they fire it up, funnels of gray smoke and circling seagulls drift in the wind and hang over that field I play in. Sitting on our low front step, I watch black ants evacuate the rotted boards. I let them walk right into my hand and up my arm. Behind me, dark green door paint bakes like melting crayons and blends with the smell of sewer mud flats and burning garbage. People know where you live when you go downtown on a low tide dump day.

Our house was built in the day when historic wooden sailing ships launched from wharf-lined banks. Schooners that sailed their way through Hell's Gate and out past Fort Popham to the ocean. Brown sewer-stained banks, then and now, overrun with cat-sized river rats I watch from my bedroom window. Daddy's dock and boathouse, a short walk through our sloped backyard, balances over that water on tide-worn, mud-licked pilings.

Over the dock, up high in a sprawling hundred-year-old oak tree, a rope and pulley hang over one branch. At one end of the rope is an eye with an old wooden ax handle threaded through it. Today Tommy and two neighbor boys stand together with their hands, as high as they can reach, clutching up on the loose end of the rope. I count twelve footsteps away from them and stand in the yard with the cross-bar between my legs. Twisted fibers, frayed and dry, bite at my hands as I get a good hold on the rope. "Ready?" I yell.

"Ready," they yell back.

I run, seized to the length. My bare feet have lightly brushed the top step of the dock staircase when the boys yank down on the other end and, tight gripped to it, fall in a head-clunking heap to the weathered floor. They fly me out past the end of the dock, over the water, like I will project right out of my soot-stamped body. I am high above it all. A bird with no weight. A gypsy spirit who longs for the wind.

Later when we slog the low tide shoreline we find driftwood and dead animals to toss back to the tide. From a hole in the boathouse wall, we watch the sewer pipe gush out over the banking to the Kennebec, as river rats lose their long, toe-nailed grip, swipe off slimy rocks, and are forced to swim for their lives. The river, fields, and woods are my whole world. I know every path and backyard. We race homemade go-karts, with dump-rummaged wheels, past Uncle Ike and Aunt Lilly's house and down over the hill to the bus stop.

Uncle Ike calls me the Barefoot Kid. Some days I run a mile barefoot down overgrown wooded dirt roads to the end of Bath where the Kennebec River meets Merrymeeting Bay. And when I do, walnut-sized rocks make dents in my bare heels, and wiry red creeping vines trip me if I don't jump high enough. One day they rip a pink wishbone shape right off the back of my leg, but I keep running. I run until I'm at the clearing we call Mushroom Palace, where chairs are made from tree stumps and a big slab-rock, mushroom-shaped table sits nearby. It feels cold on my hands when I climb up on top to look down off the ledge. Below the water sparkles like diamonds in the sun, but beyond the calm of the surface are whirlpools of dark water that suck in and drown anything within reach.

From that table I watch the seasons change. Birch leaves sprout, pine needles fall and, in the winter, rolling river whitecaps burst high with salt air so cold it freezes my nostrils shut. Potholed paths to home get covered in thick, crusty snow, slick as a bowling alley. One winter day my flying saucer races reckless and my head lands smack in the center of a burdock bush. At home Mumma lays my head on the warm asbestos ironing board cover and cusses me for not wearing a hat. My face itches hot as she pulls the round burrs one at a time from my curls, leaving sharp fiber needles that stab invisible under my skin and refuse to let go. But Mumma says I am imagining things.

In the summer, pear and pine trees bend down and open their arms for me. I climb higher than anyone else can. At the end of the road, where Mumma never goes, are blackberry bushes full of luscious fruit that drops to my hands with a touch of my finger. They stain beautiful pink satin on my palms. If I could be a hermit and live on that harvest, I would tunnel and crop-circle the bushes from end-of-summer ripeness to when red maple leaves fall across its dead growth.

We kids sit on the edge of my father's dock. We hold bamboo fish rods and watch for eels to bite raw chunks of hot dog barbed to the end of the line. One day on a back swish, the neighbor dog gets hooked in the corner of his mouth. A boy cuts the line, grabs up a handful of the dog's neck, and runs him to his grandfather's cellar on the other side of Nanny's house. When we creak open the old wooden door, the space is cold and smells of rank, wet blood. A dead fox, two skunks, and too many squirrels to count hang from hooks on the low ceiling. The grandfather takes the dog between his knees, gets a solid hold on the fishhook, and with one quick yank, rips it out. The dog whines and yelps, and we all run in different directions. In the tall, dry grass next to Nanny's house, I crunch to the ground and watch yellow-bellied black spiders crawl across my bare feet. I stare at them until I can think of nothing else.

Today we are playing in the yard when my father calls out from our cellar door. A yellow basket lamp with a long cord winds around a support pole and burns hot to a tin go-kart Daddy has made out of sheet metal. All the kids want to ride it. But today it is only one boy and me who my father asks to come in and play, and the door with the new silver latch closes behind us. The dug-out cellar under our house smells of wet dirt and beer. A wooden folding stool with a rotting orange-and-green canvas seat stands in the center of the dirt room, and behind it, my old table and chair, the one I used to do puzzles and color on. Its red plastic coating peels up at the edges. Dirty black sand is stuck to the glue of it. In the crew cut of the boy's scalp there is grime you could dig out with a full fingernail. His white T-shirt is stained, and his brown pants with the high-water hem cut into his belly at the waist. My father's glare traces to the outline of the boy's privates, squished to one side of outgrown pants too tight for underwear. Tears flood day-old sleepy seeds in the boy's frightened eyes. His small, dirty, finger-nailed hands push back against my father. The air is suffocating. Daddy's touch to my skin is like barb wire to my veins. I go away in my mind for a long time. When I come back, the boy is behind the table with his hands to the crumbling dirt wall of our under-porch. I am in the corner of the dirt room near the door. The smell of my own piss steams under my feet and puddles muddy up over them. From rotting overhead beams, spiders hang from carefully constructed webs.

The inside padlock, threaded through the silver latch, rattles in the damp grip of all ten fingers as I shake it wildly. "Open the door," I hear myself scream. "Open the door."

Daddy's grease-stained hand grabs tightly at my arm. His face is so close to mine, I can taste his rancid breath. "Don't tell Mumma. You don't wanta make Mumma mad at you, do you? You'll hurt her feelins." My father's eyes to mine say chances I will tell are slim. He counts on it, a sick victory, a free pass to the next time.

In early-morning hours of August, when the air smells musty of bloom and death, I lay on the slant of our backyard. In dewy patches, delicately woven fairy blankets balance atop green blades of grass. Frothy spit hangs from the stems of orange and yellow Indian paintbrushes. Queen Anne's lace tickles soft to where my tears have dried. Crickets sound out the day will be hot. A random acorn falls to the tin roof of the boathouse, dinging sharply before plunking into the river. Lazy waves lap the shore. Beyond the branches of the weathered oak trees, clouds drift in shapes of chariots that will take me away.

Things happen in my house I have no words to describe. They bury and hide in places forgotten. But I will remember forgetting. I am the holder of the truth.

7

Swing Time

THE GATE BETWEEN my yard and Nanny's swings open easily, even though the split-rail fence is splintered and coming apart. My grandmother's little brown-shingled house on the shore is as cozy as a doll's house and everything in it is clean and loved. When I go there, three brass bells chime from a braided gold rope on the inside of her front door. The kitchen smells of date-and-coconut squares hot from the oven and last night's butter-fried onions. When we play big band records, Nanny's soft hands clap out the beat as I twirl. We sing loud and dance like the floorboards are tickling our toes. Then she picks me up, smoothes down the ruffles of my dress, and holds me tight as we laugh. My grandmother smells like spring flowers and face powder. With her kisses she breathes me right into her, and I feel safe in her arms.

Nanny is a widow. Her husband died of a stroke in his fifties, just after Tommy came to live with us. She never learned to drive a car, but she often travels with friends to places like the Vermont mountains and the Arizona desert. One year they drove Route 66 all the way to California, and everywhere they stopped, Nanny bought a tiny souvenir pitcher. Nanny and I inspect her collection on the narrow staircase shelf. I listen closely to her stories.

"This one I got at the Grand Canyon." She picks it up and smiles. "Oh, Nancy dear, you can't imagine how beautiful it is there. Just glorious. One day you must go."

I watch her take one fragile keepsake at a time, dusting between them with a tissue she's pulled from the wrist of her purple sweater.

Purple is her favorite color. She has purple clothes and purple jewelry she says she is naked without.

Nanny loves adventure. Maybe that's why I love it, too. When the weather is good, we go by boat upriver to Nanny's camp in Merrymeeting Bay. It's the only way to get there unless you break a path through the woods from the main road at Chops Point. At camp there is no electricity or running water, so Nanny teaches me how to make do with what we have. In the morning we wash our faces in a tidal pool caught by the rocks. The water is not as polluted up to camp. And in the evening we fire up a wood-cooking stove that heats the little two-room building. By the light of an oil lamp, Nanny teaches me to play canasta. I know what she will say at every turn, "Now let me see. Oh dear." Then she flips cards to the table and we both laugh. It is late when Nanny wraps a blanket around my shoulders and, with a small flashlight, walks me to the outhouse. Back inside the camp, she snuggles me up in a bottom bunk with wool blankets as old as World War I. The kitchen wood stove crackles next to me. "Have a cozy sleep," she says, then rubs her kisses to my cheek.

When Nanny's husband was alive, he worked on Merrymeeting Bay as a duck-hunting guide for wealthy men from all over the country. In years to come, Uncle Ike will tell me he worked for the wealthy women as well and had a long-time affair with one of them. Uncle Ike says my grandfather had a mean disposition. Nanny will never let on to that. Mumma says Nanny wouldn't say shit if she had a mouth full of it.

It was after her husband died that Nanny went to work at the hospital. And now, four days a week after our teatime, she walks to work down over the hill to Park Street. Sometimes I go with her and sit quietly on a stool next to the rack of Teaberry gum and *Life* magazines. I watch her lift the headset from a hook on the side of the upright switchboard and carefully nest it into her white wavy hair. She speaks with perfect diction. "Bath Memorial Hospital. How may I direct your call?" Her graceful fingers scan a row of long black cables, then pulling one from its base, she lines the end of it up with the correct hole and nods for me to plug it in and connect the call.

Nanny comes home from work late at night, after most people are asleep. In the morning I go next door to visit and sometimes we take a picnic lunch outside to her table at the end of Daddy's boathouse. For dessert, my grandmother makes ginger ale and vanilla ice cream floats in tall green glasses. I study the white etching of a swing dance couple on the side of it. One corner of the girl's skirt is blown up with the breeze of her spin, and her toes are perfectly pointed in a high-heeled shoe. Sweet creamy foam runs down over it with the stir of my long-handled spoon.

"I'm going to dance like that someday, Nanny."

"I know you will, Nancy dear, because you are determined and you can do anything you put your mind to." She wipes her lips and reaches for me with one hand. "You remember what Nanny tells you, won't you, dear?"

Her eyes are the bluest I have ever seen. Above them her graying lashes are long and soft. "Yes, Nanny, I will."

But that will be a tough promise to keep. As the years go by, Nanny and Mumma will come to all my dance and theater productions. Each time, I will stand in the glare of the stage lights searching the black auditorium for a reflection from the frames of my mother's cat-eye glasses. Somewhere, silent in the darkness, my mother is watching.

8

Passing Ships

AUNT LILLY AND Nanny are like sisters. They walk back and forth from one side of my house to the other, exchanging recipes and plant slips, things Mumma says she has no time for. Aunt Lilly wears polished gold jewelry and Pendleton wools and smells like good cooking. She and Uncle Ike used to be friends with my parents, but now that Uncle Ike works at the bank, Mumma says they put on airs. Aunt Lilly says, "If we'd had a daughter, we would have wanted one just like you, dear." Then she bends to hug me and her knees crackly snap.

Every spring, Aunt Lilly takes me with her to buy big red geraniums at Hawkes Greenhouse. That makes Mumma mad. Mumma takes me to Old Nanny's house down over the hill. But that is never a good time. My father's mother, Old Nanny, lives in a little house that used to be an office building back in the early 1800s when towering pine trees, one day to be sailing masts, were floated in the cove behind it. She and Mumma's mother are the same age, but Old Nanny looks worn out. In the winter her pipes freeze, so Daddy sends her to Florida where she works as a waitress, carrying heavy trays on her shoulder at a big hotel in St. Petersburg, the Sunshine City.

Today at Old Nanny's house, a hand basket full of medicine bottles sits on a table next to her bed. I watch her shake the pills into her hand and count them out. In the living room she sits in a red wing chair, leans over on one hip, and with her bony knees crossed, takes long drags from her cigarette. Smoke blows out in a line from one side of her thin lips. Then she crushes the butt in an orange ashtray and takes her pulse with two fingers over one wrist.

"She's checkin to see if she's still alive for God sake," Mumma tells me, then she gargles throaty phlegm and shakes her head. "She's had a damn miserable life, that's for sure. Her husband ran on benders with women for weeks at a time. It was an aunt that raised your father down on the family farm in Arrowsic, because your grandmother always had ailments."

Old Nanny used to be a school-teacher. Her foot-stool is piled high with books about crime and history. I think Old Nanny likes to live in her books more than anywhere else. Her husband left her a long time ago and moved upstairs to a one-room apartment over Daddy's shop, but Tommy and I have never met him. The day of his funeral, Old Nanny takes care of the grandchildren while my parents, aunts, and uncles go to the service. Old Nanny's elbow points hard into the arm of her chair, and holding her cigarette high, she watches out the window like she's waiting for a long-lost schooner to sail up the river. Tommy and my cousins play old maid on the floor in front of a card table covered with dark, unconnected puzzle pieces. I sit quietly beside Old Nanny and watch the smoke curl its way to the ceiling, searching for a way to escape.

9

Milky Way

AFTER NINE CONSECUTIVE years, the summer I turn twelve is the last year we take a family vacation to Sebago Lake, Maine. During those three weeks every August, my mother becomes someone else. Everything about her seems different. Maybe it's because Daddy is with us only on weekends.

Early in the morning we leave camp for the beach. Mumma pulls the inside door shut behind her and lets the wooden screen door go. It slaps three times at the frame. Nanny's big hat, the one she bought in Mexico, is balanced on her gray waves. Long flowered ties hang to each side of her neck. Tommy walks behind her with two flippers in one hand, a diving mask in the other. He wipes the front of it on the hip of his red swim trunks. Mumma pats his head and laughs toward Nanny. "Thank God for those red trunks. He's under the water more than he's up."

In the sandy parking lot between our camp and the beach, my bare feet dance around dead June bugs and clumps of sharp grass blades. A greasy industrial fan on the side of Currier's Store blows out the smell of bacon, eggs, and homemade donuts. At the lake, boat engines rev on water as smooth as a window pane. The smell of two-cycle oil coils like incense through the air. Pools of iridescent green and purple orbs float next to the runway gas pump.

Nanny spreads her old yellow plaid blanket out over the sand, then sets a green, webbed lawn chair next to it. Mumma steps out of her flip-flops, sets her straw beach bag on the blanket, and sits down. I watch her rub Coppertone up and down her white freckled legs and around the straps of her bathing suit. I lean close to her. "I love that smell, Mumma."

She puts her face close to mine, brushes hair out of my eyes, and rubs lotion across my nose. Then she takes my chin in two fingers and smiles around rose-colored lips.

Every beach afternoon, Mumma sends me back across the street to Currier's Store. Sometimes I buy candy watermelon slices made of pink-and-green coconut, sometimes mint julep taffies, three for a penny. But always I get Mumma the same thing, a Milky Way bar. On the blanket, I sit beside her and watch her savor each bite as sweet caramel pulls from her front teeth. When half the bar is gone, she wraps the paper around it and drops it into her beach bag. Then with her white rubber swim cap snapped snug down over her hair, she walks barefoot into the water. Swimming beside her, I keep my eyes open and watch the sandy bottom as I dive down, weaving through and around her legs. Mumma scoops handfuls of clean, clear lake up over her shoulders and lets it roll down over her back. Then she begins to whistle from a tiny pucker in her lips. Without hardly taking a breath, she whistles "Tammy" by Miss Debbie Reynolds. It's the prettiest thing I've ever heard. "Do it again, Mumma."

As she does it, she holds my hands and gently swishes me from one side of her to the other, the water holding me weightless and free. The sun is bright on her pink cheeks. Freckles appear in the glow. There is a suntan line at the top of her forehead. A brushed-back wave of gray is hiding under her swim cap, and below it her hazel eyes look blue. In this moment I believe she must be the most beautiful lady in all of Maine.

I DON'T know why we never went back to the lake. All I know for sure is four months later I started my period, and that's when my world took a turn.

It was the twelfth of December. I remember that. It was after supper. And it was dark. Mumma had a church meeting to go to. She was in the bathroom with the door open, combing the one long back curl that stretched across her neck up around her finger. I reached to hug her, and as I did, she grabbed my hands and held them back. Then she made a loud sipping sound, sucking air in over her red lips. "I'm late, Nancy. Let go of me." I pressed my cheek to hers, closed my eyes, and breathed in the sweet scent of her Evening in Paris perfume. I begged her not to leave.

When she came home two hours later, I was in bed with a big wad of toilet paper between my legs. My face flushed embarrassment. "What do I do, Mumma?"

With one long, disgusted sigh, she left for her bedroom, then reappeared with a box of sanitary pads. She dropped it onto the bed beside me. "There's some pamphlets in there too, so you betta start readin." As she was leaving she stopped in my doorway and turned back around. "It's a damn curse, that's what it is, and your father says there's no need of you shavin your legs, so stop askin me. He says once you start you'll have to do it the rest of your life. So you betta just forget about it right now. God, I pity the man that marries you. I don't know who would ever put up with all your foolishness."

My childhood curls have darkened. They lay long and wavy below shoulders of an hourglass body I cover in tights and long sleeves, even on the warmest days. I am not a little girl now, but Mumma and I never say "young woman," because to Mumma, that's like saying a bad word.

10

Validate Me

FOR THE NEXT three years my body screams to be validated by my mother. At night, with a clenched fistful of blankets at my chin and a nightgown hem pulled between my legs, I pray the pain will end, beg for Mumma's comfort when it doesn't. Inside me, bladder infections burn like fire and the curse clamps everything female about me like vise grips pinch sheet metal in Daddy's tin shop.

Mumma says she's sick to death of hearing me complain, so she has taken me to Daddy's friend, the family doctor. In his office, Mumma sits in a straight-back chair next to the examination table. I am sitting at the end of that table dressed in a cotton gown wrapped twice around me.

"Lay back and put your feet in the metal loops," the doctor says. Then he lifts up my gown and rolls his stool closer. My knees lock tight together. I push myself up the length of the table and away from his hands. "Nancy, open your legs. I need to see what's going on and why you are having such pain."

Heat is rushing up my body in a wave of panic that starts at my crotch and ends in my throat. I can't breathe. "I . . . I have to use the bathroom," I stutter.

He takes my hand and pulls me back to his end of the table. "Oh, I see, you have a tampon in. I'll take care of that." He pulls at the string between my legs, my muscles fighting its release. Tears run hot down my neck and into my ears. I am shaking all over.

Mumma sits silent with her hands stone-like over the purse in her lap. Her eyes make the slightest pinch at me, then search the room across blank walls and out the window. I lock my eyes on the corner of her blue metal glass frame. My mind and body begin to separate. I can hear the squeaking of my grinding teeth. Everything in the room is vibrating and changing size, like I am Alice down the rabbit hole.

I leave his office that day with drugs. From age fifteen through eighteen, per his prescription and my survival, Darvon and Demerol will dissolve into the cells of pain and hidden memories. Twice between my fifteenth and sixteenth birthdays, I will be admitted to the hospital, put under anesthesia, and have my cervix and uterus scraped. Mumma said there were things inside me that needed to be removed.

Painkillers, prescribed by the family doctor and refilled by my mother, keep me numb. I carry them like candy, a pocket-full of green-and-black jobbies, capsules of synthetic opioids given to me without question. Pills that absorb pain like the stuff the school janitor throws on the floor absorbs vomit.

THE winter night I dump green-and-black jobbies across my white bedspread, my eyes are drooped and glassy. I watch my hand sweep them flat to the bed like valuable coins. I think about swallowing them all at once. But instead I walk two miles in thirty-degree weather to the dark side entrance of Morse High School and drink wine with a bunch of kids until I tip backward off the step, smacking my head on the icy tar. When I sit back up, my friend's voice vibrates in and out of my ears. She yells my name and pulls at my arm with both of hers. The red glow of a half-smoked butt pulses from the corner of her mouth. When I get to my feet, my flat-ironed hair falls into my eyes and my coat drags off my back and hangs from my elbows. Foggy breath as thick as our cigarette smoke makes clouds between us as we snicker. Then, in snowmobile boots heavy as cement blocks, I walk the two miles home, gripped to my friend's arm and laughing.

When my mother sees me, her chin pits up and the lines between her eyebrows make a deep *M*. She is mad as she dials up the family doctor on the kitchen wall phone. Her finger pulls so hard around that dial, it looks like her pointer might break off at the knuckle.

When the doctor arrives, I am sitting up straight in the kitchen chair at the edge of the living room next to Daddy's book divider. Daddy is leaned back in his spot on the couch trying to read the *Bath Daily Times* and clearing his throat in that nervous kind of way. After Mumma brings the doctor in through the living room, she sits back down next to Daddy, folds her arms tight over her chest, crosses her legs, and begins swinging one foot.

The doctor bends close to my face, shines a small flashlight in my eyes, and asks me to follow from side to side. He looks in my mouth, takes my pulse, and listens to my heart. Then, packing his stethoscope back into his black bag, he turns to my father. "She's fine, Jimmy, just a slight concussion. She'll feel better tomorrow."

The alcohol reeking from my breath is not mentioned.

11

Don't Leave Me

MUMMA STANDS BESIDE my bed. Her hair is perfectly in place and her lipstick is fresh. "I'm not gonna fight with you, Nancy. I have to go to work. I can't stay here and waste my time tryin to get you outta bed. If you're too damn lazy to get yourself up and off to school, that's your problem. You'll just never amount to anything, that's all."

I reach up over her shoulders and pull my body close to hers. "Please, Mumma, don't leave me."

"For heaven sake, Nancy, what is the matter with you? I have to go to work. Now let go of me." She pries my arms from her neck and pushes strands of misplaced hair back into waves as she turns and walks out.

I wait for the rumble of her car to disappear down over the hill. In the top dresser drawer under red knee socks I only wear if nothing else is clean, I reach for a prescription bottle. The top pops off easily. I shake the capsules into my hand. My tongue sticks to one, like I am eating popcorn from an overflowing movie container. I go back for another, then wash them down with a gulp of two-day-old grape Kool-Aid from my nightstand. Back in bed, I bring the covers to my chin and wait for the drugs to hit me.

I am spiny and fuzzed, numbing out with the drugs, when I finally pull back the covers. My big toenails catch and bend backward against the sheets. I have danced them almost off. Mumma says I should forget about dancing on pointe, because every time I do my shoe pads get soaked with blood. But I will dance with my feet sore and bleeding just to spite her.

In my fingers, the left big toenail bends back and forth. It twists and pulls from skin that barely holds it alive until finally it is completely detached. I flick the small, insignificant piece of me at the window. My eyes pulse. They scan orange walls I have smeared with thick black paint. I watch my naked toe make squishy steps across stained beige carpet that looks like sewer water has washed over it. I stand at the window, slide it open, and look down the four-story drop past the kitchen, past the laundry room, past the dirt cellar door to the ground. I wonder, if I jumped, would I be lucky enough to die on impact? My knees fold to the floor next to the discarded toenail.

Now it is afternoon, not long before everyone will be home. The front living room desk drawers slide out easily toward me. When I let go, their thin brass handles ding like the cash register in my parents' office. Mumma keeps important papers here, things she says are none of my business. Dozens of old black-and-white photos are strewn with no order. Crinkled Christmas bows sit under double packs of playing cards in cardboard holders. Below insurance paperwork, bank statement envelopes, and recycled wrapping paper is a dark folder bent over with a single snap holding it together. It opens fast with the weight of bursting documents.

"City of Boston, Health Department Registry Division, Commonwealth of Massachusetts, date of record June 6, 1955. Birth record of Deborah Lee Dawes. Deborah," I say it out loud. Proof that I had a name and somewhere, maybe still, a mother.

The paper shakes in my hands. I read it over and over, each word again and again. Then, suddenly realizing I could be caught, I quickly re-bury it deep below forgotten things, like all secrets in our house.

I WILL be a mother myself before I understand my right to know where I came from. However, my parents have agreed with the so-called experts of the decade that an adoptee searching for her birth family is not only an act of ingratitude to the adoptive parents, but also a sign of emotional imbalance. Kooky, Mumma calls it, and says for the life of her, she can't understand why I would want to look for someone who didn't want me to begin with. "Don't open a can of worms," she warns. "For once you do, there's no goin back."

Tommy and I had been the chosen ones in an era that condoned secrecy. We were born to women who Mumma said had sinful pre-marital intercourse with men who didn't want them. She said giving birth to us had been the punishment for that. My brother and I were the throw-a-ways, now living a blessed life in a house of lies where our father's calculated process of devalue would keep us shame-based and our mother's blind eye would enable it.

12

On the Run

IN MY BEDROOM, morning sun reaches through the river window and gently brings me back from sleep. My body is tense and contorted from Daddy's predawn visit. I make a low groan, turn to the brightness, and release the tattered quilt from my grasp. Musky smells and the sound of a fast zipping of Daddy's work pants are my only clear details of memory. The rest have fled like a beaten dog. My legs are liquid as they slowly pool to the low end of the bed. I pull at my flannel nightgown, twisted tight and strangling my waist. I wait and listen. Tommy's feet stamp heavy up the stairs, then back down. Mumma yells, "Hurry up for God sake. You'll miss the bus." I study the air for the energy of my father. He's gone.

On top of my bed, I lay down a blue bandana and smooth it out under the weight of my shaking hands. I wrap the folded triangle to my head and tie it back under my long dirty hair. I step into my only pair of hip-hugger-bell-bottom jeans and pull them up my lanky legs. The hems are frayed from ground dragging. A week's worth of mud-puddle water marks have made wavy white lines at my ankles. The crotch has dampened and dried several times over. I yank down over my head a navy blue sweater, the one with the pilled armpits from scrubbing the stink out and the cigarette burn over my right boob.

The school bus stop at the foot of the hill is halfway to Old Nanny's. I can see her little wooden house across the swampy cove. Here on the corner of Washington and Harwood Streets, at the bus shack, is where we kids used to wait for the ice cream truck, and where I skidded my bike and fell after pedaling straight down the hill like I was a bandit on the run. Today it is where I ditch the bus, run ahead of the kids up over the crest of Harwood Street and into the woods.

Drooping pine boughs bend easily as I make my way through the trees, pitchy secret arms that hide me in a fort of green. Up the hill, we call it, where stolen scrap wood becomes lookout towers over moss-covered rocks and thick blueberry bushes, where near-death apple trees drop fruit fit only for deer. Searching down through the field, up over a burnt-out farm plot, and across the street to my house, I watch. Waiting for Mumma to come out of our house, a purse and Daddy's lunch box hanging from one hand and her car keys in the other, like every work-day just before nine o'clock.

Mumma's car begins to slowly roll away from the front of our house. I am standing tall on a flat slab of rock, then lean over my toes like a ski racer. I do it every time. And I run. Blood swishing, pounding at my eardrums, my feet sprinting choreographed steps, weightless down through the open field and across the rotten gully plank. Then hand over hand, I crawl up the steep hill, grabbing stalks of dry field grass and pulling myself to the street. At our rock wall, I slice through the lilacs and jump down into our yard. The downstairs shed window rattles in my tingling hands. I lift it high enough to fit under and roll into the house, just short of the furnace. Cobwebbed empty shirt boxes crush under my butt. A scattered pile of *National Geographic* magazines slide under my feet. Then up the laundry room staircase, both hands climb each tread. In the bathroom, my clothes peel and drop to the floor, and in the hot spray of the shower, I begin to scrub my skin of morning filth. But there's no brush that goes that kind of deep.

13

Bleeding

MUMMA'S BLUE CHEVY Nova fills the space between the gas pumps and the front of Daddy's shop when she pulls in. It clunks as she turns off the engine. Then she gets out and looks up at the four stories of red brick. "Those damn pigeons." She shakes her fist at them, then at me as I get closer. A history text book, a notebook with a sheet of carbon paper sticking out, and an unread copy of *Catcher in the Rye*, rest on one hip. Carbon ink has bleed into the bottom of my tan cardigan sweater during the walk down over Centre Street hill from the high school.

In the showroom window, a five-foot stovepipe tin man holds a bent arm. In the space behind it are white cardboard boxes of various sizes holding heating and plumbing supplies. Sun-faded price stickers hang loosely from the boxes.

Inside the office, Mumma lays an empty deposit bag on the desk and puts her pink smock on over her yellow three-button jersey. I pull down the side handle of the cash register next to her. It makes a ding as the drawer pops open. I put my finger to the buffalo and slide the nickel out against the wood compartment. "I'm going out back for a Coke, Mumma."

She doesn't look up. She speaks out of pursed lips. "Yeah, okay, Nancy." She is tracing perfectly-squared numbers in the column of a ledger page, then gets up and slides the black leather book back to the dusty shelf. "Keepin up with the mess of dirt around here is an endless job." She lets out a long sigh and wipes down the front of her.

Out back, next to the Coke machine, are towers of foul-smelling rubber tires and a car lift heavy with grease. On the wall over the tin bench, where my father bends sheet metal, is a calendar with one naked woman for each month. Daddy pulls a bottle opener from his pants pocket, takes the Coke from my hand, and pops the top off. The flower shop man, who is important at church like my father, is there too. He is always happy when I see him. He asks me how school is going and taps my arm as he talks. We all stand next to Miss March, half-sitting on a chair with her legs spread open. Daddy, the important church man, and me.

My father is the go-to man for problems at the Methodist church, where on Sundays he likes to squeeze my hand while the pipe organ moans "How Great Thou Art." Daddy is a devout Christian. He says no matter what we do, each week at church the sins of man are washed away in the blood of our savior Jesus Christ. I guess that means come Sunday, if you believe in the wash-away, important church people like my father get a do-over.

Daddy and the flower shop man have been friends since they were teenagers. They used to do community theater together. Now I do community theater with his daughter. When my friends and I go to the Spudnut Shop after school, we see her sitting by herself at a center table full of sandwiches, donuts, and drinks. Under the table, her mini-skirt hem is up to her lady parts, and her feet propped up in the seat across from her. On the tabletop is a *Playboy* magazine. She flips pages while gorging the food, then burps loudly, goes to the bathroom, and throws it all up. As she strides to the front door, her go-go boots click and her hips sway side to side. Sometimes when she walks past my booth, she looks down at me with a faint curve of her puffy wet lips and I get a chill that rides across my insides. People say she is weird, but I think behind her heavy black eye-liner and mascara there is a tragic story waiting to be told.

Many years from now, a young man will come into her father's flower shop and shoot that important church man in the back. The accusation will be pedophilia. At the funeral, that daughter will tell an overflowing congregation that her father lived a violent and fearful life. She will be shut up and removed from the pulpit, and my father will get up and walk out. People in Bath will call her a liar. They say a man so loved by the community like he was would never do anything like that. She will speak her truth, but people don't like to listen to things that make them question their own consciousness. I think that's what destroyed what was left of her spirit. She will put a gun to her head, and the little girl inside who painfully kept her family's shameful secret will take exit.

14

The Bathroom Door

I AM STANDING NEXT to the blue chair, arms tight across my boobs. Again, tonight, I am sweaty and stinky from being a teenager, and being with him. Layers of clothes don't hide the foulness of that. Daddy sits straight across from me on the end of the couch with the *Bath Daily Times* spread open in his lap. He bites a pipe between his stained teeth, then makes three quick puffs at a time. In a wide glass with an *S* etched on the side, he swirls vodka in clinking ice cubes, then takes smacking slurps with his poison mouth.

The smell of boiling potatoes blends with cherry tobacco and steams up the kitchen windows. Sweaty tears run to the white sills and puddle next to a lead-weight fish-line sinker and a red-and-white plastic bobber. Mumma pulls the pan from the stove top just as it boils over.

Still wrapped to myself, I call to her from around the corner of the blue chair. "Please, Mumma, I have to get in the shower."

I can hear the splash of hot potato water hit the sink. "Once a week is plenty. You were just in there a couple nights ago."

Daddy lays everything down. He stands up and walks across the living room to me. One side of his mouth is curled to the top of his teeth, which are stained dark yellow at the gums. His hands are on me, running down my shoulders and following my arms across my blouse. He leans close and takes a long breath of me. "No shower," he says. Bristly eyebrows wire out from his face like weeds. Gray hair sprouts from his ears.

"Please, Mumma."

Her voice comes quick. "Your father says you don't need a shower, Nancy, so never mind."

Daddy goes back to the couch, his eyes glancing between the paper in his lap and the folded wooden door I have now closed and stepped behind. It hangs from an overhead track with wide voyeuristic gaps between its two panels and the doorframe. From the middle gap, I see him watching me at the sink as I reach up under my sweater and run a wet washcloth over my arm pits. I rinse out the cloth and turn my back to him. Again, today, with my stomach sucked to a hollow, I reach into my pants and wipe at my crotch.

When I come out of the bathroom and walk toward the kitchen, Daddy is on the other side of the blue-chair wall, refilling his glass inside the freezer compartment of the refrigerator. Mumma is peeling whole cooked potatoes over the sink. She holds up a fork with a hot potato stabbed to the end and looks at him. "Jimmy, don't you think you've had enough?" She gargles phlegm and turns her back to us.

My father steps close to me and stares over the top of his gold wire-rimmed glasses. Then he bends his knees so we are eye to eye and licks his lips.

"Mumma, can't you see how much he scares me and how it gets worse when he's drinking? I'm afraid of him, Mumma. Why won't you ever listen to me?"

Daddy's smile twists. His tongue flicks in and out of his polluted mouth. He lays his glass on the kitchen table. His callused, soot-stained hands grab at my breasts, then slowly move down my hour-glass sides. I look away from eyes the color of a thick algae-covered swamp, the kind you don't dare walk near for fear it will suck you to the bottom and eat you alive. "Mumma, please."

The aluminum cover slams onto the potato pot. She turns fast to us. "For God sake, Nancy, he's just relaxin. Stop imaginin things. Your father would never hurt you. You're some damn kooky. Now stop thinkin so crazy. There must be somethin wrong with you. God."

I run the stairs two at a time ahead of him, shaking the thin banister in my speed, and brace myself against the back of my bedroom door, a door with a latch that years ago Daddy painted over. His awkward body pushes heavy as the cracked wooden panels groan for mercy against his hands.

"Move away from that door now. Do you hear me, Nancy?" He bellows.

I jump up on my bed, step bouncing from one side to the other to avoid his lunging grasp. Scum-covered words fire from his mouth with such force, I white-knuckle my clothes in fear they will be torn from my body with the power of his salivary blast. "You're nothin but a fuckin slut. Do you hear me? A fuckin slut."

I scream my throat raw. "Mumma, help me. Please, Mumma, make him stop." But there is no rescue in a house with no boundaries.

Some nights, after everyone is asleep, I sneak out the back shed door and run barefoot through the neighbors' yards in my nightgown. I slippery slide over wet, chilly lawns and jump weightless over thorny puckerbrush. I am drunk on midnight summer air, fragrant with blossoms of beauty that have opened just for me. Moonlight glows softly overhead and laughs like a childhood friend as I stand in the middle of the road, lift the hem of my nightgown, squat down, and pee. I watch it run between my feet and into the gravel. There is some kind of deep freedom that comes with that.

In daylight, pine trees scoop me up one pitchy branch at a time, until I am swaying on top and hidden in the green. From our river dock, I race the Crestliner swishing and cutting sharply around rocks and buoys, full speed jumping the waves. Sixteen feet of aluminum slams over and over. I do it until the rhythmic banging of the boat and jarring of my body are all I feel. Down the Kennebec, through Hell's Gate, out past Fort Popham to the open ocean. Then, with the cut of the engine, I drift far away.

15

Tossed and Tidal

In my junior class at Morse High School, I hold the record for most missed days. Senior year will be the same. With Daddy's money and Mumma's car, it's an easy thing to do.

When the four o'clock whistle blows at the Bath Iron Works, people pack Ma Roy's Market for beer and cigarettes. That's always a good time to go, because the owners are too busy to ask for an ID. Virginia Slims are my favorite. I hold a fresh one in front of my shoulder. My fingers feel long and feminine as I do it. I put a match to the end, inhale all the way to my toes, then blow the smoke back out in two pointy streams from my nose and off my pouted lower lip.

In Mumma's blue Nova, my girlfriends and I drink Old Milwaukees and drive every street in Bath. Most nights we make at least one trip to Popham Beach, fifteen miles of dark winding ocean road. When we pull into the fort parking lot there, my tires crush heavy in the loose granite rocks. I love that sound. Then I run to the shore, like she is a waiting friend ready to soothe my pain. Numbing curls of icy relief swallow my feet in salty foam. My toes dig into the hard, grainy sand as it drops out under me with the wash of the wave. Seaweed laces between my toes. My jeans soak heavy, wave-licked clear up to my knees. In the pre-Civil War fortress, I climb to the top on protruding stones of the inner wall. Sometimes I use the winding turret staircase, like a scene from a fairy tale, but not often. It smells like piss.

I walk the top of the crumbling fort walls, like the balance beam in gym class. Small pieces of rock break loose and dive into whirlpools below. Seals disappear in swirling circles, then pop their black, shiny heads back up, playing hide-and-seek on the pull of the tide. My bare toes are wrapped to the edge. My eyes closed, arms stretched to the sides. My body rocks with the ocean wind beating at me as if I am a sail in a ship with broken steerage. Seagulls cry as they fly past me, and sometimes, I cry with them. Then I sit down, light a joint, and let its honey-syrup warmness move through me, melting my pain like a blistered sun dropped into a dark ocean.

Back in town, we park at the library, where long-haired, hippie kids gather on the front steps, passing a joint and watching carloads of kids loop the circular driveway and down Summer Street past the YMCA. Officer Haines pulls up in his police car and shouts out his window. "You kids can't sit on these steps every night drinking, ya know. Now, toss those cans into the trash barrel and move along."

When we are not in Bath, we are at parties I will not remember the location of the next day. One night I drunk-sat on the edge of a picnic bench and peed, unsure if my pants were up or down. I have spent hours retching up alcohol with my arms pasted to filthy toilets, been best drink-and-drug buddies with people I didn't know, and once at a J Geils concert fell down a full set of bleachers and landed in some guy's lap at the bottom. He shot a wineskin to my mouth and passed me a joint. Then I drove everyone back to town.

I COME home long after everyone is asleep. I pull Mumma's car to the front of the house. Forward, backward, forward, backward, until it lines up even between the lilac bushes, the way she does it. Standing at the front door, I run my fingers over the edge of the house key. "Straighten up," I whisper. It's how I remember the flat side of the key must be facing up for it to fit into the lock.

In the dull light of the kitchen range bulb, two hot dogs sizzle in black, smoky butter, then lie in rolls toasted greasy and crisp. Chunks of raw white onion are sharp on my tongue and mix with tart yellow mustard that drips down my chin as I bite.

Up the dark staircase, plate in one hand, ginger ale in the other, I step around loud creaks that never seem to be there in the light of day. I hear Mumma let out a low, disgusted sigh from her bed. "Well, finally, she decided to come home."

In my room I pull the rolling television stand with the small black-and-white set close to my bed. I lean to its glow and take the last bites of hot dog. My blurry eyes watch the door, and again tonight I pray I will pass out before my father pushes it open.

Out my bedroom window, the morning sun teases the Woolwich tree line across the river. My eyes have startled open. My body is locked in sweaty panic, with the rip of bedding from my grasp. Daddy's face is stubbled with a thousand spikes that stab at my cheek. His greenish, front-tooth implant is the color of snot you blow from a cold. His cherry-tobacco-stained breath forces its way down my throat. Through my flannel nightgown, the one that Nanny made me, his hands knead at my breasts. His hips push to mine. My own blood grips a choke hold on my neck. And then I am gone, leaving my body behind like I am running from a burning building. I am gone until the smell of bacon and coffee wafts up from the kitchen. On the damp bedsheets, I curl into the smallest ball I can make. Staggered breath releases from my contaminated mouth. My lungs beg for air. It's a lie. I made it up. It never happened.

I want to die.

Mumma's voice booms up the staircase. "Nancy, get out of that bed for God sake, and get yourself to school. You're never gonna amount to a damn thing. You're gonna be good for nothin."

But today is just like the others. I wait for the ting of the wire hanger as Mumma pulls her jacket from the hall coatrack. The front door slams hard, and I am alone. As I slide off the edge of my bed, my strong dancer legs are like overcooked noodles. In the hall, I grip the trauma-stained railing. My fingernails dig into its gummy grime.

In the bathroom, Listerine swishes over my tongue and dribbles down my throat until I can no longer stand the sting. I spit into the sink, then pull sticky underpants down over my feet and bury them in the wastebasket. I am so dirty, inside and out, I don't know what to wash first.

With the front door locked, I lean against the television set, out of sight of the windows. Pills wash down with grape juice. Seeds snap from the end of a perfectly rolled joint. Fire sucks down my throat. Mumma was right. It is better to be unconscious. That way you don't feel the pain.

16

Groomed Unconscious

MY MIND CHOOSES to forget what my body remembers. Fear seeps out every pore. It stings, it smells, it screams to be noticed. Yet, no one notices. If I could form words defining what it is like to be the chosen one, if there were anyone to listen and believe me, then I would destroy my family. And who would love me then?

"I'm going to tell everyone what you've done to me," I cry.

"No one will believe you," he says.

Thirty years will pass before the family knows, and Daddy's brother will say, "It doesn't surprise me."

THROUGH the picture window in our kitchen, I watch the Crestliner being thrown from side to side, tossed up and down, in the salt spray of the storm. It begs to be unlocked and freed to the ocean current. Waves crash wickedly against it. But it will never get loose on its own. Daddy has bound the lines tightly.

My father has taught me the kind of knots that hold a boat when high tides rise to the very under-edge of our dock, then stretch back out to dead mud low. I know how to replace the cotter pin in an engine, and the proper way to eat a lobster, by sucking the meat clean from the shell.

People say Daddy and I are two peas in a pod. I will agree with them, praising and minimizing my father's behavior, blaming myself for the shame in still wanting to be loved. Maybe all families live like this and no one ever talks about it. Maybe others are better at dealing with it than I am. Shame, a disease that will spread throughout my body, taking root without me understanding its source. Every word, every touch, every experience, locks into places in my body and encodes every cell. It festers in wait of rediscovery. I am groomed to live a life of shame in a body fighting against itself.

Some would say he took my power away. But it was my body and control of my belief system that were of value to him. He taught me to fear. He convinced me I was without worth. But he never took my power, like the dark will never take the light. If I believed he had something of me that I valued, then I would need to retrieve it. There was nothing he was or had that I required. Fear is not power. My true power never left me. Many years of self-abuse will pass before I even begin to understand that.

17

Stewed

SOMEDAY I WILL marry a boy named Michael. At six years of age, I was in love with Michael Babish, the kindest boy I knew. In fifth grade it was Michael Roba. He was beautiful, Maltese, and exotic. That crush would last for years. Michael Bridwell was the third, the high school basketball star, tall and gangly, with fast feet and faster hands. But it was Grant who would turn my world without me remembering how. That was the summer between my junior and senior years.

In the front dooryard of my house, Grant makes a wide, sweeping turn with his motorcycle, then stops between the end of Mumma's car and the mailbox. My hot pants are pink and tight. The hem just covers my butt cheeks. A macramé bag flung to my shoulder blade bounces off me as I swing my long leg over the bike. I lay my bare feet to the side pegs, wrap my arms low around Grant's thin body, and put my hands flat on the top of his thighs. With my chest to his back, I kiss him lightly on the neck. He smells like burnt rope and four-stroke engine exhaust. The bike jerks forward, shifting gears, as we gun down over the hill, my long hair and pink halter top strings blowing back to the sissy bar.

For three months there are countless shots of tequila that burn all the way to my stomach, and bags of pot I roll to perfect joints. Each time, I watch Grant's pale face fire red when he inhales hard, pulling it from his lips, swallowing it down, then going back for one more toke and blinking away smoke with his strawberry blond lashes. One night we drive home in the rain from an Old Orchard Beach bar, shitfaced and passing cars in the dark, and my long, straight hair pulls out of the stick I have it wound around and slaps at my face. There are bongs, and hash pipes, and blowing smoke to the northern lights somewhere out of town on a dirt road. And drunken dances atop tables at Andy's Bar, where I scream the words to "Layla" out over the crowd. Sex happens in dark places, but I am disconnected from where or how. I'm not really there. Grant and summer fade at the same time. My memories of him are like shards of sea glass, foggy and mysterious.

SENIOR year has started. I will stay as far away as possible. Again, tonight, Nanny has left her front door unlocked for me. Slipping into the house on my best drunken behavior, I feel safe when I hear her brass bells chime. The house smells of fried onions and butter. Nanny is already in her bed when I sneak up the stairs and slide into the clean starchy sheets of the spare bed. A night-light glows between the two doorways.

"Good night, Nancy dear. Is everything all right?" she says in a whisper.

"Yes, Nanny. I love you." I whisper back. I can't tell my grandmother the truth. That would erase the last piece of me being her little girl.

The next morning I am still in bed when I hear Mumma at the front door. Her voice bangs at my head. "She needs to get up outta that bed and go to school for a change. I'm sick to death of her pullin this stunt."

Nanny's voice is soft and sad. "Let her sleep, Doris. I'll take care of it. You go on to work."

When Mumma has gone, I wrap up in Nanny's old blue nylon bathrobe and go downstairs. In the kitchen, she holds her arms out to me and I melt into them. "Well, okay," she says. "Let's have some breakfast, dear."

My grandmother's small kitchen table is connected to a metal arm that collapses to the wall. Two wooden chairs painted the same color as the picnic table sit with it. At my place, there are three stewed prunes in a Memory Lane bowl from Nanny's A & P collection, and next to that, a plate with buttered toast cut into three strips. Nanny picks up a cup and saucer and pours boiling water over a tea bag. I suck the butter from the middle piece of bread and sigh.

"Maybe you'll feel better tomorrow, Nancy." She pinches her tea bag with two fingers and lays it on the saucer. Then she reaches for my hand. "You know your mother loves you in her own way. You must have patience with her."

Mumma will never know how I love the way the leaves blow backward in a shift of cool breeze just before it rains, or how dusk is my favorite time of day because shades of earth seem deeper. She doesn't know that green is my favorite color, or how magical I feel when I drive our snowmobile at night under low, icy branches of heavy, frozen snow. I will never tell her that I took her best white sheet from the ironing pile to bury a dead seagull in the field, or that the dandelions I dug for Daddy's supper with her paring knife were the same dandelions earwigs crawled through and the neighbor's dog peed on.

I finish my breakfast, wait for nine o'clock to pass, go home, take some pills, and light up a joint. It's one more day.

18

Zig-Zag

ON MY BEDROOM floor, the Ouija board lies flat. Ten fingers rest lightly on each side of the plastic, heart-shaped planchette. I start. "Who will I marry?"

With our fingers still attached, it slowly begins to inch across the board, its center nail pointing to letters and numbers underneath a clear plastic window. B O B. "Do you know anyone named Bob?" my friend asks. I keep my eyes to the board and shake my head no.

"How many children will I have?" I continue. The planchette scatters back and forth, then holds on the number 1. "Only one?" Then with a frantic scratch from one side of the board to the other, it comes back to the number 2.

THE first time I saw him he was standing in our front hallway. He was a senior and I was a sophomore. He and his uncle had just delivered a television set from the family appliance store on Front Street. My mother made small talk. I sat halfway down the staircase watching. His frame was small. His cotton shirt was perfectly pressed, buttoned at the lapels, and tucked into tight-fitting corduroys that stopped short over his white socks and penny loafers. His large, brown eyes were the color of Mumma's suede coat, and his teeth sparkled white like first snow. I must have seen him before in the halls at Morse High School, but I didn't remember. He was in the popular clique, and would be voted nicest smile, and best personality in his senior yearbook. We only nodded to each other that first day.

It is two years later the first time we talk, February 1973. Coming home from an away basketball game, six of us are squished into Bobby's green 1968 Camaro. The headlights are shining like lighthouse beacons down the dark, icy highway. Snow is breaking against the windshield. It looks like an endless tunnel of white. Bobby's narrowed eyes stare into the storm. Smoke pulls past his curly, black, shoulder-length hair and out through a slight crack in his side window. The speedometer reads 30, but it feels like a backwards 70. Sitting next to him on the console, between the two front bucket seats, I pull a nickel bag of pot from the pocket of my dungaree railroad jacket. There is just enough light from the dash for me to see what I'm doing. Two thin papers lift from the small Zig-Zag package. I hold one up with both hands, lick the edge, then carefully lay one to the other, gluing them together. With my fingers pinching and rolling the weed, I drop it into the crease. Not too much, and no stems or seeds that will pop. Roll. Lick across top. One twisted end pulls through my moistened lips, then the other. Little Kicks pass over my shoulder from the back-seat. They empty with a couple of good gulps. The label on my bottle is glued upside down. In the moment, it seems hysterical. When we get back to town, Bobby kisses me. I turn my head and puke.

The night of our first real date, Mumma gets to the front door before I do. Bobby comes in on a couple of sloppy drunk stumbles and steadies himself against the doorway of the front living room. That next day Mumma will ask, "Does Bobby drink?" I will look her straight in the eyes, tilt my head to one side, pinch up the lines between my eyebrows, and say, "No, I don't think so."

Bobby's family is Jewish. They forbid him to date me. He lies and does it anyway. At night when he picks me up, he now waits outside the door. At the Camaro, before swinging his legs under the steering wheel, Bobby taps the insides of his shoes together to knock the dirt off. The V8 purrs while he examines the dash, searching for dust to spit polish. He adjusts the rearview mirror, checking for food in his teeth, then pulls at each sock. Everything has its place. Roaches on his side of the ashtray and empties neatly back in the cardboard holder, never rolling loose on the floor like they do in my car.

Most of the night we smoke, drink, and drive. Sometimes we go together to the Bounty Taverne, but never separately. That always ends in a fight. One of those nights he drives us onto the frozen New Meadows River. We fight all the way to the middle, as the ice cracks beneath us. Then, in a drunken seethe, he gets out of the car and walks to the shore in pitch-black darkness. I cry and scream for him to come back. "Don't leave me."

Toxic emotional sludge from drugs, alcohol, lies, anger, and neediness is the start of our relationship. Not at all what I thought first love would be.

19

I Just Know

Thunderclouds are rolling overhead, and the threat of storm is near. I watch Bobby step into the Crestliner with one foot and push off from the dock with the other. I am perched on the top edge of the driver's seat as I lean forward and jam the throttle full open. Salt water sprays my face. My hair blows back behind me. The faster we go, the harder I laugh, turning the wheel back and forth, cutting shapes in the water. Bobby sits low in the seat beside me with one leg crossed over the other in a triangle. He smiles uncomfortably as one arm tightly hugs the side of the boat.

When we get to the Merrymeeting camp, the Crestliner makes long, slow scrapes along the jagged rock shoreline. I jump to land, line in hand, and tie the bow to a small tree. Bobby follows. I stand on the porch railing and reach for the door key wedged between the top of the post and the roof of the deck. We smoke a joint. Then I butt the roach and drop it into my dungaree jacket pocket. Inside, we lie down on the bottom bunk next to the stove, and the next hour blurs by me.

Later, I move to the front of the camp, tightening the macramé belt looped through my jeans as I walk. The screen door makes a rusted screech as I open it and step out onto the porch. The last bit of sunset dips into the wild rice across the bay. A haunted shudder sweeps my body. There is someone standing next to me, whispering in my ear. Cool air turns course and blows through the porch screens and against the camp. My long hair pulls off my neck and swishes to the back of my sweater with the breeze. Bobby walks toward me, working his shirt neatly back into his corduroys.

"Oh my God, Bobby." His eyes are glassy, mine wide with fear. "I'm pregnant."

He stops, one hand still tucked into the front of his pants. "How do you know that? You're crazy, Nance. What's the chances?"

"There was a whisper in my ear. A feeling in my stomach. I just know things, Bobby, that's all. Things that are hard to explain."

There is a full moon tonight. It guides us back as we dodge submerged logs and rocks. They peek at us between ripples of glittered waves. Navigation of the boat is all we talk about on the way home. Six weeks will go by before we talk about that night again.

20

Announcement

AFTER THE DOZENS of dance and theater productions I have been involved with during my high school years it will be my absence from school I will be remembered for. On our Senior Class Day, our president stands on the auditorium stage and calls up into the balcony at me as he announces it. "Nancy Steen of the class of 1973 wills her "most skipped days" record to Nancy Quinland of the class of 1974." Everyone laughs and claps when he says it. I laugh too. But that is just on the outside.

On graduation night, when we march the aisle in white nylon robes and caps, I look like all the other girls. But I am not. I am stoned. I am numb to my future. And I am pregnant.

I HAVE never gone to a doctor's appointment without Mumma. I have randomly picked his name out of the phone book and driven alone to his office in Brunswick, the next town over. Now I am sitting in the parking lot with my head on the steering wheel, thinking I don't ever want anyone to know what I am about to do.

His waiting room is covered in dark fake-wood paneling. I speak quietly when I give my name to the receptionist. She smiles and offers me a seat. A small, low lamp lights a corner table with *Reader's Digests and Family Circle.* I sit next to the table and pick up one of the magazines. There are three women also waiting to see the doctor, their bellies rounded in different stages of pregnancy.

I am quickly called to give a urine sample. I go back to the waiting room. I wait a long time, watching women go in and out, congratulat-

ing one another on their upcoming births. I try to ignore them, looking blankly at an ad for Mop & Glo floor cleaner. I am in my dead
space, like when I am stoned, and everything seems far away and out
of reach.

"Nancy?" I hear the nurse ask. She is smiling. "It's good news.
Come on in."

I already know what the news is, and I know what I have to do. She
asks me to sit next to her desk. The metal chair is cold under my butt.

"Well, it's positive," she says, clapping her hands together, then laying them flat on top of her paperwork.

"Positive?" I say. "Positive as in. . . ."

"Yes, you're pregnant." I look down at her perfectly rounded fingernails and gold wedding set, on her left hand. A chill runs fast from
underneath me up to my head and out each strand of hair. It makes
me shudder. She lifts her hands off the paper, looks at it again, then
speaks softly. "Oh, is that not good news?"

"No" is all I can say.

"Would you like to meet with the doctor, then? I can send you right
into a room to wait for him."

The doctor's office has no windows, no sunlight, just shelves of
medical books and a desk full of papers that lie under sample boxes
of pre-natal vitamins. He walks in, taller and older than I thought he
would be. He doesn't smile as he sits down.

"Is this pregnancy unexpected?" he asks.

I stare at his brown-checkered tie. "Yes."

He leans into me from across the desk, his hands politely folded.
"Would you like to talk about options, or do you have your mind already set?"

I lean back into the wide wooden slatted chair. "Yes, it's set. I'm
sorry."

He doesn't ask again.

21

I'm Not Ready

It is the night before my appointment. As fate would have it, I am not home, but house-sitting with a friend at her sister's place. It is late, and my friend has gone to bed in the master bedroom. I am in the spare room, at the other end of the house, with a blanket pressed over my quivering lips. I cry for a long time, pleading for forgiveness.

Then I write my son a letter.

"I am naming you Michael. I just know you are a boy. I can feel it. I wish things could be different, but we have no one to help us, and it would be a horrible life for you if you come to me now. If I am gifted with children at some other time, I pray you will watch over and keep them safe. My baby, Michael, I love you. Please forgive me. I will think of you every day of my life, and look forward to the day we are reunited in another dimension. And I will hate myself forever for what I am about to do."

I hold the letter to my heart, my right hand to my abdomen. My pillow soaks with tears. Eventually, I fall asleep.

In the morning I am quiet until I hear my friend leave for work. I prop myself up on the bed pillows, read Michael's letter out loud, lay my salty kiss to the print, and rip it up. Then I dress in my friend's clothes and wait at the front door for Bobby's Camaro to pull up.

On the way to the doctor's, we are silent. My heart pulsates in my throat like hands strangling me of breath I don't deserve. In the office, just before I walk down the hall with the nurse, Bobby puts one hundred dollars cash in my hand. He hugs me. "I want to see you smiling when you come out," he says.

In the procedure room, I lie down on the table. The paper crinkles underneath me. There are small, blue diamonds on my white, johnny. I am freezing cold, covered in chill bumps. My shoulders are at my ears, and my head is vibrating in a nod.

The doctor rolls his stool closer. "Put your feet up in the stirrups, Nancy, and slide to the end, please." He adjusts the overhead lamp to my crotch. "You will feel some pressure."

His face disappears. I see only the white sheet draped up over my knees. At my right shoulder are two large, clear glass bottles with tubes running out the top, like a high school biology experiment. There is a sting as the other end of the tubing inserts up into me. I gasp for breath. My forehead breaks with sweat.

"Wait, wait, no, I'm not ready." I slide my butt away from him. I grip at the sides of the table. The nurse at my left offers her hand. I squeeze tightly. "Okay. Just get it over with. Oh God." And before I can turn away I see part of me being sucked up the tubes and into the jars. Red blood, the color of sin. Like siphoning precious gasoline from a junk car. You stupid, stupid girl. You don't deserve to live. You worthless good-for-nothin piece of shit. You'll never amount to a damn thing.

Bobby's high school class ring, with the blue stone, and pink yarn wrapped to the band, is tight on my finger. My thumb presses so hard against the raised lettering I will be able to read CLASS OF '71 on my skin when it's over.

I don't remember how long it took or what was said between the doctor and me, just that when I come back out to the waiting room, Bobby is reading a magazine and doesn't stand up until it's time to leave. I stand in front of the office window, shaking violently. Globs of bloody pus balls roll out my vagina. I pass the one hundred dollars to the receptionist. She says thank you. I say thank you. What an odd thing. I don't mean that at all.

22

Scarlet Shame

Bobby holds the Camaro door as I lower myself into the passenger seat. My legs are like rubber. We drive from the doctor's office to the corner market, just down the street. "I'll wait for you here," he says as he leans back in the bucket seat and lets it swallow him up.

I weakly pull my feet up over three worn, gray-painted steps, then grab for the front door handle. I stand just inside the store entrance for what seems like minutes. There are four aisles. Every product looks the same as the one next to it. I finally see a display of toothpaste and start down that row. Sanitary pads. Why didn't I think of that before the appointment? I take one box from the shelf and scuff back toward the register.

The clerk watches me. He nods. "Is that it?"

I nod back. One hip leans against the counter. One knee lets go for just a second. I watch the man put the box into a paper bag. I hand him money.

He looks at me. "Yup," he mumbles.

I nod again. My eyes are swollen with guilt. My body oozes shame. This brief moment in time, shared with a stranger, it scorches my soul like a hot iron singeing a scarlet letter *A* for abortion.

It takes thirty minutes to drive from Brunswick, across the bridge to Woolwich, and down Chop Point. We leave the Camaro on the side of the road and break a path through the woods. I haven't walked it since I was a little girl. But I still remember the land-marks that Nanny taught me. A half mile of overgrown brush and thick tree branches bungee back at my face as Bobby and I tunnel into it. On my butt, I slide down the rock ledge I am too weak to jump from.

When we reach the camp, I am doubled over with pain. In the outhouse I pull down my jeans. The pad is heavy-soaked. I let it drop with my pants to the rotting floorboards. I sit down and bleed clumps of flaming discharge to the earth. On the wall is a damp roll of toilet paper that has been chewed on by an animal. I wad up a handful, lie down over my trembling legs, and cry.

Inside the camp, spiders flee thick, dusty webs as Bobby unfolds the Murphy bed out of the wall. Then he covers the 1940s oilcloth mattress with a scratchy green army blanket and tells me to lie down. All night, he holds me as I shake and cry.

Through the dark hours of that summer night in 1973, I relive my scarlet shame like it is caught on a film reel endlessly rolling over and over.

23

Someday

WHEN THE MORNING light comes, we slowly make our way back out through the woods to the car.

The road to Popham is long today. Between the seats of the Camaro, next to the stick shift, is a green rubber monster that fits on top of a pencil. His arms wave out the sides of his head and bounce up and down as we drive. I watch it for a long time.

Bobby reaches for my knee. "Pretty little girl? You okay?"

I shift my eyes out the side window and sink lower into the seat. I am cried out.

When we reach the state park, it is so early there are no other cars there. As we walk through the dunes, my bare feet scrape and catch on the splintered boards of the walkway. I never noticed they were coming apart until now. Sitting in the cold morning sand, I feel my toes clench the loose grains. I dig down as far as I can, until the hard-packed earth stops me. Overhead, a gray ceiling of storm clouds holds back their tears. Far in the distance, the sun makes silver blade-like streaks in the sky. Lethargic waves wash up dirty with black silt. They break sluggish and repetitive at the shoreline, like a fading heartbeat. Tiny black-footed birds run back and forth with the surf, repeating the same path like wind-up toys.

I am numb and vacant, rocking back and forth with my knees to my chest. I tell myself there was never a baby. It was just a mass of blood and goop.

Bobby reaches around me and shifts closer. There are tears welling up in his brown eyes. "What can I do, Nance?"

Faint beach-rose sweetness floats just out of reach. "Promise me," I say. "That someday we will have other children together?"

"Yes. Someday we will." He fingers the sand.

We sit at the edge of the dunes for hours. I think about how "someday" has to be with Bobby. How we would have boys with his curly hair and my long legs. How we would keep the secret forever, and how secrets keep you locked to others when nothing else does.

24

The Route

It's Saturday morning, almost ten o'clock. I am still in bed, curled up inside my long nightgown with my feet wound to the flannel hem and locked together. Stickiness has glued my inner thighs. My hips hurt from holding one position for hours. I wish I were dead.

Mumma and Tommy are fighting at the front door. His cigarette smoke creeps away from him and up the yellowed walls of the staircase. "Where the hell were you last night? Can't you get yourself out of high school before gettin into that stuff?"

The door slams. Mumma yells at it. "Now who the hell's gettin him into that mess a booze?" The tires of Tommy's red truck peel out, and he is gone.

My brother is gone most of the time. Drinking and driving I guess, I don't know where. The day Daddy brought that truck home for Tommy, the back end was filled with cases of beer. He stood my brother next to it and told him he could have the truck and the beer too, if he promised to stop drinking hard liquor. But Tommy drank whatever he could get. It was all the same to him.

When I come downstairs Mumma is still standing in the hall looking out the front-door window. Both hands are on her hips. "Well, I don't know where the hell your father is. He left on a service call hours ago. I wish to Christ people would leave him alone." The green carpet under her feet is so stained from where Daddy has scuffed years of furnace soot, Mumma has given up on it. "He was out last night until the wee hours of the mornin," she raves. "And didn't even charge them. I was some mad now let me tell you."

I don't care where he is as long as he's not here. With a pillow and blanket I am on my way down the cellar stairs to the dock in my bathing suit.

"Now where are you goin, Nancy? Isn't it about time you get out and look for a job? I'm embarrassed to death for what Lilly and Ike are thinkin, watchin you layin around in the sun, and comin in all hours of the night. What's the matter with you? You're good for nothin, that's what's wrong. Get out and get a job."

I have a job. It's to stay as far away from my body as possible.

EACH swell of tide rocks the float up and down. The sun nudges at my nearly naked body lying across it. One roll into the swift river, that's all it would take. It could be very peaceful, sinking down into the water and looking up at the sun's rays following me on a drop to final darkness. Seagulls soar freely overhead. I am with them, swooping and gliding on the wind. I am nameless, lost with others that all look the same.

Nanny waves at me through her picture window. Tonight she will come to my house. We will eat beans and hot dogs and watch Lawrence Welk. She will use her church voice to sing "Rock of Ages" and I will memorize every dance step Bobby and Cissy make. For a while I will forget how much I hate myself. But that will end when she goes back home. I will get into my 1969 red convertible Mustang, and alone I will drive to Popham Beach, my tires wearing bald from the hundreds of trips I've made. Driving with one knee, I will toke a joint, smoke a cig, chug a beer, and change radio stations until I find something I can sing loud to.

In the fort parking lot, another beer can will hiss at me as I pull the aluminum ring. Bitter foam again will lick at my lips, ashes burning long and gray at the end of my cigarette. With my head laid back, I will watch stars turn on across the night sky, a few clouds blowing shadowy across the moon. Waves hit the shore like rhythmic nighttime snoring. The salt air feels fresh on my cheeks, like it's alive with a million tiny messages, all telling me to hang on.

And then the next night I will do it again. Into the Mustang, shoes off, radio on, light joint, light cigarette, buy beer, ride the route. Washington Street, through town, down Weeks Street past Bobby's house.

Endless until death or marriage.

25

Without a Map

BOBBY HAS BEEN home from the University of Maine at Orono since flunking out two semesters ago. Now that summer is over, his parents have sent him back for another try at a business degree and finding a nice Jewish girl. On Friday nights, my Mustang rattles at 90 when I drive the three hours north on wooded highways to see him. Big rigs loaded with logs and potatoes flash their lights, directing my cut and weave. The smell of diesel fuel makes me nauseous.

At Sigma Phi Epsilon on Fraternity Row, Bobby's room is small. Nailed to a wall of Cape Cod shingles is a homemade wooden single bed frame that feels like a coffin when we lie there. One night I turn over so hard against the boards, it takes the skin right off my kneecap, and my blood stains his sheet. In the corner, wedged in-between the windowsill and closet, is a piece of board just wide enough for a typewriter. On Saturdays, when I type Bobby's papers, he tells me I am much faster than he is. It's the only thing I learned in high school, to keep my fingers on the home row and do what's expected while looking away.

In his room one afternoon, Bobby and I fight so hard I land up against the wall. On the other side, in the next room, books fall off a shelf and onto that boy's typewriter. Bobby gets so mad, he punches a hole in the wall and plaster pieces fall onto the brown shag carpeting.

Like a tick, I have attached myself to Bobby. I am a worthless, dying shell without him, playing the game of come-here-please-love-me, get-away-from-me, I-don't-deserve-to-be-loved. Want me, need me, validate me. It is constant and smothering, played out in a fog of strobe lights, weed, and Harvey Wallbangers.

By the following September, I have been accepted into the two-year mental health technology program at the University of Maine and move into a co-ed dormitory on the Bangor campus, just a few miles from Bobby. The first term I make the dean's list, which is easier than making friends. I cry so much, my roommate moves out, and two girls leave a note on my door saying I am as worthless as a paperweight. Nanny writes weekly. Mumma sends prune juice.

My second year, I live by myself in the center of downtown Orono in a brick building that looks like a brothel from a hundred years past. In my second-floor, back apartment, the braided carpet is so packed and heavy with dirt, I roll it up, drag it into the outer hallway, and stuff it into a utility closet. Three kids live on my floor, but the only time I dare talk to them is when I get their mail by mistake.

With Bobby busy at studying and fraternity things, I wait in my apartment for him to call. "Jesus, Nance. I've got things to do. I can't be running over there with you every night."

Slumped into the couch, I watch my cigarette smoke move like a Slinky across the room to the black-and-white television I have brought from home. Static snow crackles from the one local Bangor channel I get. There is a sheet of tinfoil crimped to the top of the antenna. Every day it loosens and slips to the bottom. Every night I re-crimp it to the top. Over it hangs a paint-by-number clipper ship being overcome by a dark, stormy sea. I still remember the smell of paint and the way Daddy got real close to the cardboard with his brush when he painted it.

Behind the couch, in the kitchenette, I turn off the whistling tea-kettle and pour boiling water into a burnt-orange coffee mug. Instant cream-of-chicken soup smells buttery as I stir out the dry clumps, a Wonder Bread and bologna sandwich in my other hand. I take a bite, then lay it down and open a beer. Six cans later, suds are rolling up my throat like bubbles in a lava lamp.

In the bedroom, pulled up beside me on the bed, is a metal waste-basket. Just before puking into it, I gather my ironed, straight hair and twist flip it back under the neck of my shirt. The sound of people laughing and stamping up the outside staircase at my bedroom window is a comfort. I pretend they are my friends as I drift into nauseated sleep.

In the Orono campus library, there is a sense of respect when students quiet their voices, remove their hats, and pass through the entryway. In the high-ceilinged great room, people sit at long wooden tables in the glow of small lamps. Bobby is here to do research. I am here to people watch. I study groups of girls with shiny hair, polished and pretty, looking grown-up and confident. I imagine they are preparing for success in business and finance, but instead will marry important men.

Again, today, I see the shy girl who always arrives alone. Her long hair is dry and frizzy, brown like compost mulch. It falls messy across her big round glasses. I watch her small, precise steps map erratically through the room, always to the same corner chair. She looks frail as her head bows low to her work. I can't take my eyes off her, and even though she never looks at me, I can feel her energy call out a desperate cry for help. One day she is not there. We hear she took a flashlight, a science text-book, a bottle of wine, and climbed into an abandoned refrigerator behind her dorm. It will haunt me for decades, wondering what it was that took her very last hope away and led her to the cramped coffin where the white walls of a kitchen appliance would be her last sight.

26

Food for Thought

It is the spring of 1976, when Bobby and I both graduate from Orono and go back home to live with our parents. On Christmas Eve, Bobby asks me to marry him. Actually, he never says those words. He hands me a box. I pull out the ring. He tells me not to lose it. And a lump instantly forms in my throat, like I have swallowed a whole matzo ball.

"You marry her and we will no longer be part of your life," his parents warn. They change their minds after Bobby tells them I have been studying Judaism and plan to convert.

Tonight I am at the home of my in-laws-to-be. The house is full of people. Bobby's father has invited all the relatives, and his mother has emptied out the freezer. Half-thawed noodle kugel and runny spaghetti casserole sit in bent tinfoil, baking pans on top of the stove. His mother shovels a spatula into the kugel and jerks it quickly onto plates. I am sitting in a dining room chair that has been pulled to a corner of the living room. A plate of food balances on my lap. A cousin's wife bends down to hug me. "We are so happy for you and Robert." She smiles sweetly. I say thank you and smile with my lips down over my teeth. They all know my parents. Both our families are merchants in town. I keep my eyes on my plate, smile when I need to, and stay to myself. I don't want my new family to know I'm good-for-nothin and will never amount to a damn thing.

It is the middle of May, two weeks before the wedding. Today Bobby's aunt, the matriarch of the family, is hosting a tea for me in her home.

There are crystal bowls of nuts and candies, and the dining room table is covered with china plates of tiny sandwiches and sweets, and in the middle is a decorated cake with fancy blue-and-white icing. All the women of the synagogue are here. An older woman with a white-hair bun takes my hands and shakes them like she is pumping water. "We are so pleased you are joining the sisterhood, Nancy."

Two little ladies bent over with dowager humps have brought me gifts of pewter candlesticks and a linen tablecloth. There are packages wrapped in shiny white paper holding silver bowls and china tea sets. Bobby's mother has brought a Hanukkah menorah. "Use it well," she says, and gives me an awkward hug.

Mumma and Nanny stand next to me in the dining room. All three of us have corsages of pink tea roses pinned to the left shoulder of our dresses. Nanny is beautiful. A double strand of pearls lays over a pink chiffon dress she has made herself. Mumma is nervous. Her teacup rattles on the saucer as she shakes hands with the ladies and they congratulate her. Mumma nods and smiles with one side of her mouth lifted higher than the other, the way she does when she's not really listening.

Later, when we get home, Mumma will tell Daddy all about it, and her hand will swipe across her face like she's batting at flies. "Ya know those Jews have a lot of money, don't ya? Bobby's family must be loaded."

My father will look up from his reading at the end of the couch. His soot-stained fingernails will scratch at his day-old-whiskered chin, the sound that precedes a throat-clearing, and I will look away.

27

What's Left Behind

IN THE MIKVEH room at Beth Abraham Synagogue in Auburn, the walls look wet to the touch. There is a moldy smell, as if those who have been here left something behind that stayed unnoticed. The water is cool as I step down into the four-foot deep tub. Chill pimples rise up my body and out my naked arm laying atop the water. The rabbi's voice rolls deep like a trained baritone as he chants conversion blessings. I feel his hand on top of my head, gently pushing me under the water. It feels like I am under a long time, listening to his muffled tone and feeling embarrassed that I am about to step out with water running down over my bathing suit and naked legs. Then I am above the surface, choking and coughing up what I inhaled. The rabbi raises his volume. I look over at Mumma, sitting in a folding chair beside the tank of water. Her mouth is twitching like she needs to say something. Daddy is sitting next to her with an odd half smile, his eyes darting everywhere but at me. I am ashamed, hot and cold all at once, grabbing for a towel and wondering why the hell I asked them to be here and witness this.

The rabbi hands me a certificate. "Nahannah. The children of Israel welcome you."

Bobby is sitting next to Mumma with his fingers locked together. I wait for him to stand up and say something, but he doesn't. I thank the rabbi and get dressed. That's it, I think, as I pull my dress down over my head. I am officially an obedient Jewish wife. I read the books, know how to keep kosher, and celebrate holidays. I promised to raise our children in the faith. Done deal.

My father drives us home. I sit in the backseat with one elbow dug into the arm-rest, looking between the rows of cookie-cutter houses and at the back of his bald head. None of us have much to say.

It is Sunday, May 29, 1977. Today I am marrying Bobby.

In my bedroom I spray flowery Jontue under my ears and on my wrists. My cheeks are blushed and my lips are pink. The hot rollers are out of my hair. Fluffy curls lay on my shoulders. I step into my long white gown and reach back to the zipper. The gown fits tight around me. On top of my bed, I lay down my veil and smooth it out under the weight of my shaking hands. I lift it to the crown of my head, dig the plastic combs against my scalp, and gather my skirts in both arms. Then I turn slowly to each corner of my bedroom and say good-bye. The black paint has now been covered up with mint green, and my dolls have been dressed in their best outfits and packed in the attic.

As I sweep past the top of the staircase, one headless nail on the hall banister catches the edge of my dress. It pulls me back and asks me to take one more look at the room I spent twenty-two years in. I untangle the netted skirt and glance again. Yes, I'm all set now. The dresser has been wiped clean, and my bed is made.

Mumma stands at the bottom of the stairs, looking in the mirror and pushing waves into her hair. "All right," she drawls. "I guess we're ready."

I am smiling as I step out the front door. I am going to leave it all behind. I will walk myself down the aisle at Beth Israel Synagogue on Washington Street, and not one yarmulke-wearing person will stand. My voice will be so soft when I say my vows, no one will hear them except Bobby and the rabbi. A few miles away, at the reception hall, Mrs. Kaplan's big gummy pastries and smelly tuna rolls will be served out of bakery boxes because the plates there are not kosher, and my mother will be horrified. Then Bobby and I will drive away, and for the first few minutes there will be a silent freedom.

28

Grateful

THE NIGHT I conceived, I knew in that moment it was true. The flowers on our bedroom wall were so lovely, they bloomed right out of the paper and reached toward me. The scent of lavender lifted off the delicate pool of candle wax and filled the room like it never had before. As I smiled, the flame grew taller, and I knew my life was about to change. I would have someone to love and be loved by, forever.

Eight months have passed since our May wedding. It's dinner-time on a dark, chilly January night. I am sitting outside my in-laws' appliance store waiting for Bobby to get out of work. The car idles, the exhaust spitting bullet pops. A car rides by slowly and beeps. My wet breath frosts the window as I look quickly to see who it is. My stomach flip-flops. Through the plate-glass store windows, I can see Bobby finishing with his last customer. He grabs his coat from the office, squeezes down the narrow aisle of new washers and dryers and broken television sets waiting to be fixed. My throat is thick. It begins to close up as I swallow and rehearse what I will say. My fingers are still tight to the steering wheel when Bobby and a cold blast of winter blow into the passenger seat. I watch him tap the snow off his boots, then swing them into the car.

He looks at me. "How did your doctor's appointment go?" His full lower lip hangs separate from the top one, his mouth waiting to respond.

"It went beautifully." I sit up tall and shift into drive. "We're going to have a baby."

He sinks down into the seat, his head pressing hard against the back of it. Vapor works out his mouth and smokes to the wind-shield. "Oh, great, Nance. You know we can't afford that." His mouth purses and his lower lip disappears. I watch a marble shape roll up and down his jawbone as he tenses and grits his teeth. I smile all the way home. It's too dark to see Bobby's face, but I am pretty sure he isn't.

By the time we've finished dinner, Bobby is not as upset. The one-mile ride to my parents' house feels shorter than usual. As we get to the top of the hill, I am glad to see that Daddy's car is gone. The front doorbell has been painted over so many times, it rarely works, but this time as my thumb presses, it rings so loud the back of my neck vibrates. Mumma is coming out of the kitchen wiping her hands on a dish towel as we walk through the hall and into the living room.

"Well, what are you two doin up here?" She looks at us hard, with her brows pinched and a questioning curve to her dry lips.

I am so nervous, I feel a gut urge to run out across the street and up into the woods. "We've got something to tell you."

She slings the towel up over her shoulder. "Oh?" She sits at the kitchen table next to the trash compactor.

My words stumble and my face flashes hot, like I'm about to make a sinful confession. "Well, I've never had to tell you this before." I look at Bobby. He sits on the arm of the chair next to the bathroom door. "I'm going to have a baby."

"You're pregnant?" The word pulls long out of her mouth, like she swallowed something nasty. A scene bursts to memory of when Mumma said how disgusting it was that the clerk at Burgess Market was still working, and women shouldn't be seen out like that. "'She should be home for God sake, and not out pregnant.'"

Mumma's left hand cups the edge of the kitchen table, and her arm lies heavy, like she's anchoring it to the floor. I don't remember anything else of the conversation, except Mumma's foot was swinging hard with one leg crossed over the other when she talked about Daddy. "Yup, well, great. That's just great. I'll have to tell your father when he gets home."

When she said it, I could feel my armpits tingle, and I had to pee, scared like I'd done something wrong and I was going to get it when Daddy got home. No, not this time, I think. I will not allow you to shame me. No one will ever take this happiness away from me. Not Bobby and certainly not my mother. Nothing in the world will ever be as important to me as my babies, and Bobby will never be first again.

29

It's a Boy

Most days I go for a walk up and down Washington Street, and when I do people smile at me. My son is on his way. It's a boy, I just know it.

The world is so beautiful. I never noticed that before.

Now that the baby is almost here, Mumma seems different. Sometimes we go shopping together. From the department store shelf, she pulls blankets and sheets and soft pretty things that fill up her arms. "Babies need lots of things, you know," she says and winks one blue eye. I am transported to Sebago Lake, hear her whistling, see the sun on her beautiful face.

Many afternoons she leaves work early, picks Nanny up, and they come to my house. We drink hot Red Rose tea with Nanny's sweet, molasses cookies. "I just can't wait to get my hands on that darlin baby," Nanny says, laying her head over to one shoulder and hugging her arms across the front of her purple-figured blouse.

In the nursery, Mumma teaches me how to fold a diaper three different ways. Then she winds up the mobile over the crib, and we all listen to the lullaby and watch the yellow lambs go round. Even if Mumma can't love me, surely she will love my baby.

Mumma didn't want to go on vacation up north to Moosehead Lake with Daddy. I told her I knew I would be fine at least until July 27, two weeks before my due date. She made me promise to call, and they would drive right back to Bath. My mother hugged me tight that day and said she would miss me. She didn't even seem to care if I messed her hair up when I pressed my cheek to her curls.

For ten hours at the hospital, I wondered if Mumma would arrive before the baby did. After a nurse came in and whispered in my ear that Mumma was in the waiting room, I gave one last push, and that's when Joshua arrived. It was 10:24, the morning of July 27, 1978. Mumma said he was the most beautiful baby she had ever seen, with full pink cheeks and my long legs.

At home in the nursery, I rocked my baby and sang him to sleep, my fingers making tunnels in his soft curls. Wispy ends vacuumed up my nose. That baby smell, a combination of Johnson's baby shampoo and something you just can't describe, but I'm sure if bottled, would solve problems and end wars. As the months went by, we walked miles with the denim umbrella stroller. We did it until the wheels wore down. When the family came for dinners, I cooked all day and decorated the house. Nanny danced in the living room holding both Josh's hands, then she picked him up and breathed him right into her with her kisses. Mumma clapped to the music and danced beside them. Bobby's parents and aunt were there too, and Tommy, if he wasn't drunk.

WHEN Joshua turned two, I was pregnant again. Bobby and I prayed for another son, the only thing we had ever agreed on.

30

Ice and Fire

IT WAS THE end of December, just after Christmas, the morning Bobby's father died. The road between our house and the hospital was icy from an overnight snowstorm. Even the sand trucks had not been out yet. As we drove to the emergency room, Bobby's eyes were huge, his breath forceful, and he didn't speak until we got there. Bobby's mother sat alone in the waiting room. There were no tears, only shock. Bobby's father lay lifeless under a white sheet, just steps away. I watched Bobby pull the sheet off his father's face, then cry like I had never seen before, with his head against the gurney and his knees buckling beneath it. My mother-in-law said someone should call the rabbi, but I don't remember what happened after that, just that when we got outside, Bobby was carrying his dad's red sneakers, and against the white snow, they glowed like fire.

THE Beth Israel Synagogue is packed full from the second row back. Bobby and I are in the front row with his mother and sister. Just as the rabbi is ready to start the service, I see Bobby's old, patriarchal uncle limping fast up the center aisle. He bends slightly to me.

"You," he says, pointing down at me. "Go sit over there." He points to the empty front pew at the opposite side of the congregation. Then, leaning close to Bobby's mother, he speaks fast with tongue ticks. "She's not a born Jew. She has to sit somewhere else." I am the mother of Robert's son. Surely he can't be serious. But he says it again. "Go sit over there."

He steps back, motioning me up and across the room. I pull to my feet and stand still for a moment, sure that Bobby or his mother will say something. But they don't. I walk to the other side in front of two hundred sets of eyes, my hands across five months of roundness growing under my brown plaid jumper, and sit alone.

When the service is over, we drive forty minutes to the Portland synagogue for another service and burial in the Jewish cemetery. Once again, Bobby and I, his mother and sister, settle into the front pew. Again, the old uncle hurries up to us. He leans into me and speaks sharply. "Go to the back. You can't sit here."

This time I will not conform, stand again, and walk away. I feel a hand lightly wrap around my wrist. Bobby's mother is stretched across Bobby and stares heated at the uncle. "She is Robert's wife and she will sit with us." The old man sputters something in Yiddish and limps back to his pew. My mother-in-law smiles at me, with the corners of her mouth quivering, and I smile back.

Later, when we arrive at my mother-in-law's house, we find it filled with people. The two little ladies with dowager humps are standing hand in hand. "Oh, Nancy," the first one says with coffee cake crumbs stuck to her chin. The second one speaks. "The community will miss him so." I thank them and inch my way through the crowd and into the kitchen. Two women from the sisterhood are taking covered dishes out of the oven, on their way to the dining room table. I stand alone next to the warm stove, hoping it will calm my fuming anger toward the uncle.

Not knowing I am there, he walks into the room. He is surprised to see me, takes a half step back, balancing a plate of food , then looks to the floor and rumbles his throat. "Oh, ah, is there anything I can do for you?"

I step closer to him. Steam rises off a coffee percolator on the counter beside me. "Yes, there is. Don't ever speak to me that way again. I am part of this family, and I will not allow you to make me feel that I don't belong." He mumbles and backs away as Mumma, Nanny, and the lady with the white-hair bun come into the kitchen.

I sit down at the table. The lady lays one hand on my arm, a teacup rattles on a saucer in the other. "You already have a boy, so this time you are having a girl, I suspect."

"I don't think it's a girl," I say. Gas rolls up my chest.

Mumma speaks quickly and smiles with half her mouth. Her eyes dart between the woman and me. "I think what she meant, Nancy, is we're all sure you want a girl who you can dress up and curl her hair. You know, like I enjoyed you?"

I lay both my hands over my belly. My jaw is tense. I can feel fire coming out my eyes. "No, Mumma, I don't."

Nanny's eyes sparkle at me. She twists purple beads between her fingers, then lets them fall down across her purple cardigan sweater. "I bet someday you'll have a granddaughter and the two of you will have fun like we've had." Nanny always says the perfect thing.

31

Deliver Me

DADDY SITS AT the back of the labor room with a camera resting in his lap. Mumma is at my side, leaning toward me with her arms folded over the top of her pocketbook. "Not long now and Josh may have a little sister." She looks back at Daddy and cheers with one fist in the air.

Contractions squeeze and push at my rectum. A monitor beeps beside me. "It's not a girl, Mumma. I know it's not." I lay my head back onto the pillows. My hands grip at the side rails. Not a girl, I think, not a girl like me.

In the delivery room, Bobby pulls hair up off my forehead and wipes it with a cool cloth. Then he takes my hand and holds on tight, like he won't let go until it's over. "You're doing great," he says, kissing my fingers. "I'm so proud of you. Not much longer now. Take in a breath. Now let it out. Only a few more. You're almost there. Look up at the light. Can you see it?"

At the end of the table the light is bright, shining off a mirror angled at arrival. With a last breath and one smooth exhale, the baby slips through into waiting hands.

"It's a boy," the doctor says, and pulls him up by the feet. I hear his first cry. My eyes pinch tight shut. Tears run down the side of my cheeks and into my ears. I have disappointed her. If I had died on the table, it would have been easier than telling her it's another boy.

I hear Bobby's voice. It sounds far away. "Look at him, Nance. Open your eyes." The doctor lays Jason on my chest. I kiss his perfect face. His eyes blink to the glaring light, and he is swept from me to the nursery.

I am wheeled to my room and wait anxiously for Mumma to appear. Anticipation gnaws at my raw insides, like I am waiting for a final test score. Finally, she pushes my door open and steps just inside the room, with one hand still attached to the door.

"Did you see him, Mumma? Isn't he beautiful?"

"Yup. Well, I see the sign here on the door. Mother Nursin." The two words slide mean from her mouth. "So I guess we're goin home now."

"You're going home?"

"Well, we're tired you know, Nancy. We've been waitin here a long time for God sake."

She leaves me abandoned and punished. Undeserving and cheated of her acceptance. I pull the covers to my face and cry with heaving wails. I cry for a long time with my eyes sealed, like I never want them to open again. I cry so hard, I go away.

Hands grab at my upper arms. I don't answer the nurse who calls my name. She doesn't let go. "Nancy, you have a beautiful baby son who needs you. There is a baby down the hall who is very ill and won't make it. You pull yourself together and be grateful your baby is healthy. You have a long, blessed life ahead of you." When I open my eyes she is not there. I can still feel her fingers dug into my flesh.

Monday, May 4, 1981, 7:33 in the morning, the moment of Jason's birth. Nothing could have been sweeter, and I missed it because I allowed the fear of Mumma's words and her not loving me to steal it away.

Alone with my precious baby in our hospital room, I hold Jason warm in my arms. I run my finger around the perfect curve of his ear, then to his chin, so much like mine. I kiss his nose. I study his fingers and press my cheek to his. "I love you, my blessing from heaven. I wanted you, always wanted you. I'm going to be the best mother I can. I will protect you, and teach you, and I know that not every day will be easy, but we'll figure it out together. Your brother is waiting to spend his whole life as your best friend, and it will be amazing."

TWENTY-SEVEN years will go by before I tell my mother how much she hurt me that day. And she will laugh.

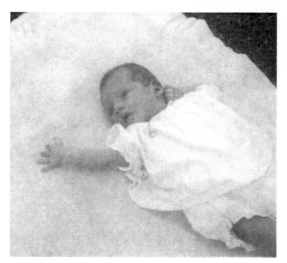

Baby Debbie. Foster home. Waterville, Maine.
Summer 1955. Wearing Mother's locket.

With my mother, Elizabeth. She came to see me several times before I
was adopted.

Mumma at home. Bath, Maine. Before the staircase railing showed signs of trauma.

Daddy. Looking like all is well. It wasn't.

Baby Nancy with Nanny. Our back yards connected along the Kennebec River.

Path to Nanny's Merry-
meeting camp. The water
was not as polluted there
as it was at home.

Sebago Lake. Summer moments in time when I believed
Mumma was the most beautiful lady in all of Maine.

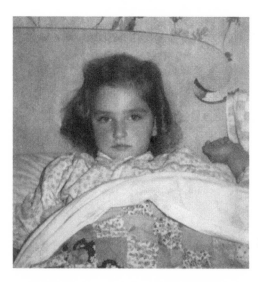

My bed 1961.
Where dolls lined
up like guards.

The man I called
Daddy. Too creepy
for words.

Old Nanny's house. Just down the hill from us. In the 1980's it will
become Tommy's home.

Nancy and Tommy. Dressed for church. Behind us, Nanny's little
house on the shore.

Tommy's 5th birthday.
Lobsters in our kitchen.
December 1961.

Looking out our
front door. Up the
hill. Where pitch
pine arms scooped
me up to safety.

Christmas 1965. Mumma, Daddy, Nancy, Tommy, Nanny. The only early
photo of all of us.

Looking down the hill to the bus stop.

Daddy's shop. Where the body hung against blood colored bricks for the whole city of Bath to see.

Tommy in front of our house. Mumma's yellow, tar stained Cadillac lined up to the lilac bushes.

Jazz Dance. It was the dance and nature that saved me.

My father's spot on the couch. In voyeuristic view of the bathroom door.

Fort
Popham.

High school
graduation night.

With Bobby. Summer 1973.

Wedding Tea. Mumma nervously rattled the teacup on its saucer.

Wedding Day. May 1977. I'm going to leave it all behind.

Waiting for baby. Summer 1978.

Baby Joshua.
Beginning the
long and
winding road.

Cookies with Joshua.
Curled around the
sharpest corners of my
truth, were perfect life
moments.

Baby Jason 1981. Loving
my babies. It was when I
saw Mumma at her best.

air

32

Little Wanderer

WITH JASON AND I snuggled to each other in the soft light of a Winnie-the-Pooh lamp, the rocking chair moves front and back. With his tiny hand locked to my finger and chocolate-brown eyes blinking softly to sleep, my heart beats in rhythm with our lullaby. I can hear Bobby reading *Make Way for Ducklings* in Joshua's room next door. Nothing could ever be more wonderful than this.

But there are questions long asked seeping their way to the surface, spilling over in my mind like mother's milk from the breast. Did I gaze up into my birth mother's face during our brief time together? Did she hold me tight while searching her soul and praying that she had made the right decision? Was there a moment that she wished to steal me away and love me forever? And had she regretted her choice after it was too late? How could she not remember? Wouldn't she want to know how I turned out? Or if she were to meet me on the street and recognize my twenty-six-year-old face so like her own from years gone by, would she just keep walking?

ON my kitchen counter lies an open three-ring notebook stuffed with wrinkled pages that have been stapled and written on in different-colored inks. It was seven years ago, in college, that I began collecting magazine articles and pages ripped from phone booths across Maine and the Boston area. Angled from each corner of the page are pencil scribblings from telephone conversations. The New England Home for Little Wanderers, Bath Court House, John Vorman, attorney-at-law, State of Maine Vital Statistics. As I study each page, pieces of yellowed Scotch tape and old newspaper clippings fall to the floor and slide under the kitchen stool.

One sheet of paper shakes in my hands as I begin to read again, a response to my inquiry from the adoption agency.

December 12, 1977

Dear Nancy,

I was very interested in the information that you inquired about with questions regarding background knowledge of your natural parents. I shall answer all that I can to the best of my ability.

The national origins of your birth mother were English and Scotch. That of your birth father was French. The religion of your mother was Protestant, and your father was Catholic. At the time of your birth, both sets of grandparents were still living.

There were no complications at the time of your birth, which occurred at 9:20 A.M. on May 26, 1955. Your birth weight was seven pounds, six and a half ounces. Your length was twenty-one and a half inches.

Because marriage was not a serious possibility, and due to your mother's conscientiousness of her age and financial status in life, she felt it was the best decision for herself and her child to surrender for adoption. Your mother's family reached out to this agency for help in planning for the future.

Your mother was a Maine native. At the time of your birth, she was twenty-two and in her first year of college in Boston. She was described as a very intelligent, poised young lady with a great deal of stability. She was very much thought of by her family, as well as the agency staff who worked with her. Your father was twenty-five, a high school graduate, and described as an excellent worker.

The reason for your birth taking place in Boston was due to the fact that your mother entered a maternity home there to await your delivery. It seemed best to all those involved. Immediately after your birth, both of you came back to Maine, she to her parents' home, and you into temporary foster care.

We do not have natural parents coming back in search of their children. Once they have decided to surrender to the agency for adoption, they don't return, since this is their own decision arrived at without pressure. We do have some natural mothers writing to hear about how the placement is going during the first year after surrender. We rarely hear from them following that.

The adoption agency does their best to match a child with an adoptive couple. At the time of the placement we seek to share any and all general information on the natural parents of the child, with the adoptive couple. In their excitement, often this material is not remembered. We have in the last few years been placing this information in writing for them to share with their child at a later date.

As you may know, by Maine law, we are prohibited from giving out identifying data. Maine law seeks to protect the privacy of the natural parents.

I trust that this information will be of help to you and will satisfy your questions.

Sincerely yours,
Harland Turner, Director

It was two weeks after receiving that letter, four years ago, that I walked through the front door of the New England Home for Little Wanderers in Waterville, Maine, looking for more answers.

Sitting in the director's office that day, I tried to imagine what my life would have been like if my mother had made a split-second decision and hurried away with me still snug inside her. And I wondered if the day they put me in Mumma's arms she thought of me as a sinful sex mistake, and if Daddy passed them a check and said thanks. The director patted my back and apologized. "I wish I could tell you more. You might want to try the state cross-match program for adoptees and birth parents in Augusta. I have really done all I can."

That afternoon, I listened as the Vital Statistics woman tapped the eraser end of her pencil against a thick directory. "Probate court records relating to any adoption decreed after August of 1953 have been sealed and deemed confidential," she said with no emotion. Her office smelled like mimeograph ink and musty books. My eyes began to water as I leaned over the long wooden counter and filled out an application. "We'll let you know if your mother applies," she said, then gathered up my papers and cracked the bottom edge sharply on the counter.

The can of worms had been opened, and no one knew it but Bobby and me.

33

Luck Be a Lady

FINGERNAILS DIG INTO my clenched palm as I dial the number of the state office. Mumma's voice screams from the back of my head, "For God sake, Nancy, there must be somethin wrong with you. Just forget about it." Jason nurses peacefully in the bend of my arm. His coos calm me.

"Vital Statistics, this is Mrs. Levoy. How may I help you?"

I adjust my position on the kitchen stool and speak up. "I am calling about the adoption cross-match program I registered with four years ago."

Her voice is polite. "I'm sorry. There was no luck with that program, not one match. I must tell you, the only way to find a birth parent would be to petition the court and have your records opened. Then I can give you a copy of your original birth certificate."

I slump over Jason, remove myself from his sleeping suction, and cuddle him close. "I have tried. I've done everything possible, everything I can think of to find my mother."

Her voice softens. "Sounds like you've come to a brick wall, dear." Her pause is long. "You know, I have worked for the state of Maine for many years, and I am just about to retire. Throughout my career I have talked to hundreds of people just like you in search of a loved one. When I hear the desperation in their voice, it breaks my heart. All the information is right here at my fingertips, and yet because of state law, I am not able to help them."

I lay my cheek to Jason's face and hold him tighter. There is a dryness at the back of my throat I can't swallow past. "Yes, thank you, I understand."

She continues in a hushed tone. "But I told myself, just once before I retire I would do it. I have actually prayed that I be given just the right opportunity. Nancy, you sound like a kind soul. So if you will wait on the phone for a while, I am going to do my best. I'm going to help you."

The kitchen wall phone cord stretches behind me as I lay Jason in the living room playpen and pull a blanket up to his little shoulders. Joshua nibbles Cheez-Its in front of the television. "Come and play. Everything's A-OK," he sings.

My left ear is a cavern of silence with the receiver tightly capped to it. Then I hear papers sifting. Mrs. Levoy clears her throat. "Nancy? I have the name of a woman I believe could be your natural mother. Her name is Elizabeth, and all the criteria matches with your birth date. We have no way of knowing for sure without opening up the sealed file, but from what I have at my disposal, she looks like a good probability."

I cradle the phone to my shoulder and watch a pen bring life to Elizabeth, her birth date, information on her siblings, parents, and, unbelievably, that her mother was born in Bath. I scribble the name of Elizabeth's husband, their telephone number, and their address in Auburn, just down the road from the synagogue where I was converted. She could have been anywhere in the world, but she is less than an hour away. It's her. I can feel it in my gut.

It is Wednesday night, October 21, 1981. Seven o'clock has passed, the time Mrs. Levoy promised to call Elizabeth. I am sitting on the kitchen stool next to the phone. My legs are crossed so tightly, one foot has wound around the other leg like a snake. My right thumbnail is ragged in my teeth. Bobby presses his dark beard to my cheek. "I know you feel incomplete, Nance, like there are a lot of shadows you don't understand." He stands back up. "Good luck." One side of his face scrunches. "I don't know how it's going to set with your parents though."

At eight thirty the phone rings so loud, both hands fly up over my chest and I can't breathe until after the second ring. "Hello?"

Mrs. Levoy's voice rises like notes on a music scale. "Nancy? She's your mother."

"Oh my God. My mother? We found her? What did you say? What did she say?" Tears fall salty in my open laughter.

"I told her I was a private investigator. I asked if she had given birth to a daughter on May 26, 1955, in Boston. I asked her, does the name Deborah Lee mean anything to you? She started to cry. She said to tell you she loved you very much and didn't want to give you up. Not a day has gone by in twenty-six years that she hasn't thought of you. She asked if you wanted to know anything about your father. His name was George, and he gave her a hard time after she married her husband. She thinks George moved out of town some time ago. Her husband knows about you, and he is fine with it. She thought she would start looking for you at one time, but never did. She is very happy that you found her and anxious to see you. Call her, Nancy. She's waiting."

My hand shakes. My finger pokes at the circular face of the rotary phone. I chicken out twice. The third time I let it ring.

Her husband answers. My tongue is thick. I carefully sound out each syllable. "I am calling for Elizabeth, please."

"Hello?" I hear her say.

"Hello, Elizabeth? This is Deborah."

Her gasp is full, with only a slight pause. "How are you?"

My heart is thumping so hard, my head bobs like a backseat bobblehead doll. "I'm fine. Just fine. You must have been very surprised to hear from me."

"Yes, very surprised. It's so strange. My husband and I had planned to go to a friend's house, but just as I was about to go out the door, something pulled me back, so I sent my husband on without me. When Mrs. Levoy called soon after, I was sitting at the kitchen table with a pencil in my hand. When she said your name I heard the pencil snap in two. Quite a surprise indeed."

Before Elizabeth and I hang up, she says she can't wait to see me. I say I will be there next week, on October 26. Twenty-six years and five months to the day since she saw me last.

I am so excited when I hang up, I tell Bobby every word I remember. Then I sit down hard on the kitchen stool again, and my stomach falls all the way to my feet. How will I tell Mumma? My God, she'll be mad.

34

Secrets

MY CHILDHOOD FRIEND, Rosie, who lives on Western Avenue in the old Adams' house, is babysitting the boys tonight. Where I am going is such a secret, I didn't even tell my best friend. I can't tell Nanny either, I want to, but I can't risk that she will stop loving me. I am afraid that when people in Bath find out the truth, they will say I am selfish and ungrateful, that it's a slap in the face to the people who raised me.

I am about to shame my family.

A dark, winding road of dead swirling leaves disappears behind us as Bobby and I get closer to Elizabeth's house. We pass occasional farms, small homes without numbers, mailboxes with only names. October air blows through the top of my window and teases at my swooped, Farrah Fawcett bangs. Coral lipstick is perfectly traced, my wrists dabbed with lilac cologne, and the tail of my pink nylon blouse is tucked neatly into the waistband of my gray fitted, knee-length skirt. Shoes are on, flat to the floor.

Elizabeth's driveway is steep. The emergency brake makes a grinding noise as Bobby pulls up on it. He asks me if I'm ready. I can see Elizabeth's husband move across the picture window heading toward the front door. The cement steps have been swept clean of falling autumn leaves, and my high-heeled sandals click the length of it. The edging smells of freshly turned dirt. A large, yellow mum plant has browned in a half-barrel container under the porch light. My legs are loose as rubber. One hand is numb from holding tightly to an envelope of my life in photos.

I knock twice quickly. The door opens up. It's her, hazel eyes glowing misty, and the top of her short, brunette perm measuring right to my chin. Her face is smooth from a light dusting of powder, and her lips, earlier glossed in red, look chewed on. A gold chain necklace lies simply over a long-sleeved, tan knit top covering her petite torso, and her A-line skirt widens over her broad hips. Her breathy words sound rehearsed. "Hello. Welcome." We stand speechless for seconds that seem like minutes, until finally she opens her arms. We hug like strangers at first, then tighter, like we will never let go.

"Sit here with me," she says, tears streaming down her cheeks. She taps the living room couch cushion. "I have spent twenty-six years wondering where you were. I didn't even know if you were still alive. But now you are here, part of our family." She takes both my hands. Our fingers weave together, all looking the same.

She asks me a lot of where were you when, and did you ever go there, questions. "You know your grandmother, my mother, was from Bath. Her family home is on Western Avenue, the Adams' house. Do you know it?" It seems impossible that it could be true, but it is. I have been visiting my best friend in my own ancestor's home for years.

As Elizabeth talks, her eyes never leave me, like she is afraid I will disappear if she looks away. "We'll have such fun, Nancy. You have a great big family now that is so excited to meet you. You'll be here for all the Christmas and Fourth of July parties, and everyone will love you."

My gut twists as she says it. I never thought beyond one meeting with her. I never planned to be part of her family. I have a family. Elizabeth slides closer toward me and wraps her arm around my back. Her lipstick has sunk into the deep lines of her smoker mouth, and her perm curl is tight and burnt.

"I'm so grateful Mrs. Levoy was willing to help you. If she hadn't, there's no telling how long it would have taken us to find each other, if ever." I shift back from her, let go of her hands, and brush the bangs out of my eyes.

"I still have your pictures," she says. "One I've carried in my wallet all these twenty-six years." She reaches for a stack of photos and holds up a black-and-white print of her sitting on a blanket spread out on a grassy lawn. I lie low in the crook of one arm. I take it from her and study us, wondering if I missed her when she never came back.

"After you went to live at the foster home, I came to visit you. I really wasn't supposed to, but your foster mother was so nice and allowed me to visit several times before you were placed in a home." She hurries through the photos. "Do you ever remember seeing a gold, heart-shaped locket when you were little?"

"Yes. There was a locket that Mumma put around my neck every afternoon when she took me out. It's in all my baby pictures." I dump the envelope into my lap and walk my fingers between photos until I come to it. Two years old, dressed in ruffles, small bracelets on my wrists, and the gold heart locket around my neck.

"That's it." She takes it from my hands, inspecting it closely. "When I gave you up, I asked for two things, that your parents tell you that you were adopted, and that they pass the locket on to you. It was from me." She holds up another baby photo. I lie on a blanket, arms outstretched to a waiting world, the locket around my neck.

Before I leave, Elizabeth hooks her arm in mine and walks me to the den. She points at a wall photo of a woman sitting in a wing chair, her posture perfect, legs crossed at the ankles. A man sits on the arm beside her. "These are my parents," she says, and lays one hand flat to the bare wall. "They loved to dance. That's probably where you got it from." She laughs lightly, then I watch her eyebrows drop to a *V* over her nose. She doesn't look at me. "My father was a very possessive man. We did as he said, and that's the way it was." She looks disturbed and transported. "He required a lot of personal time, shall we say, with my mother. I tried to stay out of his way. It was better not to be noticed. I loved the woods, so that's where I would go. My father was. . . ." Her words stop. Her breath holds, then lets out fast. She takes her hand off the wall. "Well, we'll talk about that some other time." A chill runs up my back.

My mother stands square to me and takes both my hands in hers. "I could have kept you, you know. My father said I could. But you would have been raised under his rule, like you were his own. I didn't want that for you." Elizabeth's head bends back, her neck stretching long like she's offering it to be sliced. Then her eyes come back to mine. Lips pressed, tears running wild down over them. "Do you hate me, Nancy? You must be so angry at me for giving you up. All the things I missed. I wasn't there for any of it."

Her candor startles me. "No, I'm not angry with you. Of course I don't hate you. You did your best."

As Bobby backs the car down out of the driveway, my mother and her husband stand in the picture window and wave. As excited as I am to find her, something just doesn't feel right. Part of me wants her love. Part of me never wants to come back.

TWENTY-SIX years ago, my mother was caught in a regrettable situation that sent her into hiding in an age when society saw her as carrying a disease rather than a child. She was one of those girls who were told to forget it ever happened. One of many who would spend the rest of their days dissociating from when life grew inside them, girls who grew into women with emotions buried deep, where secrets grow remorse like rocks grow fungus.

My mother and I. Two women with secrets.

35

Out the Window

I AM STANDING IN the middle of the street, halfway to the door of my parents' house, and halfway from getting back into my car and driving home. Except for the gas rolling up my chest, it is deadly quiet. The globe over the front door and the inside hallway light are dark. Mumma never leaves them on after supper is over. Through the windows of the front living room, I can see Daddy sitting on his end of the couch. His stocking feet are flat together like a yoga pose, and pulled up into his crotch. I watch him shake the paper open, then fold it back together and turn the page. Mumma is in the kitchen chair just steps from him, still covered in her apron, scratching at her elbow rash, and staring ahead at the living room television.

In my head, I can hear Elizabeth's voice. How she told me identity was by first name only at Crittenton Home for Unwed Mothers in Boston, that she sat in the Public Garden with a fake wedding band on her hand, and how giving birth to me ended her education at Fisher College. She said back then, having an illegitimate child was the worst thing a girl could do, next to committing murder, and she tried that too, with a back-alley doctor, but couldn't go through with it. I felt poison run every vein in my body when she said it.

With a letter that Elizabeth has mailed for me to deliver, I ring the bell and open the door. The house smells of boiled fish and potatoes. The dishwasher is thrashing, like a plastic cup is being slammed with each swing of the sprayer arm. Daddy's drink sits on the bookcase divider between the couch and the kitchen. He picks it up and slurps through the ice cubes. Mumma stands up, pulls the apron up over her head, lays it on the chair, then sits down next to Daddy. There is a tea stain just above the top button on her faded yellow jersey, and her nylon ankle socks have been rolled down close to the top of her lace-up shoes. With squinted eyes, she watches me. "Everything all right with you and Bobby?"

The blue chair next to the bathroom lops to one side from Tommy slamming down into it. I sit with my feet tight underneath me, my back to the folding door. My heart is skipping beats. It makes me cough. "I just wanted to come alone and talk to you about something that I've waited to say for a while. I hope you will understand why I did it."

Mumma's eyes are still pinched. Daddy rumbles his throat. We all wait. The air goes bitter and heavy between us. Their eyes feel like thousands, boring bullet holes through me. They tense as I pull the letter out of my jacket. My stomach knots. Breath barely comes with the words. "Well, a few weeks ago, I found my biological mother."

Mumma's crossed leg swings forcefully out and back, the toe of her shoe locked up to the ceiling. "I knew it," she says, staring me down and sealing her arms over her chest.

"Mumma, she is a very nice lady. I have a letter here that she wrote to you both." I lean out over the arm of the chair and hold it toward my father. One foot goes to the floor as he reaches for his drink. He drinks it all the way to the bottom, then lays it back down. His eyes skip over me, then back to the glass. "I don't want to read that. You read it."

"Well, she wrote it to you. You want me to read it?"

"Yes, Nancy, you read it," he demands.

I can feel my tongue getting fat and my shoulders working their way up to my ears. I tear open the envelope and read.

Dear Doris and Jim,

At the time you read this, you will be aware that Nancy has followed through on a longtime wish to locate and meet me. I know it must be a shock, and I do realize your feelings of perhaps betrayal on her part, and that she does not appreciate all you have done in raising her. I can assure you, she most certainly does hold dear the many things that you have provided. Her dancing lessons, her college education, and of course the many times you must have held her when she was sick, and said I love you.

I also realize for twenty-six years you have protected her and prayed this day would never come. You must know when I gave birth to her my love was also very strong. So strong, in fact, that it was for the betterment of her future that I signed those papers of surrender. It was because I loved her so dearly, wanted only the very best for her, and knowing that I would not be able to do so, did I finally sign them.

For twenty-six long years I have wondered and shed many tears not knowing if she was happy or even knew that she was adopted. I know I asked she be told, but I am also well aware when the time comes, many couples cannot bring themselves to do so. There were several occasions that I wanted to try locating her, but I gave my word not to. I could not hurt her then, and I will not hurt her now. Please try to understand us wanting to share some part of our life together. I will not try to take your place or hurt you in any way. I will be forever in your debt for the wonderful life and all the love you have given her.

In a letter I received from the social worker on August 8, 1955, she quoted you as saying, and I quote now from that same letter which I still have, "She is so perfect and lovely, even nicer than we ever dreamed our baby would be. We feel greatly indebted to Debbie's mother. If you should ever see her, tell her how happy we are and that her little girl will have a good home and be loved as much as if she was our own flesh." I read and reread that letter hundreds of times over the last twenty-six years.

Please know in your heart that I will be of no threat to you. I come with complete honesty and genuine appreciation that you did not raise her living a lie.

Sincerely,
Elizabeth

We are silent. My pulse beats double time to the kitchen clock. Coldness shrieks through the razor-sharp pieces of the broken window next to Mumma's head. My father's face is gray and clenched, with a day's worth of whiskers and soot. He gets up from the couch, moves to the kitchen window, and turns his back to us.

Mumma stands up. "I think it's time you leave for home now. Your father can't talk." As we leave the living room, her hot anger burns at my back. In her hand, the front door pulls open so fast, the attached door chime reverberates a low pitch. Hurt moves through my ears and lands in my gut like an iron spike. I step outside. Her grip is still on the doorknob.

"I knew you would do this," she says. "I always knew you would. When you were a little girl, you asked me so many questions about who your mother was and where you came from. I just knew that someday you'd find her. You've always been some damn determined, Nancy. Now get home." The door slams in my face.

I sob two miles of uncontrollable wails of pain.

THE next morning on the living room couch, Joshua is hugging my arm and Jason is reaching for his brother's thick curls as the kitchen phone rings. The stove clock reads quarter of nine, right before Mumma leaves for work. It must be her. I haven't finished saying hello when she speaks up.

"I just want you to know how much you upset your father. We had a very sleepless night and today we're both exhausted. After you left, he went to the window to pray, and he told me that you findin your birth mother was the second-worst thing that ever happened to him. I don't think he'll ever get over it."

My eyes clamp shut. They sting like gritty dirt blew under the lids. My armpits begin to sweat ugly heat. "I'm sorry, Mumma. Please don't be mad at me. I didn't mean to hurt you."

"You hurt me, and you hurt your father. Just like his father hurt him." I don't answer. I am confused. "You know when you were little, that man used to live upstairs over your father's tin shop, don't cha?"

My voice whispers flat off my tongue. "Yes, I remember."

"Well, one day your father went to check on him and found him hangin from the neck. Dead. He'd put a rope around his neck, tied it to a ceilin fixture, then jumped out the second-story window. God, there he was for the whole city of Bath to see, hangin dead off the side of the brick buildin. After all your father did for him, and that's how he repaid him."

Like someone else's voice, words crawl low and crazy out of my shame. "That's what he's comparing this to? That's what I've done to him?"

"Yes it is, Nancy, and he told me to tell you never to mention Elizabeth's name again. At first I thought I'd like to meet her. But now I can't go against your father. So you betta just forget the whole damn thing. It's nothin but a mess." The phone goes dead with a slam.

My throat feels tight and panicked, like the time I swallowed a piece of hard peppermint candy whole, and it wouldn't come up and it wouldn't go down. I don't cry as I hang the phone back on the wall. I finish dressing the boys, get them a snack, turn on *Sesame Street*, and pull them both tight against me.

Mumma's shaming voice, buried deep into the cells of my being, and with it, hid the memory of that whole day.

36

Shame

My Dearest Nancy,

How I wish I could have heard your laughter as a child and when we walk together now, I want to take your hand as if you were still that child. The only time I really had you alone was when I carried you. There I knew you were only mine, but now the dream is over. I guess we both have adjustments to make. I wish you could be here for our family reunions, the Fourth of July and Christmas. I guess it's best to let things stay as they are until you understand your feelings and trust all of us.

I am still thrilled that you found me and I am sorry that the search has put such a hardship upon you. I never wanted your family to be upset because of me. When I told my family and friends, they were delighted, and think of you as part of us. I wish you would accept the fact that we love you.

It still pains me that I gave up all the wonderful years. I lost forever the touch of your arms about my neck and hearing you say, Mommy, I love you. I exchanged all of this for you to have two parents, an education, nice clothes, and a warm, dry home. I am left heartbroken that you would believe your parents when they say I never loved you. I love you now, and I loved you then. Don't think I didn't want you, Nancy, I did. I always had you in my heart and you were always my daughter.

So, I guess our future is in your hands. Please do more than read this, try to understand my feelings. Believe me, you are not the only one who has been hurt.

Love,
Elizabeth (Mom)

I don't know my mother's pain and she doesn't understand mine. It feels sneaky to be with her. I tell the boys not to mention to their grandmother that we have seen Elizabeth. That doesn't feel right either. Whatever the plan to visit, I look for an excuse not to follow through.

I AM a taboo with a legacy of shame. I have brought disgrace to both my mothers, one a woman who secretly birthed me into a world where purity of reputation was prized, the other a woman who took me in on a year legal trial period that offered the possibility to return me like an ill-fitting dress.

The woman part of me wants to comfort Elizabeth, but the child part of me feels loathed. I think Elizabeth expects me to hate her, maybe wishing I would, to release her in some way from the past. For the next twenty years our emotions will run hot and cold, me not feeling loved by her, her not feeling forgiven by me. I'm not sure, maybe she's right.

37

Pieces of Me

THE ADOPTION NOTEBOOK on my kitchen counter is overflowing with the last four months of journaling. Through the phone receiver, I can hear Elizabeth drumming her nails on something. "I figured you'd want to know more," she says, then stops tapping. "I dated him the summer of 1954, just before I left for college. When I came back to Maine to tell my parents I was pregnant, my father was furious. When I saw George and told him, he laughed. He put one hundred dollars cash in my hand and said from then on, he didn't want anything to do with me or you."

Chill bumps run up my arms. "I'm sorry," I say, not sure I really mean it.

"He said he was already married with three children. I think I knew that from the start, just didn't want to admit it." She makes a humming sigh. "And then one day, he came to see me at work, saying he and his wife wanted to adopt you, but I said it was too late, you were gone." She swears it's true.

"He was so charismatic and handsome. God, he loved to laugh. It was infectious. He also loved to drink, and I worry what might happen if he knew where you were." For a moment, she goes quiet. "What if he shows up at your door and tries to take the boys? It could happen, you know. They are his grandsons. Anyway, I'd like to know where he is too. I'll help you find him, but for the safety of your children, don't make yourself known."

A week goes by. "Good luck," Mrs. Levoy says as she hangs up. My father's marriage certificate shakes in one hand. George and Alice, it reads, April 1951.

When Elizabeth calls shortly after, she sounds out of breath. "Are you sitting down?" I hear papers rustling. "I know where your father is. "Tupper's Trailer Park in Durham, just fifteen minutes from here. I got that information from the post office. And from the motor vehicle office, I found out his wife's license plate spells out her first name, ALICE."

THE snow-packed road to George's house is so dark and deserted that I come to a still stop right in the middle of it. I hold the paper up to the ceiling dome light and follow the directions given to me by the post office. TUPPER'S TRAILER PARK, reads the sign nailed to the thick pine tree. I tap the brakes as the car rolls, more anxious than me, on the icy path. Cold, bare windows allow me a peek in at people eating dinner and watching TV. Driveway snow piles have been pushed high with such force from the plows that chunks of dead grass and dirt teeter on the frozen embankments.

In the last lot on the right is a car with ALICE spelled out on the license plate. I pull to the opposite side of the road and shut off the engine. I tug at both sides of my unzipped insulated coat, lap them double across my chest, and stuff both bare hands under my arms. The inside of the car chills fast. Condensation begins to stream down the inside of the window. I shiver, peering at the shaded windows of the mobile home. Within a few minutes the trailer's front screen door fully opens and bangs against the porch railing. A tall man steps out and stands under the glare of the porch light. A pack of cigarettes has been rolled up in the sleeve of his white T-shirt. A young man and a woman with a baby in her arms step out from behind him. She is tall and slender, built like me, but she's too far away for me to see details of her face. I watch them closely, their breath smoky in the cold night.

I start up the car, afraid they will stop and ask what I am doing sitting at the end of this dark dirt road, and back out to a hidden side driveway to wait. When I return, no one is there and the light is out.

For now, this is all I can do. Years will go by before it feels right to look again.

38

Flashbacks

SPELLS. THAT'S WHAT my family calls it. Old Nanny had them, days she would cry for hours slumped in the chair by the window with a cigarette in one hand and the phone in the other, begging my father to come sit with her. Mumma hated that. She would throw dishes in the sink and yell at Daddy, saying someone else should go tend to her for a change. I always wondered what took Old Nanny to those dark places, what made her so different from my Nanny, and why the family dismissed it. "Oh she's just havin another one of her spells," they'd all say. Then someone, usually Mumma, would drive to the drugstore and get her pills. That's just the way it was. I was not supposed to ask questions, and when I did, I got no answers. Secrets.

My spells are happening every day now, not just once in a while anymore. Violent crying, buzzing, leaving my body with no control. I am yanked to scrambled scenes of my childhood in fast flashes of fear, and when I come conscious again I am jammed into a corner of the room, or under a table with no memory of how I got there. Every day since telling my parents about Elizabeth, something has called from deep inside me, demanding I now pay attention. Louder, closer, clearer, begging me to release information stored in each cell of my trauma-torn body. Memories, feelings, fears I fight against.

The boys see it happen. It is their normal, watching Mom on hands and knees, snot dripping, gagging, crying, corner-crawling messes. And not knowing they are even there, because I am seven years old under my bed at Mumma's house, or fourteen with blankets being ripped from my body, or a hundred other scenes that have dug wormholes through my flesh, places to disappear into and never come back from. Flashes of my life triggered by almost anything, or seemingly nothing at all, transport Daddy's chosen child to a hell that no one would believe he was capable of, unless they themselves had felt his hand.

Tonight I am sitting in the hallway looking into Jason's bedroom. My fingers ride hard up my temples. Tears drip from my chin. There is a cold sweat in the small of my back. On Jason's bed, Bobby holds a book in his hands and doesn't take his eyes off it as he reads and turns the pages. Jason sits next to him, one arm looped through his father's arm. Joshua sits on Bobby's other side, looking only at me. "Mom? I love you. Are you okay?"

Bobby pulls Jason closer. "Your mother's crazy," he says.

I think he must be right.

Mental health assistance, I believed, was reserved for people with diagnosis classifications of mild, moderate, and severe. Conditions that would be ranked and case-studied by people who were book smart and real-deal stupid. Guidelines that made no sense to someone with a handful of pills or a gun to her head. Purging of personal crap to a total stranger, I compared to taking a shit in the middle of a bus station. It would be embarrassing, rancid, and no one would really care if I felt better after dumping it out or not.

For the next two years I will fight half memories of molestation and the guilt of being a horrible daughter, wife, and friend. And most devastating of all, a traumatic disappointment to my sons.

It is Wednesday morning, March 2, 1983, my first therapy session.

I am less than a mile from home when I pull into the long driveway of the mental health center and park out back of the one-time family residence. I sit for a few minutes with the motor running, thinking I can still change my mind. I am afraid to reveal to myself, and the therapist, what may lie entombed, like she is going to grab my outer layer and keep pulling until I am spun down and bare-naked. Tears run tracks in my foundation makeup. Black mascara brushes marks across my fingers. I blow my nose, ball up the tissue, and drop it to the car floor mat next to an empty pink Tab can.

The sky is heavy with clouds. I step around a frozen puddle in the dirt driveway and tap on the door window. A "PLEASE COME IN" sign is hanging from a suction hook. The door opens. Justine shakes my hand, ushers me to a small office that feels more like a dining room, and asks me to sit down across from her. Her brown wool, tweed skirt rides up the sides of her stout thighs as she lowers to the chair. She appears uncomfortable from the tight waistband, as she leans forward and pulls at it.

"Let's start with why you are here, Nancy."

I start slow, then there is a pouring out like she is my savior. Tears flood my face. I pull my feet up under me in the boxy, cushioned chair and clutch my coat to my chin. The more I talk, the fuzzier the room begins to look, vibrating in and out like it is alive and about to squeeze every last ounce of strength from me.

"Breathe slowly," she says, then reaches behind her for a box of tissues on the desk.

"Something is wrong with me, but I don't know what. I can't control myself. I've been having these hysterical spells. I cry so hard, I think my eyeballs will explode. The pressure in my head is so bad, I tingle all over like I'm about to pass out. Then all of a sudden, I'm somewhere else, in places I haven't seen for years. Dark, scary places."

"Flashbacks," she says. "That's what they are called, and it is for sure a real thing. So real, you feel like you are actually reliving those childhood experiences again. Is that correct, Nancy?"

"Yes, then I realize, I remember that, why didn't I remember that before? Then I'm on the floor pushing myself into places I can hide, like I'm being attacked, and my husband is yelling at me to come back. As everything blurs out, I can hear myself screaming 'Mumma.' I wake up at night screaming for her. I've done it my whole life. Kids used to tease me at sleepovers. That's crazy, isn't it? I never really thought about that before. I mean, that's not normal, is it?"

Justine says I am dissociating from my body. It's my survival mechanism because I have not learned adult coping skills, and I'll keep dissociating until I remember what happened and why I've buried it. She says there are ways to change how I view my past. But I must reach way down into the depths of my soul and bring the most painful scenes into the light. Only then can I safely view them through adult eyes. I can't do it. It's like I've been asked to reach my hand into a dark, wild animal cage.

When I tell Justine about Elizabeth, and how my parents are so mad that I ruined our family because I found my birth mother, she leans back into her chair and thinks for a while.

"I have some homework for you to do this week." She pulls at the hem of her skirt and sits up taller. "I think it would be a good idea to have your mothers meet. Introduce them. You may find that they would enjoy the opportunity to share with each other." Then she says I must choose. "You can only have one mother, Nancy. Elizabeth keeps coming up smelling like a rose, but is that who your real mother is? It's one or the other. You can't choose both."

I am in complete panic as I leave her office. All the way home, I grip the steering wheel tightly and shake so hard my foot slips off the gas pedal several times. "The boys, the boys, the boys," I cry over and over until I pull into my garage. I call my friend who is babysitting and plead that she keep Josh and Jason until Bobby comes home from work. Then I go to my bedroom, wedge myself between the bed and the wall, and scream so hard I think my whole body will combust.

That was the last time I saw Justine.

39

Brown Paper Packages

THE NEXT DAY I telephoned both my mothers. I knew Elizabeth would agree to come to my house and meet Mumma. I was shocked that Mumma agreed to meet Elizabeth.

"Don't you dare tell your father about this," Mumma said quietly. "I'd never hear the end of it."

THE following Monday morning, I deliver the boys to my friend's house, then drive home to clean up the box of Cheerios that slipped out of my hands during breakfast. Dozens of little oat circles have rolled across my fake-brick linoleum floor like shooting dice. I am still picking up broken powdery pieces when Elizabeth rings my doorbell.

"I'm always early," she says with a laugh. "Hate to be late for anything." She wanders my living room, studying knickknacks and humming unrecognizable tunes while I finish in the kitchen.

The bell rings again. I hear the front door open. As I enter the living room, I see Elizabeth facing the door. Fear clenches at my throat. Mumma wipes her feet on the inside mat and pushes the door closed behind her. Mumma looks first at me and asks where the boys are, then at Elizabeth, now standing square in front of Mumma and smiling anxiously.

I am about to introduce my mother to my mother.

"Mumma, this is Elizabeth." Elizabeth extends her hand in a polite, careful way. "Elizabeth, this is my mother."

Their hands meet loosely. Mumma pulls hers back first and rests it on the books in the crook of her left arm. "It's nice to see you, Elizabeth. I've thought about you a lot over the years."

They both sit on the couch, and their conversation begins like I am not there. It's hard to believe what I am seeing. Mumma with two photo albums, full of my baby pictures, turning each page, and pointing out my ruffle dresses, curly hair, and straight legs. Every few minutes she gives Elizabeth a nudge with her elbow, and they both laugh.

"I wanted to show you how cute she was when she was a baby. Just like a little walkin doll. Everyone said so. I had the best time dressin her up. Here's the locket the children's home sent with her." Elizabeth scoots closer to Mumma, looking down at the photo. "I put it around her neck every day, and when I did, I thought of you and how sad it was you had to miss out. Ya know, I never told my husband where it came from." Mumma looks up from the album. She smiles with her lips tight together and blinks her eyes slowly at Elizabeth.

When it's time for Mumma to leave, she stands up and asks me for a brown paper grocery bag, then slides the albums into it. At the front door, she stands with the bag tight against the left side of her chest, and reaches her right hand out to Elizabeth's. "Well, I need to get to work now. Jimmy will wonder where the heck I am. I told him I had some errands to do." She chuckles. "We had a real nice visit, Elizabeth."

"Yes we did, Doris. Thank you so much for meeting me. I know that wasn't an easy thing for you to do." She lays her other hand on top of Mumma's.

"No, it wasn't." I hear the words catch in Mumma's throat. I feel my stomach flutter. I hug her tight and say thank you. Then I watch her step out the door and slip back into her old self. "Yup, all right, Nancy," she drawls, then calls back at Elizabeth, standing behind me at the door. "Well, at least when I'm dead and buried, Nancy will still have you."

40

My Favorite Things

CURLED AROUND THE sharpest corners of dissociative spells, of crawling in corners on hands and knees, of half memories of being molested by my father, are soft, perfect life moments. So perfect, it feels near impossible they could all be part of the same life.

In the kitchen, Joshua, Jason, and I stir up big pots of homemade Play-Doh dyed in different colors. And when we make chocolate chip cookies, we never care how much flour lands on the floor. The walls are covered with bread baskets, small wooden folk art pieces, and a collection of tin gingerbread cookie cutters. A calendar hangs next to the telephone. Each square is filled with birthday reminders, swim lessons, and library story times. In the bathroom, there is a vanity drawer just for tub toys, and on the mirror up over it I have written, I LOVE YOU JOSH, I LOVE YOU JASON, in thick pink lipstick. On the floor of the boys' bedroom closets are bins of art supplies, where every day we sit and do projects like finger painting and peanut butter birdseed pinecones.

When the boys go to school, I slip kisses into their pockets to save for later. Then we all hug tight and say, "I'll miss you all day."

On snow days, I bundle them up in layers of clothes and we build huge, white animals in the backyard, then climb up on top and ride them away. And when the snow is packed in the streets before the plow comes, I wrap the boys in blankets, sit them together on our wooden sled, and with rope in hand, run down slippery corridors of sparkly magic. "Faster, Mom, faster," they yell.

In the summer, we go to Popham Beach almost every day. For

hours we boogie board in the rolling ocean waves, and when the sun is high overhead, I spread an old sheet on the sand and make sandwiches with layers of ham, cheese, and veggies. At night I bathe sand from their sun-kissed bodies, dress them in super-hero pajamas, and tuck them cozy into bed.

On Saturdays when Bobby is working, the boys and I go visit Mumma. For lunch, she steams hamburger buns, then spreads them with Miracle Whip and carefully lays bacon, lettuce, and tomato over them. She sets the plates in front of Josh and Jason, gently pulls curls off their foreheads, and kisses their tanned faces. For dessert, we have chocolate cake she's made just for us, and after lunch we play Candy Land on the living room floor. When Mumma sits in the blue chair next to the bathroom door, she lets the boys climb up beside her with a wide bristle brush and work her hair up high into gray fuzzy peaks. We laugh about good times, like when we all went to Disney World and the boys talked Mumma into riding Space Mountain. When she got off that coaster her hair was blown crazy to the sides and she didn't even mind that it wouldn't go back into place. And the time we went to Busch Gardens in Tampa and the pickpocket pygmy goats buried their noses so deep into Mumma's purse looking for food, I couldn't get them out. Then they dragged out papers and tissues that fell to the ground and other people came to help us. Mumma and I laughed so hard we had to cross our legs so we wouldn't wet our pants, and that made us laugh harder. It was the best laugh Mumma and I ever had together.

Bobby, the boys, and I love to hike wooded Maine trails, jumping off rock ledges into chilly rocky gorge streams, and at Old Orchard Beach we ride carnival rides all night until Palace Playland closes for the day. Everything we do as a family, I meticulously record and catalog in photo albums, knowing someday when the boys are grown, despite what is to come, it will be important for them to remember that there were precious moments and favorite things, and most important, that they were loved oceans by their parents.

41

Jeepas

AFTER OLD NANNY died of a ruptured stomach, Daddy legally signed her little house at the edge of the gully over to Tommy. It's where he drinks and drugs with people who steal his money, under-age kids he buys beer for, a homeless woman he sleeps with, and a cousin who stole his truck and sold it for scrap, while Tommy was in jail again, for drunken driving.

Each morning Tommy walks up the hill to Mumma's house, where she cooks bacon and eggs and packs his lunch before they both go to work at Daddy's shop. That's where my brother bends sheet metal, but mostly just shoots the bull with whoever comes in, or wanders by the back tin shop door. Everyone seems to like Tommy, and he loves to reminisce with them about things that have happened in Bath, things that mean the world to my brother, shipbuilding history, fishing at Nequasset Dam, Morse High School football, and the time Haystacks Calhoun wrestled at the Portland Expo. Once in a while, Tommy talks about the time three of his football teammates blamed him for making prank calls to an old lady. He just couldn't understand why they would do it to him. The day after it happened and the police finally caught these boys, those little shits knocked my brother to the ground and pissed on his head for telling. But Tommy forgave them right away. My brother loved everyone, no matter what.

Downstairs in Mumma's house, next to the washer and dryer, are two old stuffed chairs heaped high with Tommy's clothes, where she tosses them after laundering, and where he dresses each day. With a seventh-grade basketball uniform on the bottom and, cigarette-burned T-shirts on top, those piles get higher each year.

Today as I walk through the front door of Mumma's house, I see Tommy sitting in the lopsided blue chair next to the bathroom door. Across from him, the television loudly blares. My engagement portrait hangs over it. Tommy's face looks wild and wounded, his skin hot and red. Blood expands the veins in his neck. He sucks hard off a cigarette butt and blows the smoke at me as I walk by.

"Jeepas, Nance. How could you do that to Mom? You know you just about broke her heart in two. Why'd you have to go lookin for your real mother anyway? She didn't want you, remember? What you've done to Mom and Dad is wicked bad." His sunken eyes bug out and his head juts quick at me, like it may slide right off his shoulders and drop to the floor. "Jeepas," he says again. He stares me down, his head looking like it will pop like a ripe zit and smoke steaming out holes where teeth used to be.

"Just something I had to do, Tommy. I had to know the truth."

He picks a beer bottle off the floor, puts it to his mouth, takes a long chug, then burps. "Jeepas."

THE first time Tommy got arrested for drug possession was just after Bobby and I got married and lived across the street from where kids partied in the Episcopal church parking lot. I pleaded with Bobby to let my brother come live with us, knowing in my gut as long as he was home with our parents, he would never stop drinking and drugging. Bobby and I screamed and fought so hard about it, I threw a glass of milk at him and he threw a tuna sandwich back at me, skidding oil marks across the new wallpaper. He got so mad, he stood up and ripped his shirt open with both hands, popping white buttons all over the floor. That night I sewed them all back on and cried, knowing I could not save my brother, only myself.

IT is the middle of February, a Thursday afternoon, and my parents are at their winter mobile home in Florida. Because Tommy is staying at their house, I haven't been there in weeks, but today while he is at work, I have come looking for videotaped movies to borrow. As I open the front door, the smell of rotting food and sour piss is overwhelming. Littering every room are empty beer bottles, ashtrays full of stale cigarettes, strewn newspapers, and dirty dishes. Polaroid pictures of no one I recognize are scattered across the kitchen table. I pick them up one at a time, a drunken girl sitting on the counter next to the stove, some guy with a red beard and a beer bottle up over his head, another toking a joint on the couch. I lay them back down.

In the living room, I reach under the stereo for a stack of videotapes and see a large brown paper grocery bag with the top folded over. I look down into it. There is a scale, razors, a mirror, small folded squares of paper, and a large plastic bag of white powder. I fold the top back over the brown bag, take it to the cellar, and hide it in the shed near the furnace. Then I call my brother at our father's shop, where now every day he sits on the tin bench, smoking butts and selling pot out the back door, whether my parents are there or not.

He is furious when I tell him what I found, but doesn't ask where I've put it. "Come on, Tommy, you're so much better than this."

"Mind your own fuckin business, Nancy. You left, so it's none of your business what happens at home. Just leave us the hell alone. We don't need you." The line goes dead.

THREE weeks later, when my parents get back from Florida, I go to their house. They're both sitting at the kitchen table, just finishing supper. I stand next to Mumma with one hand on the back of her chair. "Tommy's in trouble and I need you to listen to me."

Mumma slams her fork to the plate, vibrating tiny needles off my eardrums. "What kind of trouble? You don't even live here. How would you know that?"

"When you were away, I came up to borrow videotapes and found a bag of drugs. Lots of drugs. He's selling."

Mumma's eyes go mean. "Look, Nancy, just because you've been to college, you think you know it all, don't you? You don't know a damn thing. He wouldn't do that. He may be stupid, but he's not foolish."

I go to the cellar, retrieve the paper bag, and over the middle of the kitchen table, I turn it upside down. The scale makes a slight bounce, the mirror breaks, and the package of cocaine lands heavy next to the dish of boiled potatoes. My father clears his throat, leans back in his chair, and lays one hand to his thigh. He doesn't look up at me when he speaks. "Flush it."

One of Mumma's legs is crossed over the other. It is swinging hard. "Yeah, well, ever since his hair started fallin out, he's changed for God sake. Now who the hell got him into that mess. God."

In the bathroom, I lift the toilet lid, dump the bag, and watch it swirl away.

The next day Mumma calls to tell me Tommy wants to babysit for Josh and Jason. "Absolutely not, Mumma. What kind of mother leaves her children with someone who is drinking and drugging?"

"For God sake, why won't you let Tom watch the boys? Now you've hurt his feelins. He's got nothin else good in his life. Are you gonna take that away too? Why do you have to be so mean to him, Nancy?"

Tommy is lost to me now. I will only see him in passing at our parents' house and business. There is nothing I can do to save the precious little boy I used to know. He left a long time ago.

42

Apple Pie

MUMMA SAYS NANNY and I are just alike. Neither one of us can sit still. When Mumma drops Nanny at my house in the mornings, we always have a good time. Apple pie making is the best.

"Don't work the pastry too much. You want it to be nice and flakey. Lots of sugar and serve it warm, that's the secret." Just thinking about that sweetness makes Nanny's mouth water and her lips pucker like she's sucking pink lemonade from a straw.

Nanny likes to fold my laundry and help get the boys ready for the day. She says it's good to be useful. We sit on the back porch watching Josh and Jason climb the swing set tower and drive trucks in the sandbox. Nanny takes turns sipping hot Red Rose tea from one hand and nibbling bites of a date and coconut square from the other. "Those boys are so sweet, you could eat um right up. You've done a nice job, Nancy dear. You're a good little mother." I look into her pale blue eyes and think, how can I survive without her?

Now into her eighties, Nanny's perfectly straight posture has disappeared and her clothes hang looser with each passing month. The day I went to her house with the cancer test results, the brass bells chimed hollow against her front door, and when I came in, she was sitting in the gray recliner in the corner of the living room waiting, knowing what I would say. Her eyes were wide when I told her, then she looked away. "Well, I figured as much. I guess it's time to wind things up now." She lifted a photo of the boys off the coffee table and held it in both hands. "I knew the end would come some time. I just had prayed it wouldn't be like this. Those boys are so cute." Then she brought the picture close to her face and sobbed piercing wails I had never heard before. My gut growled empty in an alone space that nothing else would ever fill the way she did.

43

Waiting

THE HOSPITAL WAITING room is sparse and cold. Nanny's hand is in mine. We stare weakly over outdated magazines and half-empty paper coffee cups. With each chemotherapy visit, she repeats the same story.

"I lost my baby boy. Curtis was his name. He was beautiful. Died in my arms at two months old. They said it was a heart condition and there was nothin they could do. I'm lookin forward to seein that darlin baby when I get to heaven." Then she closes her eyes and sighs long.

IT's been three months since Nanny began treatment. Now too weak to be home alone next door, Mumma and I have brought her to Tommy's bedroom. A homemade afghan in three shades of pink covers a pile of childhood books atop an old red toy box. In the corner of the room is one bent blue snowmobile ski, from when Tommy hit a tree, and on the dresser next to it, dusty basketball and football trophies. I sit on a three-legged wooden stool between Nanny's bed and the sloped wall. Beside me is a nightstand that Mumma has cleared off and laid a clean dish towel over. A water glass and a box of tissues have replaced Tommy's ashtray and the stack of ten-year-old handwritten letters from a high school girlfriend.

Each day I sit with Nanny and watch her body slowly emaciate, her speech wilt weak, and her impeccably groomed white hair fall out by the handful. We talk about playing cards on the Merrymeeting camp porch while duck cooked delicious in the wood stove, about how she loved to wade into crystal-clear Sebago Lake and watch me swim, about the time we stayed up all night to sew netted petticoats on my can can costume, and about last year's Morse High School alumni banquet.

That evening Nanny sat at the head table with the honor of being one of the oldest graduates. When her name was read in recognition, and mine was also called as her granddaughter, we both stood up, her from the stage and me from the sea of alumni overflowing the school gymnasium. She looked regal in a cream-colored suit and red-figured blouse I had picked out for her that afternoon. She held a red rose from her place setting. She waved it high over her head while we blew kisses to each other across the room. "It was the proudest moment of my life," she told me later. "I just didn't want to sit back down."

The days are long as I watch Nanny go in and out of sleep. I wish for her to wake up feeling better, but I know she won't. I lay my head next to hers on the bed pillow. Her skin smells toxic and metallic from the drugs. I think about how she always said she and I had been brought together as part of a greater plan. There's so much I never told her. I never wanted to let go of how safe it was with her.

"Nancy dear." Her eyes are heavy and the light in them is leaving. "Nanny's been watching you go round on a carousel all afternoon. You kept going round and round. Every time you swung past me I tried to pull you off, but I couldn't grab you. I kept trying to tell your mother that you needed help, but she refused to reach out to you." I bring Nanny's hand to my wet cheek and kiss cold fingers unable to grasp around mine. Her smile is sweet, her whisper soft. She asks me to bend down near to her. My tears fall onto her pale cheek. "I'm not scared now," she says, smiling. "I'm ready to go. It's okay. Thank you, dear, for all you've done. You've been the best granddaughter. Always remember, and never forget, I love you."

Those are her last words to me. For three days Nanny's knees stay drawn up to her chest, her eyes locked in an open stare.

It's almost 5:00 P.M. on the third day when her breathing becomes more labored and crackles into the death rattle. Mucus gurgles wet in her throat. I run a moist lemon-and-glycerin swab over her pale, cracked lips. "That pesky nose," I say as I wipe the dripping wetness.

124

I've heard her say those words a thousand times while pulling a tissue from the sleeve of her purple sweater.

Fifteen minutes have gone by. Nanny suddenly draws one huge gasp into her lungs. It frightens me to hear her frail body pull in with such force. I drop to my knees and wrap my arms over her. Mumma is sitting in a straight-back chair on the other side of the bed, nervously running fingernails over one knee of her navy blue, nylon slacks. I hear the dryness of her fingertips catch on the material. Mumma and I hold our breath, waiting for Nanny to let hers out. Then, what seems like every last ounce of air, slowly escapes my grandmother's lips. She brings one more full, smooth breath into her lungs. Cool, spring air breezes in through the window screen, like it's being ushered on angel wings. Time stands still in this very moment. Nanny's beautiful face, which has held a stone grimace for days, is now glowing with light. The corners of her mouth lift to a smile. Her eyes spark open, like she is looking at the most amazing sight. And then, with a gentle exhale, she is gone.

44

Brown and Blue

TODAY IS MY twenty-ninth birthday, May 26, 1984. I am standing in the front hallway at Desmond Funeral Home, giving weak hugs to old friends and relatives I have not seen since the last funeral. They all somberly slough through and crane their necks down over the blue-lined box.

"Your grandmother was such a lovely lady."

"She was a wonderful friend."

"We had a lot of great times."

"Doesn't she look good?"

Why the hell do they say that? How can you look good when you are dead? Mumma has said it at every goddamned funeral we've ever been to. "Your father's family sure have loved the drink, for supposedly bein Christians." Then she hung her head over Uncle Otty's cold, dead body and said, "Doesn't he look good?"

No, Nanny does not look good at all. Her hair is not the way she liked it, her lipstick isn't right, and her hands are cold and rubbery. The two-piece dress she is wearing, the brown-and-blue-checked one that I picked out, is all wrong, and it's my fault. What was I thinking? It should be purple, and it's too late to change. For all eternity, my beautiful grandmother will lie in that mahogany box with a brown-and-blue dress. I want to die.

WHEN Nanny's service is over, the funeral goers gather back at home, in Mumma's living room. They all eat finger sandwiches and talk about the shipyard, and the weather, and things that don't matter at all in this moment of grief. Aunt Dottie gossips about some lady at church, and cousin Beverly fills her plate with brownies. "Where the hell were you?" I want to scream at them. "Why do you people only show up when someone dies? Why didn't you see how Tommy and I needed you? You call this a fucking family?"

The grass is muddy and slippery under my bare feet as I run down through the backyard and then the length of the dock runway. It bounces me up and down as my feet pound on it. The nuts and bolts grind and rattle, like they're coming apart. On the float, I lie down across the splintered boards and pull my knees up to my chest under my funeral dress. The river rocks me in swells of tidal water. Salty tears drop between the boards and disappear into the murky waves. And overhead, seagulls cry.

45

Listen to the Gut

FOUR YEARS HAVE gone by since Nanny died of stomach cancer.

Each morning since then, my body has repeated a flushing-out routine, like when the city taps the water main and rusty sediment blasts from the faucet into the sink. The coiled piping of my bowels sends crap rolling so fast that my first wakeful reflex is to tense and hold it in until I can get to the toilet. With diarrhea-pressuring release, I push a damp handprint to the full-length mirror on the back of the bathroom door until I hear the lock click. My legs shake weak. My thighs hit hard on the toilet seat. The pink plastic hospital pan I have grabbed from under the sink slaps cold on my lap. My arms squeeze around it so tightly, the sides bend in. Slimy bile chokes up my throat. Watery shit pours out my ass. Sweat slicks all the way down my chest to my belly and collects in the folds of my skin. It draws teardrop shapes down over my hips. I cough and spit heaves of bitterness as the toilet bowl splatters.

When nothing else will come up my throat, my finger jams past the back of my tongue until my teeth leave bite marks on my fist. My face burns with frustration. Tears pinch out the corners of my eyes. My body shakes angry in want of ripping out every whimper and scream that remains in formless shadows within every organ and cell of my body.

When the purging is over, my head pounds in silent failure. In a mirrored reflection, spit hangs from my chin. The air is sour and secret. Another day begins.

In my bedroom, five days a week, my thumbs walk down the inside leg of dance tights, scrunching the nude spandex in my hands until I am at the ankles. Snugly they snap up over my legs. A high, hip-cut leotard pulls to my bony shoulders, like a cloaking device, transforming me the way Clark Kent goes into a phone booth and comes out a super-hero.

In eighteen years of teaching dance, I have taught myself that once I am in those clothes, I must be on, smile, look people in the eye, project my voice. It's easy on the dance floor. What I have to say matters there.

Our new studio is on lower Washington Street, a three-mile drive south along the Kennebec River in the opposite direction from Mumma's house, but just a mile from mine. Over the outside studio door hangs a wooden sign. DAVID CHURCH SCHOOL OF CLASSICAL BALLET. NANCY STEEN GREENBLATT DANCE INSTRUCTOR AND CHOREOGRAPHER. It is everything I wished for. A big, polished sprung dance floor, walls of mirrors, dressing rooms, and an office.

Through the office two-way mirror, I watch David teach ballet while I do paperwork. Not too slight in build, he sports a neatly-trimmed beard and a small handlebar mustache. His posture is perfect as he plies at the barre in faded navy blue sweat-pants rolled down at the waist and up at the shins. His three layers of mismatched socks are worn with holes from thousands of chasses across the floor. An old stereo sits on the dance floor side of the mirror, with stacks of records next to it. During class when they need changing, David does a short run and skids to them across the dance floor, like he's sliding into home base. Knowing I am watching, he picks up the record player arm, drops the needle into the circular groove, sticks out his tongue at me, then turns a proper releve, and slides back to the barre with his students. He makes me laugh every time he does it.

Tonight, David and I are teaching a Fox-trot class. Couples squeeze into the small front lobby, change shoes, and step up onto the raised dance floor. I greet everyone and call them by name. David is preparing music selections at the stereo next to me. One woman shakes my hand with both of hers and looks at David. "Now, are you two a married couple?" David turns fast and precise on the balls of his feet and laughs at her. "Oh, God no, we'd kill each other."

My boys say David is the sister I never had. David laughed so hard the first time I told him that, spit flew out his mouth. Everything is funnier when David and I are together.

David and I have stood together in ballroom frame and given the same spiel to so many classes, we know exactly what the other will say, and when. David starts. "Ladies love to lead. And gentlemen, if they think for a moment that you don't know what you're doing . . . they take over." He makes one loud clap with his hands. Everyone laughs.

On the dance floor, I am the me I love. Secrets of self-annihilation hide deep in my gut with fizzy Tab and peanut butter crackers that I will eat if no one is watching. I dry heave at the smell of food, and shudder with chills I don't warm from unless I am loving my babies. My hair is cut short. It is dull and dry above my ears. My nails, trimmed down so far there is only a thin layer of skin before the bleeding starts. Using the bathroom is a reward that comes only when earned.

Pain. I so deserve that.

46

Dance Moves

It was a year ago, just after David and I opened the studio, that Bobby started a new job as manager of the L. L. Bean outlet, two hours away in North Conway, New Hampshire. Many nights he doesn't get home to Bath until after ten o'clock. Other nights he doesn't make it home at all and sleeps in his office. He says he wants us to move to New Hampshire, but I say I can't leave the only place I've ever known.

Today I have taught a full day of classes at the studio, and tonight I will go back to teach ballroom. It is dinner-time. While David is teaching ballet, I have come home for a break. Mumma meets me at the door with Josh and Jason running up behind her. Exhausted, I collapse onto the couch. The boys climb into my lap and kiss both sides of my face.

Mumma stands beside us with her hands firmly planted on her hips, watching me snuggle them. "Nancy, this isn't right," she says. "You and Bobby should be together. You can't raise a family apart. It's not fair to the boys. You go call Bobby right now and tell him you'll go to North Conway. It's time you were happy." Words that release me like a death pardon.

Within three weeks I close out my dance classes, make arrangements for the boys to switch schools, and we buy a house in Conway. Our Bath home will be rented for now, and once a week I will travel back to teach ballroom with David. I can't believe we are actually going, but it feels more right than anything ever has.

Tonight is our last night in Bath. The movers are on their way to

New Hampshire with a truck as long as our house, now empty except for the sleeping bags on the living room floor. It feels cold. The late November wind is blowing through one wall and out the other. There is a smell that reminds me of when we first moved in ten years ago, kind of sad and lonely. It doesn't feel like home now. Bobby and I slide into the sleeping bags. Our fingers lock to each other, over the boys cuddled between us. As I fall asleep, I feel like I am on a boat floating away from my secrets. In the morning we will drive away from here, leave it all behind, and start over.

47

New Hampshire Woods

It's Wednesday, November 23, 1988. The day before Thanksgiving.

The moving truck is beeping as it backs down the narrow, wooded Beechwood Drive to our brown saltbox tucked and hidden in the corner elbow of the pine-and-birch-lined dead end road. As we follow it into our driveway, small granite rocks crackle under the tires of our car. An old stone wall runs the side length of the backyard. The snow-covered summit of Mount Washington gleams bright in the sun beyond us, and the air is fresh winter clean.

Inside there is a wood stove waiting to be filled, and at the end of the house a den with two walls of windows that reach to a cathedral ceiling. The pine-wood panels still smell fresh cut. When the movers have finished a full day of unloading, they climb back into the cab. At the end of the driveway, drooping pine boughs sweep the top of the truck as it pulls away. Under its tires, fragments of broken granite push deep into the dirt. Bobby, the boys, and I stand on the side porch watching. They're leaving us here. It feels peaceful to think it. Bath will never be home again.

Two weeks before Christmas, we pick out a nine-foot tree from Weston's Farm, tie it to the top of our car, and laugh all the way home as the branches hang down over the windows. In our den I watch Bobby, high on the step stool, string white lights. Josh and Jason hang some of Mumma's forty-year-old ornaments, and one strand at a time, I lay tinsel over the branches like Nanny used to do. When we are done, Bobby turns off the house lights. Tiny white tree bulbs illuminate colored ornaments and gently moving silver strands of tinsel. The four of us sit on the floor in front of the tree, huddled in each other's arms, a big puffy down blanket around us. Outside, the moon is full. It lights up the snow-covered branches of the trees with a million tiny crystal sparkles. All is quiet except for the wood crackling in the stove. A cast iron pot on top simmers orange peels and cinnamon sticks. I will never have a best life moment more loved than this.

The weeks go by, and every day feels like vacation. From the living room beams I hang baskets and dried field flowers. I sew curtains for the dining room, and in the kitchen I make apple pies and meals I now have no problem eating. I sip hot coffee, watching from our back porch for the occasional deer, moose, or bear to wander through our yard. On the weekends we hike Arethusa Falls and other trails off the winding Kancamagus Scenic Byway. We ski Cranmore Mountain, and from the back of our car we winter picnic with sandwiches and hot chocolate.

LIFE on Beechwood Drive began like a wooded storybook dream. As a family, we were the strongest we had ever been. As a couple, Bobby and I were at our best. But for me, six months of amazing, perfect happiness was all I had.

48

Hidden

ALL SUMMER I live in my nightgown, unable to tolerate clothes against my stomach. Pain stabs like a knife to the right side of my abdomen as pressure builds against my organs and I bleed clots so large and dark, it feels like giving birth to small beings. Three months of bed rest, missed family outings, and waiting for an appointment with the gynecologist.

Now it is the last week of August. I am sitting on Dr. Morin's examination table with a paper dress pulled tight around my nude body. I hear nurses talking in the hall and my chart slide down into the outside pocket of the door. On the exam room wall is a photo of Tuckerman Ravine, a deep glacial bowl below Mount Washington, where hikers brave massive amounts of snow dumped there by record-setting wind gusts. I imagine what it might be like to be caught in an avalanche of cold, buried, with no one to hear your screams. Desperate and disappeared, wondering if fighting for your life would only bring the weight heavier, or if just giving up would be a more peaceful ending.

With a slight knock, the door opens. The doctor steps toward me. He looks young, maybe mid-thirties, not much older than me. The stool at the end of the table makes a depressed *whoosh* as he sits down. "Now, let's see what's going on." I lie back. He adjusts the overhead light to my crotch. "Move to the end of the table, please." I pull the paper dress down over my hips and inch my butt closer to him. I place my feet in the stainless steel stirrups.

"Okay, now I need you to open your knees." Heat radiates against my nakedness. I hear the ting of a metal instrument. I hold my breath. Ice-cold gel-covered metal spoons luge fast up inside me. My heels brake against the stirrups, quickly pushing me to the top end of the table.

Gone. Like a rat fast picked off the ground by a swooping owl, I am somewhere else in an instant. The body I leave behind shakes and cries out high-pitched slivers of fear, tearing at the paper table covering with gripped sweaty hands. I am seven years old under my bed, dust bunnies up my nose and my father's hand gripped to my ankle. I am fourteen, lying in sticky sheets that smell like furnace soot. I am seventeen, screaming for Mumma as the springs of my bed groan under my father's weight. I am all of it in this moment.

Dr. Morin stops the examination, rolls his stool back to the wall, and pulls off his gloves. He reaches for my hand. "You can sit up now, Nancy." The rustling of the stiff paper dressing gown fades in and out of my humming ears, now full of hot tears. I pull the gown tight around me and grab for his help. "Nancy, I must say something. We've gone over your personal and medical history, and I feel that something has been left unsaid." He stares at me, waiting for a response. I am shaking cold. Stunned and fighting to come back to consciousness.

"Nancy," he pauses slightly, holding his eyes to mine. "You've been sexually molested, haven't you?" My chest tightens. Embarrassment tingles panic across my breasts and arcs to my crotch like frayed wiring. "Nancy, this isn't normal. Women don't have this reaction unless they've been assaulted in some way."

My nose is running wet to my lip. My throat coughs dry, as my words stumble. "No, I'm sure lots of women do this."

"Yes, some women do react this way. But the only ones that react to your extreme are those who have been assaulted. Molested."

My body goes numb. Spiky tingles race out my arms and legs. I can't move. My ears deafen. I can see Dr. Morin's mouth moving, but I hear nothing coming out of it. My heart pounds hard in back of my eardrums. I watch Dr. Morin stand up and leave the exam room. He closes the door behind him. I slide down off the table, crouch onto the floor, and crawl behind the chair that my jeans and blouse drape over.

In my mind I float between the office and my old bedroom at Mumma's house. I am being swallowed up, lost in an avalanche, about to disappear. Please, God, don't let me have a spell and dissociate, not until I am home safe.

I think all of my clothes are buttoned and zipped when I walk out past the receptionist. I don't turn to see her reaction, and I don't know who I pass on the way. My legs step rubbery, like I am in a different dimension and have no idea where the floor is.

Then I am in my car. I have locked the doors behind me, and I am holding the keys in my hand, not sure what to do next. My back teeth are grinding. I am studying each ridge and curve of the car key, my only clear piece of reality. I hear the house key clink against the key chain, a metal square with a map of Cape Cod on it. I remember when Bobby and I rode bikes there, next to the ocean, on our honeymoon. That was a good day. I start to come back to consciousness. I can still feel the sting of being pried open by the shoehorn speculum, and my vagina still slippery from the gel. Dr. Morin's spoken word *molested* brings truth to a sick past I had defined as my normal.

Molested kids live in poor homes, like the girl in grade school who wore cut-off tights for underwear that showed when she swung up high on the swing, and the gang girl who hung out just beyond the junior high smoking cigarettes, the one I was afraid to walk past. They were the women-girls with mental problems who drink and drug, and go to jail, and kill themselves. I had pretty clothes and toys. We lived in a nice house and had a boat. My father held my hand when we walked into church. I was the chosen one.

A LIGHT had literally been shone on my truth. I had buried memories of incest. Everything will change from now on.

49

Crazy

My stomach is flipping and I have to pee as I pull into the parking lot of the women's health center in Portland, Maine. I am a half hour early to see Dr. Thorne, who Dr. Morin has contacted for a second opinion. I roll down the car window. Late-summer heat rises from low tide mud flats in the boatyard across the street. Seagulls circle and screech at one another. Next to me on the passenger seat is a folder of paperwork. I pick it up and begin to flip through Dr. Morin's records. I pull out a letter written to Dr. Thorne. The car engine snaps and knocks as I turn it off and begin to read.

"I have found a psychological component resulting in severe anxiety and apprehension about pelvic exams. I have offered counseling and evaluation, which was declined by the patient. Her exam was impressive of severe apprehension with spontaneous tearful episodes, and I have described these findings to you in our telephone conversation. I did not initially proceed with an exam until further discussion and reassurance. I was unable to elicit any history of abuse, assault, or bad experiences with previous health care providers. Details were difficult to obtain, and she is non-receptive to psychological counseling, but I suspect underlying psychological components. The patient is aware that there is no guarantee that surgical intervention will relieve her, neither of her pain symptoms, nor her other multiple underlying emotional and psychological problems. I am in hopes that surgery would be the initiated step to provide control of any pelvic pathology, allowing a more appropriate referral and contact with a psychological referring system."

⁓

HE thinks I'm crazy. She will too.

Five wooden steps lead to the front door of the Victorian house. It isn't long before a woman in a long gauzy dress comes to the waiting room and asks me to follow her upstairs to Dr. Thorne's office. Books of all sizes jam shelves, many hanging halfway out, and on the floor, a pile spires up as high as my knees. In the middle of the room is a medical table, and over it is a skylight.

After a few minutes, Dr. Thorne comes in. She looks hurried as she pulls her bangs back out of her eyes. The exam is fast. I watch for seagulls through the skylight, as she pushes on my stomach and quickly looks between my legs. Then she moves to her desk and asks me to sit down. Across from me, her bosom rests atop her folded arms. She speaks with seriousness. "Nancy, if you choose to leave here pain-free, you are certainly capable of that." She leans back in her chair, rolls a pen between her fingers, and waits for me to speak. She looks deeply at me. "Women who have been adopted typically will have this problem. You have held the pain of being given away by your mother in your pelvis all these years, and that pain will bring up other painful life issues for you."

Uneven breaths divide my words. "I don't mean to be rude, Dr. Thorne, but I really don't think that is the cause of all this pain in my stomach. There is a growth on my right side. I can feel it."

"Well, it's possible you could have a little problem there." She picks up the pen again and scratches it loudly across a script pad as her unkempt hair falls across her right eye. "Here's the name of a book that deals with pre-menstrual syndrome, and I'm giving you the name of a woman to see about dream analysis. You also might want to try hot cod liver oil packs on your abdomen." Her red matte-lipsticked smile looks generic as she rips the page from the pad and hands it to me.

It shakes in my hand. "I don't see how reading a book will take my pain away."

Her eyes narrow in frustration. "I know Dr. Morin has suggested that you have a hysterectomy. Do you want me to write that I feel a hysterectomy is in order? Is that what you prefer?"

"If there is a mass in my body, I think it would do more for me than castor oil and dream therapy." Her eyes make one slow blink. I can see her tongue run the inside of her mouth and up over her top teeth. My shoulders round forward as I slump into the chair. I am shamed and stupid. She says Dr. Morin will be in touch.

My knotted fingers make fast strangling grips on the stair railing as I hurry out of the building. I slam the car door behind me and start up the engine. My foot stamps heavy to the pedal as I pull out of the parking lot and scream back at her. "Yes, rip the whole fucking thing out. I don't want it."

My hospital bed is against the wall. The bed next to me is empty. The hallway door is half-closed and seems far away from where I lie shivering in twisted sheets and a thin white blanket. I can smell the strong odor of anesthesia, and my throat is scraped. Two fluid bags hang on a pole dripping into a line that is connected to a vein in the bend in my arm. I hear a slow beeping of a machine behind my head. Bobby leans down over me and kisses my forehead. "Hey, how are you doing?"

"I don't know. There's something wrong with my right leg." I wiggle my toes. They tingle pain, like the time I stayed out too long on a below-zero-degree day and got frostbite.

"Well, you probably won't feel great for a while. They took pretty much everything, except for one ovary. There was a large hidden fibroid that Dr. Morin hadn't seen on the CT scan. I guess that's why you were having all that pain."

"Bobby, help me stand up." He reaches under the covers and swings my legs out over the bed, then takes my arm. My bare left foot tingles cold on the linoleum. My right foot fires electricity, burning hot, sharp pins and needles all the way to my knee, like I am pressing my 130 pounds into broken glass.

I am in bed crying when Dr. Morin comes into the room and stands at the end of my bed, one hand on the footboard, the other on his hip. "There is nothing wrong with your foot, Nancy. That's your emotions taking over. We'll get some morphine into your drip line, and you'll be fine."

For five days I remain in the hospital, my body flooded with drugs, foot pain unbearable, skin swelling and stretching like a water balloon, the color turning to dark purple, and Dr. Morin holding to his original diagnosis, that I am imagining things.

50

Avalanche

At home, day and night, my bare foot lies on top of the rose-colored bedspread. Any contact with the sheets or floor is like holding the bottom of my foot to the flames of a raging fire. The only time I leave the bed is when I crawl on my hands and knees to the bathroom, while holding my right foot high and digging my nails deep into the fibers of brown bedroom carpet. The more hand steps I count, the more I cry. The more I cry, the deeper I dissociate, dragging my child self to hiding places my adult body does not fit. Truth follows me like a lit match dropped to a gas line.

From my bedroom window I have watched the end of summer turn vibrant, green leaves to withered death, listened to my sons skid their bikes into the driveway and the basketball repeatedly bounce hard and hollow on the tar. I've heard dishes drop to the kitchen sink, the television shout from the den, and my family go on without me. With the sensation of needles being shoved under my toenails, I grab at a leg I want to rip off. I slam my body repeatedly to the headboard and pull at the roots of my hair so hard, I think my scalp may lift off.

A basin of icy cold water is all that brings relief. When my foot is completely numb, sleep comes ten minutes at a time. Water sloshes back and forth as Bobby again lays the pink plastic hospital pan on the bed. From the medicine bottles that stretch across the dresser, he counts pills into his hand.

"I can't take this, Nance. It's been a month. I've watched you scream into your pillow and dump drugs down your throat. I am missing work to take care of you and the boys, and you're making me crazy.

When is this all going to end?" He picks up a small notebook from the dresser and records what he has given me. I see his jaw tense. Veins throb in his temples. He goes back downstairs.

It is late that same night, when Bobby can no longer stand my cries for help and takes me to the emergency room at Memorial Hospital. On the gurney, I am drugged and delirious, rocking back and forth. Hugging my bent leg to my chest. Dr. Morin comes into the curtained cubic. "Now what?" he says as he flumps into a chair and folds his arms over his chest. His face looks disgusted and bothered. Mumma's face flashes at me.

Bobby rubs my back. "She can't live like this any longer. What are we supposed to do?"

Dr. Morin turns to Bobby. His words are cutting. "I thought she'd do this. There is nothing wrong with her foot. She's just transferred the pain from her stitches to her toes. The only thing I can do is admit her and try some drug therapy."

For a week, I lie in a hospital bed crying, disoriented, terrified, and alone. As much as I miss Josh and Jason, I don't want them to see what a mess of a mother I am. The more I cry from the foot pain and the hormonal imbalance of having my female organs removed, the more it triggers flashbacks of my father's molestation, which I now must face as truth. When one drug doesn't stop my pain, another is added, until I am knocked out and limp.

The nurse who stands at my bedside seems rushed as she injects fluid into the line in my arm. "Nancy, after I give you this dose, I am going to have to shut your door. You are making too much noise and bothering people."

The door is pulled to the frame. I am alone again, buzzed, and on the way to unconsciousness. Desipramine, amitriptiyhline, Tylox, Thorazine, Valium, morphine, Xanax. None of it took my pain away.

It's the last full day of my hospital stay. Bobby sets a bag of clean clothes on the end of my bed. He looks exhausted, with dark circles under his eyes and stubble from a missed shave. I reach for his hand. The coolness of it feels comforting on my forehead.

"Bobby, I can't do this anymore. No one believes me." My breath feels shallow. "I miss the boys so much. We were so happy. Now I'm laying here thinking I am no good to any of you. I just want Nanny to come get me."

Bobby turns to the nurse, who is adjusting the medication drip bags. His voice snaps at her. "Isn't there something else you can do besides give her drugs?"

She pauses, both hands holding a fat yellow bag of fluid. "No, there isn't. We can't help someone like her here." Bobby's eyes are wide and lost.

The psychiatrist is dressed in a tan, baggy, wool sweater, worn jeans, and brown Birkenstock sandals. He smiles and introduces himself as he pulls the metal chair close to my bed. It makes a loud tin scraping that vibrates my brain. He leans back and crosses one leg over the other, then, with his hands at his chest, matches the tips of his fingers together in a tent shape. He speaks with conviction.

"Dr. Morin never thought a hysterectomy was a good choice for you, Nancy. Now you're addicted to the drugs. My suggestion is to begin detoxing, starting with the Valium. I've made arrangements for you to see another neurologist in Boston. You'll have an MRI, and when you return, you will move to another facility that can offer the help you need."

"You think I'm crazy, don't you? Why won't you listen to me? There's something wrong with my foot. Look at it. Can't you see it's dark and swollen? I can't put weight on it."

"Nancy, Dr. Morin says there is nothing wrong with your foot. Tomorrow morning you will be discharged from here." He stands, flattens his palms together at his chest like a yogi, and wishes me well.

It's true. I'm crazy. I drop under an avalanche of shame, and it swallows me up.

51

With Time

Boββy AND I are sitting in the neurologist's office at Massachusetts General Hospital. The doctor pulls a script pad out of his desk and begins to write. "Your nerve conduction studies showed a lumbar restriction that happened during anesthesia, and a sciatic nerve injury, called reflex sympathetic dystrophy syndrome." He looks up at us and nods. "It is a disabling short circuit of the nervous system."

My good foot taps fast at the floor. The doctor brings two fingers up over his mouth, his thumb pressed under his chin. He looks one last time at my chart, hands Bobby a drug prescription, then stands. "Well, it was nice to meet both of you. Your foot will get better with time, Nancy. These things just happen. God's will, you could say." I say nothing. Bobby shakes the doctor's hand.

The ride from Boston back to Conway will be a long three hours. Bobby keeps both hands to the wheel and his eyes to the road. We are in Saugus on Route 1, when he finally tells me. "Nance." His lips make a clamped frown, and his nose twitches like he is about to cry. "The doctors and I have decided you need some mental health care. I've already packed a bag for you. We'll go home first, but then I'm taking you to an inpatient psychiatric facility in Portland."

On the car floor sits the pink hospital pan. Cold water sloshes to my ankle and spills up over the side. I watch it run across one straight groove of treading and onto the carpet. "No, Bobby, don't send me away. Please don't make me leave the boys again. Please."

"Nance, you can't do this to them. They're scared. They don't understand what's going on and neither do I."

"I can do it, Bobby. Please let me heal on my own. I know I can do it for the boys." Bobby's jaw tenses. One huge tear rolls fast down his cheek.

It is just before Josh and Jason get off the school bus at the end of the road when we pull in over the crushed rock of our driveway. Bobby unlocks the side porch door. Inside, my tan suitcase sits on the deacon's bench under the kitchen window. Next to it is Jason's basketball and Josh's ski jacket with the Cranmore pass hooked on the pocket zipper. The house hums in stillness.

"Thank you, Bobby." We hug, draped across each other, both worn and confused. He lifts the bag, takes me by the arm, and helps me upstairs to bed.

52

Chicken Soup

ELEVEN YEARS OLD is way too young to be in charge of meals, cleaning the toilet, caring for your eight-year-old brother, and helping your mother detox from drugs. When Joshua comes into the bedroom, he sets the tray on the pink bedspread beside me. "Mom, I brought you some hot tea and half a turkey sandwich. Try to eat it, Mom, okay?"

My pillows are piled against the headboard, where I have been slamming myself. My bad leg is bent up to my chest. I am rocking the pain away. I reach for him. He hugs me tight. "Josh, I am so sorry this all falls on you. It will be better soon, I promise. I've just got to get these drugs flushed out of my system."

His brown wavy hair brushes my face as he sits back from me and takes my hands. "I know, Mom. Don't worry. I'll take care of everything. You just get better." He picks up the pink pan and goes downstairs to refill it with ice water. I think how brave and sad it is that at night when I am crying and thrashing, dumping drugs down my throat, my sons are living a nightmare huddled together in Joshua's bed, waiting for sleep, and wondering if their mother will live or die.

In the morning after Bobby has left for work, Joshua makes breakfast and packs lunches. Before they leave for school, Jason sits on the edge of the bed and reaches for my shoulders, his breath warm on my neck. "I'm afraid you'll be taken away from me, Mom. That I'll come home and you won't be here." My heart breaks, guilty of wasting precious time and having them see me crazy and weak.

Years from now, Jason will tell me he thought I would die and sometimes he wished I would, just so my pain would be over.

⌒

THREE weeks have gone by since the Boston appointment. Each day I get a little better, as I hop on my good foot the length of the upstairs hallway, gain muscle strength, and, as the medications decrease, regain some clarity of mind.

I am in bed flipping pages of a *Better Homes and Gardens* magazine when I hear the rattle of a teacup on a saucer, and smell savory chicken soup. Mumma stands in the doorway balancing a tray of food. "Hi, honey," she says, her eyes almond-shaped and soft, like I've seen them loving the boys. "Josh called me. He said you needed my help."

My nose begins to tickle. My eyes fill up. "Mumma, I can't believe you drove all the way up here."

"Well, of course I did, Nancy. You need help, don't you?" She lays the tray over my lap, pulls bangs from my forehead, and kisses my cheek. "Now I want you to try to eat somethin. You've got to start feelin better. Those boys need their mother back."

I watch noodles swim like worms in the greasy broth. My toes spark lines of electrical charge. My body jumps. Mumma grabs for the hot teacup. "God, Nancy, I wish there was somethin I could do to help you."

She goes into the bathroom, then comes back with a warm washcloth and wipes my hands and face. It feels good as she gently runs it over my eyelids and in the crease of my nose. She lays her hand over my toes and begins lightly stroking my skin, like she would the silky fur of a beloved cat. Her head shakes as she does it. "I'm sorry you have to go through all this, Nancy. Just doesn't seem fair."

I think I must really be sick to have her attention like this, and how different she is when Daddy's not around.

53

Smoked

IT'S BEEN TWO years since the sciatic nerve injury, months of it spent at Memorial Hospital in physical therapy, desensitizing my foot with massage and a pulsing electric TENS machine. Once a week I teach evening ballroom classes in Bath with David. Sometimes I drive the two hours home to Conway. Sometimes I stay at Mumma's house.

My parents now sleep in my old bedroom. In their old front bedroom, I lie in the middle of their sagging mattress and look around the room. Nothing has moved out except them. Their clothes still hang in the closet, and the dresser is still cluttered with things like Daddy's old cufflinks, assorted costume jewelry, and Mumma's knee-high stockings rolled into suntan balls. Dust gets thicker each year.

ON the outside I look normal, except for a slight limp from residual pain. I go to Josh's and Jason's basketball games and all of their activities, I teach dance and theater at their elementary school, and I function as wife and mother. That is, until a wave of panic takes me into a full-blown spell.

I have no memory of what brought it on last week when driving Jason to a friend's house. I know I turned onto the main road, and then I disappeared. I could hear my back teeth grinding and everything started to buzz out. My fingers locked on the wheel, but I wasn't steering. I know Jason grabbed it and yelled for me to let go. "Mom, Mom, tap the brakes. It's okay," I heard him scream. Then we were off the side of the road in the dirt, and he was crying.

One day a week I see the psychiatrist. When I go to that second-floor space, the steps feel steeper and narrower the closer I get to the top. That's when I smell sweet nag champa incense. In the office there is a framed drawing of Buddha on his wall, and an easy chair covered with a Native American woven blanket, where the doctor sits. Long-armed spider plants and wandering Jews crawl across the sill of his big picture window. I sit on the couch next to it, my bare feet drawn up under me, hugging a brown pillow firm against my chest. His voice is calm and soothing when he says we are working on layers inside me, which need to be healed. To me it feels like gnarled ropes of consti-pated shit lying heavy in my gut.

As he talks, I hear only some of what he says. Sometimes he doesn't say anything. He just waits for me to talk, and sometimes we say nothing for almost the whole hour. Before I leave, we say a meditative prayer. He closes his eyes, but I never do. I watch nag champa swirl around the room making smoky ringlets I wish to wrap up in and float away with.

54

Finished

TODAY IS SATURDAY. Bobby is at work, and the boys are at a friend's house. I am alone at home. I have dried the breakfast dishes and put them in the cabinet, swept the kitchen floor, and finished folding the boys' laundry. I am on my way to Josh's bedroom with a stack of clothes when I see a patch of sunshine on the hallway floor, one square outlined from the front-door window in a shadowy box of golden light.

I can feel my head going fuzzy, my eyes go wide in terror. I hear my back teeth grind dry, like nails on a chalk-board. Everything around me starts to disappear into blackness. The clothes in my arms tumble to the floor, except for one folded T-shirt from the bottom of the pile, which is now pinched and strung tight through my fingers. My face burns hot on the carpet as it rubs into the coarse brown fibers. My knees pull to my chest, my body fitting to the warm box of sunlight, like it is my portal to safety. I hear my breath suck in, slow and deep, then hold with no breath at all, like a free diver sinking to the depths of the ocean. Again, today, I am having a dissociative spell.

Teleported in time, like being sucked through a wormhole, I am five years old standing in the upstairs hallway at Mumma's house. It is Saturday afternoon. Daddy and I are the only ones home. I hear his voice calling me from his bedroom. "Nancy, come in here. Daddy wants to show you something." His tone is weird. My stomach twists like I'm going to throw up. In front of me I see a patch of sunshine on the wall, projected there into a square of golden light from a nearby window. It is so bright and beautiful, I know there must be something in that light that will save me, if I can only get close enough to it. "Nancy," he calls again. "Daddy needs you." My feet scuff slowly toward the end of the hall, past the patch of sunshine, and into his bedroom. He sits on the edge of his bed, his bare legs apart, and on the floor between them, an open magazine with naked ladies. "No, Daddy," I hear myself garble.

Then *whoosh*, like a freight train steaming through a tunnel, I am back, curled into the patch of light on my hall floor next to the pile of spilled laundry. Fast scenes flip through years of molestation as if a demon hand is turning the dial of the television screen in my head. I hear Mumma's words. "You'll never amount to a damn thing, Nancy. You're good for nothin." And Daddy's. "Don't tell Mumma. You'll make her mad." Words that have slimmed into pockets of my body, reminding me that I was born in shame, and shameful is what I am.

Up the stairs and down the hallway, my hands and knees scrape hot on the carpet fibers. I crawl between the sheets of my bed. Plastic tops pop off bottles of leftover anti-depressants and painkillers. Each container vomits out colored balls of poison onto the dusty-rose bedspread. One by one they swallow into my pain. Going deeper. Dissolving into my dark nothingness. My breath slows. My eyes shut. I hear only a throbbing hum waving in and out of my ears.

The pillow is soft at the back of my neck. It gently cups the sides of my cheeks, the way Nanny used to, just before she said "I love you." The humming fades into peacefulness. My body is dissolving with the drugs. I want to sleep forever.

I feel a blast of energy rush into the bedroom. Bobby's hands grab at my shoulders. "Nance, what's the matter? What the hell have you done?"

He pulls my shoulders fast off the pillow. He shakes me, then lets go. I flump back to the pillows. My vision blurred, I can see him grabbing at the empty bottles, reading one, then throwing it to the bed and grabbing for the next.

His panicked voice trails off into the bathroom. "I had a feeling something was wrong. I just had this sudden feeling in my gut that I needed to come home." Now his fingers are combing rough through my hair. "Open your mouth," he yells.

"No, Bobby, I'm finished. I don't want to be here anymore. It's too much. I just can't do it."

"Yes you can, damn it." Ipecac syrup pours sugary over my tongue. "Swallow it," he screams. "I said, swallow it."

He holds the pink plastic hospital pan in wait of my vomit. Then, he says the only thing that could have brought me back, the one thing I will forever hold on to for strength.

"I won't tell the boys that their mother gave up."

BOBBY made three trips to the toilet with pans of puke. I said I'd hang on for the boys.

55

Dooza

SEVERAL MONTHS HAVE gone by. The pill bottles are gone, except for Klonopin, which I only take a few times a month, when I feel a spell coming on. Physically I am stronger. Dull, damaged-nerve sensation in my foot will remain for years to come.

David is now traveling from Bath to North Conway once a week to teach ballroom classes with me. Our rented dance studio space is tucked into a courtyard just off Route 16, which runs the length of the village. Tonight we are beginning a new six-week session. David unlocks the double glass studio doors. I wait with a dance bag slung over my shoulder, loaded with notes and cassette tapes. Inside the studio, there is a small area with a bench and a place to change shoes. An old-fashioned wooden desk sits at the edge of the dance floor. I lean against it with the telephone in one hand, pulling the registry sheet out of my bag with the other.

"Now where exactly is this shindig?" The woman chuckles and says her name is Dooza. "You people like to laugh? Cause my friend Darrin and I are comin for the laughs." Her accent is Down East drawled. "Okay, sign us up. See ya in a few."

David is a creature of habit. Every dance class we have ever taught, he has worn the same thing. Black pants that I think he has had since high school and a faded, light green, button-down shirt that Mumma would say you could shoot peas through. He laughs and agrees when I tell him. "David, you're the only gay man I know who is missing the fashion gene."

Dooza and her friend are the first to arrive. She is my height, fiveeightish, and at least five inches taller than her friend. Her smile is luminous, her laughter infectious. "Well, Jesus, I thought you'd be an old lady teacher with a stick and gray-haired bun." She shakes my hand up and down like she is pumping water. "This is Darrin. We work at the bank together. I figured I wouldn't wait any longer for my husband to get up off the couch and take me, so I brought him instead." She hitches her thumb back at Darrin and laughs hard, raspy, like she just finished smoking the tail end of a cigarette.

Now, months later, Dooza and Darrin come to all our consecutive ballroom dance sessions. I stopped charging them weeks ago, because their entertainment value far outweighs any fee I could ask for. Before class begins, Dooza tells Maine hunter-woman stories, like how she tramps through the woods with a tampon soaked in deer scent dragging off her L. L. Bean boot, then sits in a tree stand in full makeup, reading a Harlequin Romance novel and waiting to fire her gun. I never know if people will be offended by her quick-witted humor, but as I make a fast visual pass around the room of students, I see they are always laughing, many of them doubled over and hanging to the ballet barres.

Dooza is teller manager at the bank just down the street, where she stands polished and professional behind the counter, hair shining rich like dark exotic-wood lacquer and her clothes lying colorful, like feathers on a tropical bird. When I call there, she answers politely, each syllable ringing clear and precise. "Good afternoon, North Conway Bank. This is Susan. How may I help you?" Then when she realizes it's me, she laughs from her toes and honks like a foghorn. "By Jesus, Sista, how the hell are ya?"

On Friday nights after dance class, Dooza, Darrin, David, and I go to Jackson Square next door to the studio and across from the bank. It's where I watch the floor fill up with my students. I cheer when they do a triple-step East Coast Swing, to "In the Mood." I screech a four-fingered whistle when they dance a Cha Cha chase step, to Santana's "Evil Ways." "You've got to change your evil ways, baby." I sing it loud.

"'Rhythm Is a Dancer'" this one's for Nance," the DJ says deep into the microphone. One long gulp of beer pours into me. My cigarette crushes into the ashtray. I am dancing before I get onto the floor of glass squares, lit from underneath with flashing colored lights. I watch my feet step from blue to red. Green to orange. Dozens of feet surrounding mine, dancing and pumping to the music. Swirling yellow spotlights radiate into my hair and bounce off my hip. I am in a box of light. Arms over my head, waving, clapping, rolling, pulling in the energy around me. The bass beats at my chest and syncs with my heartbeat. It is so loud, I think the glasses must be swinging from the bar rack.

It's always a good time when Dooza is with us at Jackson Square. She has everyone's attention in the corner of the club when she tells tales of her redneck grammy and hunting critters in the northern woods. We all laugh at her comical recounts, while she hard blots her red lips on a cigarette filter and blows smoke up over her head. Then she sips at her Coors Light and honks.

I laugh so much, beer spills down my hand and into the rolled-up sleeve of my tan blazer. David puffs menthols, one elbow dug to the tabletop, his legs crossed crooked away from it, like he's ready to jump to the dance floor. He pours what's left in the milk pitcher into his half-empty coffee cup like a vagabond. His mother's estate has left him a wealthy man, but he prefers to live frugally, buying meat end specials at Shop 'n Save and wearing the same old gray jacket that Dooza threatens to burn each time she sees it.

Jackson Square loses its magic after midnight when the lights come on. Waitresses with tired eyes and dirty bar rags stretch out across sticky tables, wiping up puddles of beer and dumping over-flowing ashtrays into paper towels. The last of the bar crowd stumbles out the side door and into the parking lot. Dooza and my students left hours ago.

The tall, handsome bouncer with the curly blond hair says good-bye to David and me. "You guys be careful on the roads. Cops are waiting over at Sid's market and down the end of the strip, in the Yield House lot." He gives me a concerned nod and locks the door behind us.

David walks me to my car, in the back parking lot, and we hug good-bye. "Okay," he says. "See you next week. I'll be following behind you until we get to the split over the Saco River. Drive safely."

I get into my car, close the door, turn on the engine, and roll down my window to the midnight mountain spring air. I watch David walk to his Volvo and hear keys jingling in his hand. I wrap my hands around the top of the steering wheel and lay my forehead between them. My fingers reek of Marlboros. My arms vibrate. Blood swishes a rhythmic beat in my ears. With the music and laughter ended, I track back over how many beers I drank, and how badly I flirted with the bouncer. "Uhhh, Nancy, you are so stupid," I say out loud.

My cloak of disguise is gone now, and I am back to being me. A shameful collection of fragmented molestation memories, a toxic body of prescription drugs, and the truth, that I am nothing more than a horrible mistake made by two young lovers in the backseat of a 1950s Chevy.

I put my car in drive and follow David through town.

56

Potholes

It's midafternoon, May 4, 1991, Jason's tenth birthday. The boys and I have come home from doing errands. I lay two grocery bags and my purse on the end of the deacon's bench and glance over at the answering machine. It's blinking one message. I rewind the tape and press Play.

"Nancy, it's Mom. Call me." Elizabeth's voice sounds urgent, and given that we talk only three or four times a year, I dial her number immediately. She answers out of breath.

"Mom? What's wrong?" My heart pounds.

"Well, there's no other way to tell you. Except just tell you," she blurts. "Your father is dead. I'm holding George's obituary in my hand. He died two days ago."

The floor comes hard underneath me. The telephone cord loops over and over, strangling my wrist until there is no slack coming out of the wall and red marks appear on my skin. My father is dead, and the only time I have seen him was in the wintery shadows of a run-down trailer park. "Why did you talk me out of meeting him?" I scream at her.

Elizabeth's tone is dramatic. "It seemed like the best thing at the time, Nancy. What do you want from me?" It sounds like something Mumma would say.

"What I want is for you to take me to the funeral. It will be my only chance to be near him."

She answers before I have finished. "I can't do that. The obituary says where it is, but it's closed, for just the family."

158

"I am family. Whether you go with me or not, I'm going."

My hands are shaking when our angry voices stop and we hang up.

RAIN batters the roof of Elizabeth's car as we pull into the narrow paved road of the Auburn Catholic cemetery. We move slowly past rows of granite headstones, rising and falling over potholes of loose dirt and chunks of tar. Five cars are parked outside the small chapel, their tires sitting low in muddy gutter pools of water. I look at my watch. It is five minutes before the one o'clock service.

Elizabeth stops the car and speaks quietly, clutching the steering wheel in both hands and peering through the constant swish of windshield wipers. "I don't think anyone else is coming."

My hands smooth over the skirt of my flowered knit dress. I reach into my purse, open a tin of breath mints, and pop one into my mouth. "Mom, are you afraid to go in? Are you afraid George's family will recognize you?"

"No, I'm not afraid." Her voice is determined. "It's been thirty-five years since I last saw your father's wife, the year you were adopted. With this extra weight and lighter hair, I doubt if anyone would know me now."

I turn to her. "What if they do recognize you? What will you say?"

"Well," she says, drawing it out as she thinks, her eyes still on the windshield. "I will say I'm an old friend of the family, that's all."

I lean flat back against the seat, my fingers to the door handle. "Then I will say I'm an old friend of the old friend." We both laugh silly, like sneaky teenage girls.

The car engine clunks as my mother turns it off. "Ready?" she asks.

In the driveway, Elizabeth's hand feels warm around mine, even though it is a chilled spring day. She leads us to the chapel. How strange, I think. Of all the things our joined hands have missed. My first day of school, mother-daughter talks, the birth of my babies. How strange that today our hands are tight together, ready to stand next to my father's dead body.

Dodging brown mud puddles with drowning clumps of fresh-cut grass, she hesitates for just a moment before pulling open the chapel door. In the short hallway to the service room, I walk behind her on the balls of my shoes to keep my heels from clacking on the tile floor. My mother's hand is still tight to mine as she leads us to the open rotunda.

A dozen people stand in a half-moon shape, heads down to the echoed chant of the priest, who has already started the service. No one looks up as we slide into the back of the group. One octagonal window stares down from the peak of the roof. A row of lit candles slightly flicker next to the priest. A damp chill runs from the back of my head down over each bump of my spine and all the way to my tail bone. It makes me shudder like I have to pee.

At the top center of the room is a pine casket draped with an American flag stretching lengthwise to the group. At the foot of it, to the right, an elderly woman sits quietly holding rosary beads in her aged hands. Next to her are two women, looking similar with short, apple-shaped bodies and dark blond hair. They stand facing the rest of us like they might say something, but they do not.

I survey the crowd, remembering the obituary list of surviving relatives. The seated woman must be my grandmother. The woman who stands closest, looking much like the grandmother, would be my father's sister, and the other woman may be George's ex-wife, since she was not mentioned in the obituary.

"George Levesque, 60, died at his home after a long illness. He is survived by two daughters. Nancy Levesque of Auburn and Ann Levesque of Portland. He was predeceased by a son, Raymond." Elizabeth says she saw my brother's obituary in the Auburn newspaper years ago. It said he had died of leukemia at age fifteen.

At the back of the small rotunda, my mother and I stand side by side. I can feel the heat from her body as it presses against my left arm. I glance at her face. Her lips are pursed together so hard, I can barely see her lipstick, like her teeth might bite right through the inside of her mouth. She closes her eyes. I wonder if she has traveled back to the memory of her secret relationship with my father, and how he left his family to rendezvous with her in the backseat of his car, where she says I was conceived. But my eyes are wide open. I will take it all in. This is the only time the three of us will be together, mother, father, and me.

To my right, within arm's length, stands a woman. Her body is slender, legs long in tight jeans narrowed at the calf and zippered up from the ankle. Our hair color is the same brunette shade. Our height, exact. We could be bookends. It's my sister Nancy. I can just feel it in my gut. On the other side of her stands a heavier-set woman. She looks nothing like Nancy but similar to the women at the front. Her hair is also dark blond, rolled under to her neck and tucked behind her ears. This must be Ann.

Other than the priest's voice, the room is silent and eerie. People stand with no outward emotion, their hands together in prayer. No one appears to make notice of the person next to them. No one speaks and no one cries, until the shorter sister, with the blond hair, moves to the front of the room. Ann walks slowly to the casket with one hand woven to the other at her chest and stands with the two blond women. The dark-haired sister to my right begins to whimper. The sounds of her quick, abandoned sobs lift above the stillness of the group. I watch her from the corner of my eye, shifting my position repeatedly in excuse to look at her. She dabs her cheeks with a tissue, then lets both hands fall loose to her hips. Tears begin to well in my eyes. I feel pulled to comfort her as she stands alone, only two feet away from me.

As the service concludes, Ann returns to Nancy and people quietly nod condolences to them, unaware that a secret sister stands at their side. This is my chance to reach out, or risk never knowing them. Adrenaline pulses as I step toward the dark-haired sister, my right hand inches from her shoulder. Then the fast, tight grip of Elizabeth's hand on my left wrist pulls me to a halt.

"Not now, dear," my mother whispers close to my face. "Not here. This is not the time, nor the place."

I study every detail of my sisters as they are escorted down the hallway by a man in a dark suit. He holds open the door as a gust of wind sweeps Ann's blue two-piece dress flat to the front of her sturdy legs and back behind her like a boat sail. Nancy follows at a slower pace to Ann's determined gait. Nancy's short black jacket fits her curved form as it would mine, her boots clicking across the tile and away from me. Under the cover of two black umbrellas, I watch them step into a waiting car. Elizabeth and I file out with the others. People group into cars, never asking who we are. I can feel the cold rain in the part of my hair. Mucky water soaks through the side seams of my shoes. I knew exactly who they were when I saw them, like there was some kind of bonding thread between us.

THE next morning, at home, I sit on the kitchen floor. In front of me is the adoption notebook that ten years ago mapped my path to Elizabeth. I have opened it to a new page and taped George's obituary to it. I read it again. "Arrangements made by Pinette Funeral Home." I will start here.

A woman answers. "Hello," I say. "I was wondering if you could help me. You did a service for George Levesque yesterday. I wasn't able to attend, and I so wanted to send a card to his daughters. Would you have their addresses by any chance?"

"Oh, yes, of course. I'd be happy to help you." I hear papers shuffling. "Hmmm. Well, I don't see the girls' addresses. But I do have addresses and phone numbers for Mr. Levesque's mother and his sister. Would you like those?"

I write down what she tells me, then ask again. "Do you have any idea how I might contact his daughters? I'd so appreciate that."

"I'm sorry," she begins. "The only thing I know is, after their parents divorced, one girl moved out of town and the other one stayed in the area."

I thank her, finish making pencil notes next to my father's obituary, and hang up. I look down at where I've written my grandmother's name and think how upsetting it would be for her to hear from an illegitimate granddaughter, especially the day after her son's funeral. I start to dial the aunt's number, then stop and lay the receiver back on the wall rest.

My gut says no. Elizabeth is right. Now is not the time.

57

Drama

IT IS MAY 2, 1993. A year and a half since Glenn and I founded Arts In Motion, community theater and education company, where rehearsals keep me out at least five nights a week. Josh and Jason are always with me. Bobby never is. He says watching me drag crap in and out of the house for props and costumes and hearing me sing the same annoying songs over and over is all he can handle.

It is midnight when the boys and I get home from striking the *Plaza Suite* set at Eastern Slope Playhouse. They drop their backpacks onto the kitchen bench and head to bed.

"I'll be right in to kiss you good night," I call after them, then flop exhausted onto the den couch. In one corner is a big pile of laundry waiting to be folded. Across from it, my desk piled high with plans for upcoming projects with Glenn and dance classes with David. Now that I am busy with the theater, I no longer go to Bath. Glenn and I have moved along so fast with our productions, there is hardly time for anything else.

The muscles in my legs feel knotted as I step down over the cellar stairs and open the refrigerator we keep stocked with drinks. I sit halfway back up the staircase, crack open a Coors Light, and look out at the mess. My cellar has filled, as flats, props, and costumes from one show pile up on those from the last. Somewhere underneath it all are antiques from Nanny's house and Jason's collection of Jolt bottles. Next to the washer is a tower of dirty laundry, some of which the cat has peed on because I have neglected to empty his litter box.

Half the beer pours down my throat as I think about how financially things are spiraling off the edge, but Glenn and I are the only ones in the company who know that. I have been borrowing thousands of dollars from my parents and Bobby's credit cards to keep up with the bills. Even though we are playing to full houses, before the run of the show is through, our proceeds have been spent many times over on venue rent, staff, and supplies.

The upstairs hall light is off. Bobby has been in bed for hours. In the boys' downstairs bedroom, Joshua is already asleep on the top bunk. I step up onto the edge of the bottom mattress, pull the blanket to the back of his curls, and hold my cheek against his. "Sing to me, Mom," I hear Jason whisper from the bottom bunk. I pull the blanket up over his shoulder and crawl over him to the wall. I lay my head on his pillow and scoop him in closer to me. My chest vibrates in song against his back. I kiss his curls, pull Nanny's handmade afghan over us, and go to sleep.

THE next morning I am sitting at the dining room table, sipping coffee and staring blankly out at the woods when Glenn opens my kitchen door. "Good morning, Sunshine." He booms from his six-foot, three-hundred-pound body. He lays a clean new manila folder down next to me, kisses the top of my head, then walks over to the coffeepot. I watch him spoon three sugars into a blue mug. "I love the start of a new show, don't you?" He sits next to me, carefully puts the mug to his lips, and takes a slurp from the top. "Nance, I've already sent for scripts, and I just talked to a guy I know from Plymouth State College who will do our musical direction. I told him we'd pay him a stipend of . . ."

"Glenn," I interrupt. Steam rises off my coffee. My hands are hot to the cup. "We can't keep making commitments to staff, charging up expenses at local businesses, and spending money we don't have. I know your money source is limited, but I have pulled money from every direction I can. I have even emptied the boys' bank accounts. Something has got to change. We've got to get this money back."

He looks surprised as he sits up tall and lays one hand over my arm. His fat lips pucker up as he says it. "Nance, don't worry. This next show is going to bring in big money. Big money." Then he waves his arm up between us, flicks his wrist over his balding head, and theatrically projects his voice. "It'll be beautiful. Don't worry."

AFTER a full day of planning, Glenn has gone back home. Bobby has worked late, past dinner. I have fed the boys and I am sitting on the screened porch drinking wine and watching them bounce on the trampoline when Bobby pulls the living room slider open and steps out next to me. His dark, thick eyebrows are pinched. I think his black mustache and connecting beard make him look like a 1960s cartoon villain.

"Nance, I've got to talk to you about this money situation."

I put the wine glass back to my lips and don't look at him.

"How are you and Glenn planning on paying me back, anyway? You know the interest charges alone are so high, I don't know how you're going to do it. You need to start some kind of payment plan with me."

"I don't know, Bobby. I keep waiting for the next show to finish, then the next, and the money goes out so fast, I can't keep up with it." I pour what's left from the wine bottle into my glass, watching it stop just at the rim. I bend down and take a long sip. "I can't talk about it right now. Leave me alone." I pick up the glass, chug half, and head for the stairs.

"Come back here right now. Do you hear me, Nancy?"

I am rushing to the bedroom, my eyes on red wine swishing from one side of the glass to the other. His feet pound up the stairs after me. "You can't do anything right, can you, Nancy? Not without your father or me bailing you out. You never have, and you never will."

That was the last thing I heard him say before my back teeth started grinding and everything buzzed out. When I came to, I was in the bedroom closet curled into a ball on top of a cardboard shoe rack that had broken down under the weight of my body. I am still whimpering like a dog that's been attacked when I realize where I am.

Bobby's voice sounds far away. "It's okay, Nance. Can you hear me? You're almost thirty-eight years old, and you are in your own bedroom. Remember?" I shake circulation into my hands and crawl up to the bed and under the blankets. His voice is patient now. "It's been two hours since you came upstairs. I watched you crawl on your hands and knees, crying and babbling from one corner of this room to the other, looking for a place to hide. It was like you didn't know you had an adult body. You tried to get under the bed, but when you wouldn't fit, you crawled into the closet. Do you remember that?"

My ears are still humming, like I am waking up from anesthesia. He takes my hand and moves closer. "You kept screaming like I was going to beat you, and you were pleading that I not take your quilts away." His voice goes lower. "But it wasn't me you were talking to, was it, Nance?"

I let go of his hand, push back to the headboard, and pull a pillow to my chest. Baked exhaustion has soaked the armpits of my white blouse. I now feel cold in all the wet spots, under the back of my hair, in the crease of my stomach, the small of my back, under my butt cheeks. Round circles of sweat mark the kneecaps on my cotton khaki pants, the way my tights used to get when teaching aerobics.

"No, Bobby. It wasn't you." I wipe my face with a handful of tissues. "When I was a little girl, I used to hide in my closet. It had a sloped wall, and on the wall was a shelf where Mumma stacked old quilts. I used to climb up on that shelf and get in-between them to hide." I can clearly see myself there with both feet braced to the doorframe, my head not much higher than the white porcelain doorknob in my tight grip. I hear the metal shank drawing back at me. "No, Bobby. It wasn't you I was running from. It was my father."

Bobby hugs me, neither one of us understanding how it could be true. I hug him tighter.

"I keep telling myself it didn't happen. It couldn't have. People in Bath respect my father. My parents have helped us with financial things. They bring us bags of food when they visit, and they seem so happy to see the boys. They took us to Disney World. God, people who abuse their kids don't do all that, do they?"

"I don't know what to say, Nance. Something happened, that's for sure, or you wouldn't be like this." Bobby holds me for a long time, until finally, worn and confused, I fall asleep.

⌣

I HAVE been pretending that things are fine. But they are not. My thoughts are consumed with what will make other people happy, and I will go to any lengths to protect them from the results of their consequences. I must solve all the problems, and put out all the fires, and relieve all the pain of everyone else, no matter what it costs me. If I don't fix it, or ignore it, then it will be my fault if it fails. And when it does fail, that will prove my point. That I am good for nothin.

Love me, want me, need me. I have set myself up for failure.

58

Birthday

THROUGH THE BEDROOM window, I can hear the neighbor's dog barking and birds chirping. The bedspread is still locked at my chin, and my body is curled tight to the edge of the bed. I stretch one leg in back of me in search of Bobby before opening my eyes. He is not there. My bedside clock reads 6:15. Still time to make breakfast for Josh and Jason and help them get out the door for school. With my temples throbbing, I pull myself up to the headboard and look over at the flattened cardboard shoe rack. Two pairs of Bobby's sneakers, my tan sandals, and three pairs of pumps line up on the opposite side of the open closet where Bobby must have arranged them last night. I lean forward and lay my chest flat to the bed. My heart beats so hard, it takes my breath away. I pull the neck of my nightgown off my throat, sit back up, and swing my feet to the floor.

In the dining room, several gifts wrapped in Star Wars paper lie on the table. A white envelope leans against one of the boxes. "HAPPY 12th BIRTHDAY, JASON, I LOVE YOU" is written across the front of it in my scribbled handwriting. Just beyond me, in the kitchen, Bobby is waiting for a bagel to pop out of the toaster.

"Bobby, did you see me get up last night and wrap these? I don't remember that I did." I pick up the card and run my finger over the ink.

"Yes." His eyes are sharp on a knife full of cream cheese. He works it back and forth over the bagel until it is completely covered in white. He takes a bite and speaks to me between crunches. "How do you feel this morning?"

I walk to the refrigerator and take out a box of eggs. "Scared. How do you feel, Bobby?"

"Scared." His eyes are wide as he slowly nods and looks down at the floor. He finishes his bagel, kisses me on the cheek, and leaves for work.

After the boys eat and Jason opens his gifts, they grab their backpacks from the kitchen bench and head out the door for the school bus. I stand on the side porch watching them, my pink flannel robe wrapped snug under my folded arms. Rays of sun stream broken at me through the pine branches. A small icy patch of snow lies in a cold shadowed spot, just beyond the woodpile, waiting to be melted. Granite rocks crunch under Josh's feet as he starts out the driveway, with Jason close behind him. Then Jason stops and turns to me. "I love you, Mom. I hope today will be better for you."

With my arms outstretched to him, I step barefooted down off the porch and into the granite rocks. He runs back and wraps his arms tight around me. He smells like maple syrup. "Happy birthday, honey. I'll see you when you get home, and we'll have a celebration dinner. Okay?"

Josh is yelling for his brother from the mailbox. "Come on, Jason. We'll miss the bus."

As they walk out of sight down Beechwood Drive, I hear the kitchen phone ringing. Pointed pieces of gray rock poke jagged into the arches of my feet as I step across to the weathered porch.

In the kitchen, I grab for the receiver on the fourth ring. "Hello."

I hear the tail end of Mumma's yawn. "Nancy? Are the boys still there?"

"No, Mumma, they just left for the bus."

"Well, did Jason open the gift I sent him?"

"Yes, thank you. He's wearing the skateboard shirt today."

"Oh good. I thought he'd like it. Sorry I missed him. I'll have to call him tonight."

I sit down on the kitchen bench and pull my purse on top of my lap. "Mumma, I've got to get into the shower. I have an appointment in Portland this morning."

"Oh? Are you goin to see that new therapist again? For God sake, Nancy, why don't you just forget about all that stuff?"

"All that stuff? You mean whatever happened in our house, Mumma? Things I only have partial memory of?" I can feel my back teeth start to clench, and my eyes fuzz into a tunnel. The room begins to fade as my fingernails dig into the leather strap of my bag.

Mumma's voice is quick. "Nothin happened, Nancy. Stop bein so foolish."

My hands are shaking as I reach into my purse for the bottle of Klonopin and put one under my tongue. I can't allow myself to dissociate. I have got to get into the car and drive an hour and a half to Portland, Maine.

"Yeah well." She pauses for a moment. "Is it rainin up there?"

"No, Mumma. It's not raining. The sun is out, but I have to go. We'll talk to you later."

As I place the receiver back onto the wall rest, my head shakes from side to side. Everything vibrates so vividly around me, the baskets hanging from the living room ceiling appear to be swinging. I say it out loud. "Pull it together, Nancy. You can do it. You've got to do it for the boys."

59

Locked Up

KAREN'S OFFICE IS in the front living room of her red Victorian house in the historic district of Portland. The sign on the front door reads, COME IN. As I open it, I expect to see her walking down the front hallway toward me, but today I only hear her voice. I tap on the half-open office door and peek in. She is sitting at her desk with phone in hand. She stands when she sees me.

"I will call you back in a bit," she says, then hangs up and asks me to sit down. Her eyes are pinched. She doesn't shake my hand.

The room is huge, with tall ceilings. Large, gold-framed paintings hang on the wall with spotlights over them. A mahogany bookcase with glass doors holds shelves of medical books. A wooden sailing ship model sits on top. The leather couch smells like the inside of a new car when I sit down on it. It is much too fancy to put my feet up on. Here there are no pictures of Buddha, no incense, and no piles of tangled plant vines on the windowsill.

Karen sits back down at her desk. The full width of an Oriental rug lies muted between us. "How are you feeling this morning?" she asks. I can tell by the pensive look on her face, she has already spoken to Bobby. I don't respond. My breath feels shallow.

"We have a lot to talk about today." She looks down at the papers on her desk, then back at me. "In reviewing the records your last doctor has sent, I have a suggestion to make, and I do want to tell you that I have spoken with your husband this morning. He feels you are not safe in your home, and he is very concerned about your two young sons. Remind me how old they are."

The sides of my mouth quiver nervously. "Joshua will be fifteen in July, and Jason is twelve. Today is his birthday."

She crosses one leg over the other and leans back. "Nancy, you've got to start making some changes in your home. What your husband and I feel is best for you is that you go away for a while and get some help. What you have is called post-traumatic stress disorder. There is a facility in southern New Hampshire that specializes in addiction and trauma issues. You will be a patient in their psychiatric unit. Do you feel you could do that today?"

My arms and legs are tingling. I slide to the edge of the couch. I want to run, get back into my car, drive home, and hide under the covers of my bed. "Today? No, I can't go today. I just told you. It's my son's birthday."

Karen stands. She slowly walks closer, her fingers laced together, hanging even with her crotch. "Well, I understand that, Nancy. But it will be today. Arrangements have already been made."

The red dress she is wearing vibrates in and out of my vision. The Oriental rug burns through the knees of my black cotton leggings. When I come conscious again, I am in the corner of the room with a desk lamp and a wastebasket pulled tight to my chest, and Karen is sitting on the floor in front of me with the phone in her hand.

Later, when Bobby arrives, I am sent to sit in the hallway so he and Karen can talk privately. On the straight-back wooden chair, I pull my knees to my chest and start to sob. My brain suddenly floods with the memory of being in the high school principal's office. I was so stoned that day, he had called Mumma to come get me. After she picked me up, she took me straight to see Daddy's doctor friend. The next day I went back to school with an absentee note that Mumma had written. "Please excuse Nancy for being absent from school yesterday. I took her to the doctor. She has a bladder infection. Sincerely, Doris Steen."

Karen's office door opens. Bobby says he will be driving me to the facility, immediately. I am sweaty, confused, scared, and, in this moment, too tired to argue.

I DON'T remember the ride to the detox facility. My first visual memory of the place is of a lone metal chair pushed flush against the end of the nurses' station in the psychiatric ward. I drop down onto it. It is cold underneath me. My body shakes uncontrollably, like the legs of the chair are wired to a low-voltage charge. I am prickly with fear. My shoulders shiver up to my cheeks.

The nurse's gray eyes peer over half-moon, red-framed glasses. They hang on the end of her stub nose. She pulls my arm under her armpit before I realize she's done it and holds it firm against the side of her breast, intent on the blood pressure cuff around my arm. She pumps the bulb tight again and again and watches the dial.

I fight her grip. "Don't touch me. Get away from me," I yell. Her arm squeezes tight over mine. Another set of hands fast grip and anchor over the back of my shoulders. "Leave me alone." I twist away from the second nurse. As her fingers dig into the soft spots between my bones, I am fired to fight.

Velcro rips long and loud as the first nurse swipes the cuff off my arm. "Okay, Nancy." She picks up a clipboard and watches her pencil record my vitals. "We will need to take some information from you. Then we will get you settled in." She pulls a clump of graying hair from her eyes, runs it through her fingers and up over her head.

Bobby stands off to one side. My leather purse hangs from his rigid fist and against pressed khaki pants he ironed with a perfect leg crease this morning. He says nothing, waiting for the nurse to instruct him. The first nurse steps up and reaches for my bag. "Mr. Greenblatt, I'll take care of that. We just ask that you take her wallet with you, and if you would stop by the office on your way out, there is some paperwork you'll need to do."

Bobby leans down. I feel his beard brush fast at my cheek. "No, Bobby, you're not going to leave me here, are you? Please don't leave me here."

"You've got to try, Nance, just try, okay?" He doesn't wait for me to answer. I watch the back of his yellow fleece jacket as he moves fast to the double doors with a nurse behind him.

I am still anchored to the chair. Fear presses against my chest. "No, I can't stay here. Don't leave me." Bobby doesn't look back. The heavy doors lock behind him with a tight slam. He disappears.

I jerk my shoulders from the woman's grasp. She lets go. The nurse

A VOICE IN THE TIDE

with the red glasses stands in front of me, still holding her clipboard. "Look, you've got to calm down. We're only here to help you, but you must follow some rules. Now take some deep breaths, and this cup, and go to the toilet and give us a urine sample. Then we'll need to search you."

I wrap my arms tight to my chest. "What does that mean, you need to search me?"

She stands firm, like both shoes are glued to the floor. She passes me a small plastic cup and a cotton gown. "I mean, you'll need to take off all your clothes and put this on."

Behind the nurses' station is a bathroom. I go into it alone, pee in the cup, and put on the gown. When I open the door, both nurses are waiting, blocking my exit.

The first nurse straddles the doorframe and speaks abruptly. "Now drop the gown. We need to see your body."

I wrap it tight, one hand to my breasts, the other near my crotch. I step farther back into the bathroom. "No. I won't."

"We need to make sure you haven't concealed anything, and we need to check your body for bruises."

"I won't."

She removes her red glasses and slides them into her shirt pocket, her patience waning. "If you refuse to take off the gown and prove you are not hiding anything in or around your body, I must ask you to spread your arms and legs out to the side and jump until I tell you to stop."

Humiliated with the thin, oversized robe hanging off my naked body, I straddle my legs, hold my arms parallel to the bathroom floor, and jump up and down. I don't count. It must be more than twelve times before she says stop. I am trembling cold and unprotected without my own arms to comfort me. My back teeth clench. My ears are humming with vibration. The cotton robe begins to ball up in my gnarled grasping fingers. Oh shit, no. I'm having a spell. I sit on the toilet, my shoulders to my ears and my body hunched over so far, my boobs are touching my thighs. I smell alcohol swabs and urine. I can hear other people, just out of sight, behind the second nurse. She talks to them, then looks back at me, the abandoned suspect.

The first nurse questions me. "How much alcohol do you drink? What do you take for drugs? What are your sexual habits? Have you ever had food issues? Who lives with you at home?" Words fire from her mouth like bullets. I am spinning dizzy. Garbled answers that run together and make no sense come through my chattering teeth.

Now back in my own clothes and sitting in the cold metal chair, I see the nurse with the red glasses digging into my purse. She holds it out in front of me.

"We need to look through your bag. Anything you could potentially injure yourself with will go into the sharps bin behind the desk. You may take whatever is left with you to your room."

Perfume, folding scissors, tweezers, breath spray, mirror, cigarettes, and matches all fall into a bin with my name taped to it.

She walks me to the end of the hall, last room on the left. A droopy-eyed woman scuffs past us. She calls the nurse by name and asks who I am. The nurse remains silent and nods. I look at the woman from the top of her matted hair down to her mismatched socks and sneer in her face. She smiles back at me.

My bed is near the window. There is a blond-haired woman reading a book in the other bed. I don't speak to her, and I don't see her look at me. The nurse asks me to take some pills that will calm me, but I refuse. I curl at the top of the bed frame, feet flat under my butt, my shoes and empty purse tight to my chest, and cry so hard, I go away.

This time I go so far away in my dissociation, I go all the way back to Mumma's house. It is summer and the sun has not set yet. From the front door, I can see streaks of orange reaching up from a golden ball about to disappear behind the trees. I can hear the theme song from *Perry Mason* coming from the living room television as I start up the stairs. Then as fast as the turn of a television dial, I am under my bed, my fingers tight to the wiry springs of the frame and Daddy's rough-skinned hand locked to my seven-year-old ankle. Dust sucks up my nose. He pulls on my leg. As he yanks harder, my favorite white undershirt, the one with the tiny blue flowers, catches on a gold metal seam tacked to the linoleum. My belly burns. I scream for Mumma.

I am not sure how long I hysterically cried in the corner of my bed that night. I just know that fragmented scenes of rape flashed like horror movie trailers in front of me. Snippets of my life from pre-school to college age stabbed and tore at my being, and never once did Mumma save me.

I guess when it is all they can take, a nurse finally decides to put an end to it. It's not the nurse with the red glasses who comes to me. The new nurse shouts my name. I hear her clearer and clearer, as I trans-port out of Mumma's house and back to the psychiatric bed. The sheets are now wound around my legs, and a pillow covers my purse and shoes at my chest. The new nurse bends to me, with a paper cup of water in one hand and two pills in the other.

"This has gone on long enough, Nancy. You have to quiet down. You are disturbing all the other residents. Come on, put out your hand and take this sedative."

I was glad she was there. It had been a long day, Tuesday, May 4, 1993, Jason's twelfth birthday.

60

Working the Program

I LIE SLEEPING WHERE the edge of the bed meets the wall. The handle of my purse is looped in the crook of my arm, my shoes inside it where other things used to be. The bed pillow in my arms is snug to the purse. The morning nurse stands over me, both fists on her fat hips. Her voice is quick and loud. "Nancy. Wake up, it's six thirty."

In the moment before my swollen, crusty eyes open, I hear Mumma yelling up the stairs and the rumble of Daddy's throat as he rips the covers off. I sit up fast, my brain rewinding to yesterday. I remember I crawled across the doctor's floor. Bobby left me. I missed my baby's birthday. Everything else floats in and out on the edges of broken thoughts.

"Get up and come to community meeting with the rest of the women." She takes her hands off her hips and steps backward, pointing to the bathroom cubic in the corner of the room. "Get up," she shouts again. "You'll feel better once you wash your face."

I pull the covers to my chin. "I'm not going anywhere with you. Leave me alone."

Her hands go back to the bulging elastic waist of her polyester pants. "Look, Nancy, when you arrived here you were told about our schedule of meetings and classes. You signed a form in agreement. That's just how our program works."

"Yeah, I don't remember any of that, so get the hell away from me." One hand digs into her short, formless hair-cut. I listen to her nails scratch at it. She lets out a long, disgusted sigh.

My voice is hoarse and thick. "Did you hear me? I said I am not going to your damn meeting." I push down into the bedding and pull the pillow over my head.

"Get yourself out to the lobby as soon as possible. We do not put up with this kind of behavior."

I yell at her as she leaves. "Then let me out of here. I want to go home." Both eyes feel like they've been punched in a drunken brawl. I rub the crusty gravel from them. "I want to go home."

My roommate sits on my side of her bed, smoothing out the lap of her aqua dress. "I'm Carrie. Sorry you had such a hard night. You cried in your sleep for hours."

"Sorry." I scan blank walls to a window that looks one story down at a mechanical building. I hear industrial fans whirring. A tall chain-link fence stretches full behind it.

Carrie pulls a brush down over her shiny, yellow hair and flips it behind her ear. Her blush and lips are deep pink. "It's okay. Eventually, they put me into another room. I was a mess the night I got here too." She lays the brush on the nightstand.

I think she looks too normal to be in a place like this. "You look fine to me. Why are you here?"

At first she doesn't say anything. Then stands and moves to the door. "I was gang raped. I didn't have full memory of that until this week. I just didn't want to remember. But I got to the point where it stopped me from living. Then one day I had a total breakdown and my husband brought me here. I'm doing much better now. You'll be fine. Trust me, they're good here." She tells me she's going on a job interview and will see me later.

I close my eyes, wanting to be lost in sleep, terrified of what secrets will be purged from me, and how long the pain will last.

"May I come in and sit with you?" I hear a woman softly say. "They tell me you don't want to come to community meeting. Is that right?"

She points to the edge of my bed. Her eyes are kind, her hair dark and silky. Dangly silver earrings shaped like birch leaves hanging beneath it. Her long green, earthy-crunchy dress wags between her legs as she steps closer. I smell patchouli oil.

I sit up, my jeans cutting into my crotch and my bra riding sideways under my black sweater. I pull the cuffs to my wrists. "I don't even know what community meeting is."

She sits on the edge of my bed and lays her hands on her knees. "Well, every morning the ten to fifteen women on this ward gather in the lounge next to the nurses' station. They talk about their expectations and goals for the day, what their low was from the day before, and take turns reading affirmations. They also practice breathing exercises. Then everyone has a class schedule to follow, depending on what you are working on. They keep you really busy here. After dinner we all get together for a wrap-up meeting, and everyone shares their high for the day. After that, we have popcorn and movies. Do you think you could do that?" She smiles.

Tears run down my cheeks and wet the slit of my dry lips. "I just want to go home."

Her eyes tell me she understands. "I know it's not easy. But I think we can help each other. This is my first day of work here at the facility. I'm a little nervous, and I bet you are too. Shall we try this together?" She reaches her hand out to me.

We walk the full length of the hall to the lobby. With my hand in hers, just one person to trust, I think it is possible.

My aching body sinks low into the couch cushions. I pull my stocking feet underneath me and survey the group. Women of all ages joke with one another as the meeting begins. I sit unresponsive in protest as the facilitator reads today's mantra from a well-worn book. "I have the freedom to choose my thoughts. I choose to focus on that which nourishes and supports a healthy lifestyle."

When the meeting is over, the woman with the matted hair and mismatched socks comes up to me. Off to the side of her thin body she is holding an unlit cigarette in her fingers like a game-show host. "Sweetie, nobody really wants to be here. But these are all good women, struggling to live. We help each other, so whatever you need, you just ask. The room next to yours is for therapy, but it doubles as a smoker. So get a butt from the nurse and let's go."

In some wild way, it makes me feel loved.

61

Sleep Until I Die

THE POLYESTER-PANTS NURSE takes a chart from behind the nurses' station. "These are your classes." One fat finger points to yellow-highlighted boxes. "You must sign in and out when traveling between the locked units, and you have no more than three minutes to get to where you're supposed to be. See here? Nine o'clock is your first class. Substance Abuse. Get moving."

The room is already full of men and women when I step into it. Two women push together on a bench to make room for me. Everyone watches. The facilitator's long, frizzed hair lies below his shoulders. One leg is folded up over the other, and a clipboard balances on it. His arms are crossed over a brown wool sweater. I have barely stopped fidgeting when he asks me what I expect to gain from the class.

"Pass," I say, looking at my black socks.

He leans forward. "Oh, you can't pass. We are here to participate. How are you going to stop abusing if you keep ignoring the problem?"

My arms and legs start to buzz, my face flushes, my heart races.

"Nancy, that's your name, right? How's your plan been working so far? Not so good, huh? Otherwise you wouldn't be here. Be grateful we are going to teach you how to work the program."

"No thanks. I don't need your program. I'm not staying."

"Ohhhh." He sounds it long with his eyebrows lifted. Some low laughter comes from several of the residents. Two male staff members sitting in the doorframe glare at me, then stand up at the same time, like a well-rehearsed piece of choreography. One motions me into the hallway.

With my back pressed against the cement wall, I tremble so hard my knees give out. I pull myself up again. The first man leans close to my face. I can taste his garlic breath. "Do you think you're better than the rest of these people?" His squinted eyes don't leave mine. "You think you already know it all, don't you?"

The second man tilts his head to one side. A tiny bit of spit shoots through a space between his top teeth. He raises his voice. "Why aren't you participating, Nancy? Do you realize, with no participation, you will not earn the privilege of going outside or having your family visit? Understand? It's your choice." I cry rippled, snotty sobs, with one side of my face turned flat to the cold wall. They back away and allow me to leave.

I don't want to participate. I don't want to try. If I remember my truth, what will I do with it? If I speak my truth, who will stop loving me? Maybe staying sick is easier.

There are classes in multiple disorder treatment, nutrition counseling, eating disorders, medication education, dual diagnosis, expressive therapy, assertiveness, work issues, relating to families, music therapy, relaxation, and crafts. Of all the classes, survivors group is the toughest. They talk about incest, and several times I have stood up and begged to leave, but every time they make me sit back down, sometimes calling staff for drugs to calm me.

I worry I won't make it to class on time, and will be reprimanded for going over the three-minute limit while in the bathroom puking and shitting out toxins. I am watched all the time. Ward doors lock behind me. Windows don't open. Room doors don't shut. There is no television during the day. No caffeinated coffee, ever. No food, drink, or wastebaskets in the bedrooms. Because I've had food issues, I must eat alone with my feet on the floor near the nurses' station, while the other women go to the cafeteria. If I have to use the bathroom after I eat, someone comes with me to make sure I don't throw up my meal. When I shower, someone stands outside the curtain.

At night I wake up in a cold sweat, screaming for Mumma. During the day I have diarrhea and vomit. I am detoxing. I am dissociating. I am diseased, crazy, and scared. I don't want to stay, but strangely, now that I have been here a week, I am not sure if I want to leave. I am protected. I am trapped.

I just want to sleep until I die.

62

Bucket of Nails

W<small>HEN MY CHILDREN</small> come through those metal doors, I am going to try not to cry. I will hug them so tight, they won't notice the sound of the lock banging, or see the disheveled lobby women talking to themselves. My boys will smell like home. Tide detergent and Doritos.

It is four o'clock, Mother's Day afternoon. We are being led to the psychiatrist's office in an institutional basement maze of sealed doors and wet paint. People pass us. I'm not sure who is staff, who are residents. If one of them yelled "Run," I would have no idea which way to get out. I have no memory of how I got in.

In the psychiatrist's office there are no windows, no decorations on the walls. Pipes run low over our heads. There is a desk with a phone, and four folding chairs in front of it. The nurse asks us to sit down and says the doctor will join us shortly.

Joshua hands me a Mother's Day card with a pink rose on the front. Inside, both boys have signed it. "We Love You Mom. Hang in there. Josh and Jason." Tears flood my eyes. Josh's voice sounds deep and closed off. "Mom, everyone at the theater hopes you feel better soon. I just said you had a flu bug. I didn't tell them where you were."

"Tell them I send my love, honey." What I really want to say is, don't let anyone know your mother has lost her mind and got tossed into the nuthouse.

Jason passes me his favorite white teddy, the one that used to dance on his tummy while I sang him to sleep. His smile quivers. Huge tears roll to his blue sweater vest.

Bobby takes a long breath. His lips purse together.

The doctor's manner is clinical. Her dark bangs lie over the top of her perfectly arched eyebrows. She is young, too young I think to have experience for this. She shifts papers from one hand to the other. She looks back and forth at the boys.

She speaks to Joshua first. "Do you know why your mother is here?"

Bobby is silent. A marble shape rolls up his clenched jaw. One vein pulses in the center of his forehead. Jason looks at the floor as tears pour down his face and between his knees. One foot taps nervously.

Joshua speaks up bravely. "I think so. Because she was drinking too much?"

It feels like a dagger to my heart when I hear him say it. Jason cries out loud, and Bobby hangs his head. I grip the sides of the folding plastic seat so hard, I think my body might break right down through it. I want to reach over and choke this woman for expecting my twelve- and fifteen-year-old sons to answer a question like that. I want to scream, "How the hell would they know why? I don't know why. Do you?"

I don't remember anything else we say after that. I only remember thinking I have destroyed all the relationships I've ever had.

It is a short visit. The nurse waits at the office door to take me back to the ward. Bobby hugs me good-bye. "You better call your mother, Nance. She's been calling every day, wondering where you are. I told her you were at theater rehearsal. I am not going to be the one to tell her the truth."

Josh is fighting back tears after we all hug good-bye. He puts his hand on Jason's shoulder and leads him down the hall. I watch the three of them walk away, not knowing when I will see them next. Jason turns back and calls out to me. His smile is wide and proud. "You can do it, Mom. You're tough as a bucket of nails." And I believe my son is right.

NEXT to the lounge is the laundry room. The community telephone hangs on the wall over the washing machine. I jump up to its white aluminum cover and sit with my legs folded under me. I reach for the phone and dial Mumma's number. After two rings, both my parents answer, each on a different extension.

"I know you've been wondering why I haven't called you, Mumma."

"Well, we wondered what the heck was goin on and why Bobby seemed so secretive."

"I want to explain to you what's happened." I am steady in breath, determined not to allow them to trigger me into a dissociative spell. "I am in a psychiatric facility in southern New Hampshire."

"Well, I told your father you've been workin too hard. What the hell's the matter with you, pushin yourself like that for God sake? Let someone else do it. Look what it's done to you."

"You don't understand what I'm trying to tell you. This isn't just from work. What I need to say may surprise you. Maybe it won't." There is silence on their end of the line in wait of my words. "I've been diagnosed with three things." They say nothing. "An eating disorder, alcohol dependence, and post-traumatic stress disorder." I take in a quick breath. "From sexual abuse."

Mumma's response is fast and fiery. "What? For God sake that's just foolishness. Who told you that?"

My father clears his throat. Each word rumbles dark and slow. "We never should have adopted you."

The receiver drops from my ear. I calmly place it back on the wall cradle. My sweaty palms make a tinny squeak as I slide down off the washer. Process as an adult, not as a child, I hear myself say.

The hallway lights have been dimmed. Residents are in their rooms preparing for bedtime. Through the window at the end of the hall, there is nothing but blackness. I see my reflection in the pane. I am moving forward to meet myself. Back teeth dry grinding. Ears ringing like a chain-saw gnawing at a tree. Then I am on the floor, in a corner, my head pressed to where one wall meets the other. I push so hard at the cement with the top of my head, it feels like I may push all the way to the other side. Groaning demon sounds boil and spill from a place inside me that has never been purged. Long slats of aluminum Venetian blinds snap and slice in my fingers. I hear feet run toward me. But I am already far away from the detox facility. I've gone home to Mumma's house.

63

Lies

AFTER FIFTEEN DAYS at the psychiatric detox facility, today is the day Bobby will be here to pick me up. I am scared to go home. The woman with the matted hair told me I would feel this way, and I didn't believe her. I am sitting in the psychiatrist's basement office. She half sits on the front of her desk, one foot hanging midair, shuffling through discharge papers.

"Okay, Nancy, now that you have a better understanding of your disorders, and tools to deal with them, you will have to work very hard to stay sober. I have spoken to your classroom facilitators, and they say you did well participating. However, you still have a lot of work to do on grounding and not dissociating from your body." She pulls out some papers for me to sign, and three scripts for antidepressants. "Do you have any questions before you leave?"

My voice is stronger now. "I have a concern. I only drank at night when I was out, or at home after my kids went to bed. You know, they never saw me intoxicated, ever. But I am afraid if I'm not busy I'll start drinking again, and be sent somewhere else."

"Understandable." She passes me the paperwork. "You have severe PTSD, and you can never drink again, ever. You are powerless over alcohol. Do you understand? You must go to AA meetings daily and get a sponsor immediately. And if you are going to heal from the incest, you must confront your father." I cringe. There is nothing worse she could have said. "But don't do it alone, Nancy. Have someone you trust with you."

All the way home, I think about what I will say to my father, and how mad Mumma will be when I do.

THE next morning, things feel normal again. Before Bobby leaves for work, I watch him iron perfect creases down the arms of his oxford shirt. I pack the boys' lunches, kiss them good-bye for the day, and stand on the side kitchen porch waving as they go up the driveway.

The late-May morning air is crisp coming in through the dining room window. I put my face to the screen and breathe in deeply. My coffee cup is half-empty before I remember the doctor's words from yesterday. My stomach begins to pinch, but I am going to do it. I pick up the phone and dial the number to my father's shop. He answers on the first ring. I ask if he is alone. He says he is.

"Daddy, I want to talk about something, and I need you to be honest with me." He is silent. "I have been working really hard to heal, and I have to ask you about when I was younger, about what happened." The dining room chair is slippery under my knees. My head presses into my free hand, and my elbow leans so hard on the table, a prickly sting goes up my arm. I hear him clear his throat.

I close my eyes tight and see people I trust. The earthy-crunchy nurse, my roommate, Carrie, and the woman with the matted hair. I speak louder. "I mean, I remember some very inappropriate things. I need your help to remember the rest."

Again, he rumbles his throat. "I don't know what you mean, Nancy. You're talkin foolish."

"Daddy, you hurt me. I remember. My body remembers. I've always remembered. I just didn't want to see it for what it was."

"Is that what they told you in that hospital? Nancy, don't be stupid. That's what they do in those places. They convince you that somethin happened to you in your childhood so you'll keep comin back. That's how they make their money. It's all a scam."

My chest lies flat on the dining room table. Both kneecaps grind to the seat of the chair. "It's not a scam."

"Honey, after all I've done for you, you can honestly say to me that you think I would hurt you? Well, I'm hurt. You've hurt me. Your mother and I took you into our home and raised you as our own daughter. We sent you to dance lessons, and paid for your college education, and I've given you money whenever you asked for it. I am disappointed in you, Nancy."

I slide off the chair and onto the floor. My butt inches back until I am under a corner wooden chair. The telephone cord strangles my wrist with each fist circle I make. I listen to words coo seductively from my father's poison mouth.

"When you were a little girl I used to watch you sleep. I'd look down at your golden curls and know you were here just for me, all mine. Of course I wouldn't hurt you. Daddy would never hurt you, honey."

"What about all the prescription drugs I took in high school? Bottle after bottle of Demerol and Darvon. I was high all the time. Didn't you ever wonder why I drugged myself?"

His shout startles me. "You're lying. That never happened."

I grab the leg of the dining room table and pull myself out from under the chair. "You're telling me I never took them? It went on for years."

"There is no record of drugs, because you never took them, and I never hurt you."

I am not conscious of what he is saying as I hang up the phone. I sit back on the chair with my head in my hands. You stupid girl. Stupid to think that he would want to help. You worthless piece of shit. I hate you. Both fists thud at my forehead, until I hear nothing but the dull, throbbing ache of failure.

I know the facility staff told Bobby to get rid of all medications and anything containing alcohol, but there must be something here, and I will find it.

In the cellar, underneath the workbench, are boxes of tools, an old train set, and an antique milk delivery box. The tin cover lifts without effort. Jackpot. A bottle of Tylenol, a bottle of rubbing alcohol, and a full bottle of champagne.

My fingers are panicked and clumsy with the plastic cork top. I am screaming like a wild animal caught in a trap, ready to chew my own leg off to be free. Finally, with both hands gripped to the bottle and my lips locked to the top, I become lost to the alcohol as it pours over my pain. The more I drink, the farther I step back to the cellar corner, until I am sliding down the cement wall, collapsing through spider-webs and onto the top of a rusty paint can.

When the bottle is empty, I lie down on the damp cement floor, curl into a ball among the dead bugs, and cry myself somewhere beyond my father's lies.

64

Emergency

Almost two years have passed. It is March 1995. David and I are still teaching dance. Glenn and I are in a rented office space, rehearsing two or three different shows at a time, and I am still borrowing money to keep us going. The afternoon is cold and already dark when our assistant, Noreen, gaits closer to my desk. I can see her chin pulled back into her neck the way it does when there is trouble. Her lips part and clamp repeatedly without words, until she has laid the papers in front of me.

"Bills," she says, then sighs long, and hugs her chubby arms around me.

As I stand up, pain stabs at my left side and doubles me over. "You'll feel better after tomorrow, Nance. Go home early tonight. You need to get some rest." Then she hugs me again and goes back out to her desk in the front office.

I pick up a cigarette just as Glenn comes in. I ask him to close the door behind him, so we can talk privately. He sits down next to me and lights both our cigarettes. Smoke curls in gassy waves around us. Glenn's full lips pucker to the end of his cigarette, then he lifts a bottle of Coke to his mouth with the other hand and takes a drink.

"I don't know how long I'll be out of work, Glenn. It shouldn't be more than a few days." A pen scratches across my check-book. I rip out the check and pass it to him. "Here is seventeen thousand dollars. I think that takes care of all our outstanding company bills. I had to borrow it from my parents. With everything totaled, this brings my personal debt to more than fifty thousand dollars. God, I don't know how we're going to do it."

We both take long drags. A wall of smoke builds between us.

THE next morning I am admitted to North Conway Hospital. While I am having my remaining ovary removed, Bobby contacts an attorney to inquire about his rights in retrieving the money. Because I have signed no legal paperwork proving what I have put in, Bobby is told there is nothing that can be done, except to contact our board of directors in consideration of a payment plan. But I am not aware of Bobby's legal consultation until days later.

Two days after my surgery, I return home under the influence of morphine, Ativan, and amitriptyline. I fall asleep that afternoon and don't wake up until the next morning, when Bobby and the boys come to say good-bye. Again, huddled in bed, I lay stunned, aching, toxic, and depressed. I hear a beeping noise. I see a moving truck backing down over the crushed rocks to the cellar bulkhead, directly under my window. Three of our board members get out of it. They open the bulkhead door and disappear from my sight.

I hear the kitchen door slam and heavy feet coming up over the stairs. Glenn and Noreen stand at my bedside. Glenn leans down and kisses my cheek. The loud volume of his voice makes my ears ring. "Good morning, Sunshine. Nothing to worry about. We borrowed a truck and we're moving the scenery flats out of the cellar and to the office."

I am in a narcotic fog of confusion, but without question I agree. Noreen's tears trail over her mounded rosy cheeks and wet my face. They leave. I go back to sleep.

The next morning I am clearer of mind and begin to wonder why they would need a full-sized moving truck to take scenery flats less than a mile down the street to our office. Still bent over from the surgery, I wrap my pink bathrobe around me, go downstairs to the living room, and open the cellar door.

Sitting mid-staircase, I am staring at a half-empty space. Not only have the flats, props, and costumes been moved out, also gone is the rack with my ballroom gowns, wedding gown, and maternity clothes, and many of Nanny's antique pieces. I climb back up the stairs to the kitchen and dial Glenn's home number. "You rest, Nance. We'll talk later when you feel better. Love you." And that was the end of the conversation.

I don't know what happened after that. Morning turned to evening. Bobby and the boys came home. Bobby made a panicked phone call to the psychiatrist from our bedroom. When he hung up he said we would have to go to the closest psychiatric hospital, and I was being admitted on an emergency basis.

Oh God, not again.

65

Am I Dead Yet

THERE IS A snowstorm tonight. It beats against the car windshield in an endless tunnel of white, as Bobby drives gripped to the steering wheel, fifty miles up Route 16, past the base of Mount Washington and around Dead Man's Curve in Pinkham Notch. We reach the hospital just at midnight.

A woman meets us at the psych unit door. There is a loud buzzing sound as she unlocks it, and in this moment I am sucked through a time warp to 1965. Mumma, Tommy, and I are standing in the lobby at the Bath YMCA, waiting at the door with the wire-screened window. "Buzzer," I hear Tommy yell across the billiard tables to the desk. In his hand is a denim bag, holding his red swim trunks and towel. He is laughing, with Mumma gripped to the back of his blue-plaid flannel shirt as they buzz us in.

Bobby doesn't go into the psych unit with me. I don't think I even say good-bye this time. I am led to a room with a bed and a chair that later I will have no memory of being on. On the floor, in the corner of the room, I watch a half-dead black fly lying on its back. Its legs wiggle, and it makes a vibrating noise trying to right itself back up. Then there is silence, and just when I think it's dead, it starts kicking and vibrating again. I'm not sure how long I watch it die. It seems like forever.

When the fly dies, I cry and scream. I flash back and dissociate. And then, at some point, I find myself standing in the hallway at the nurses' station asking a nurse for a cigarette. The lamp on top of the counter has a green glass lampshade. It is the only light. The hallway is dim. I see no other patients or staff except for this nurse who let me in. I hear no other noises but my own. The nurse's head is down in her work as I say hello. She doesn't move from her chair, and she doesn't answer me. I rattle a newspaper that lies next to the lamp. I say hello again. "Hello, can you hear me?" She doesn't look up. Maybe I'm dead.

I don't think the sun has been up for long, but Bobby has come back for me. I am still in the same clothes. I don't think I have eaten anything, and I don't remember using the bathroom.

When we get outside and into the car, Bobby asks me, "What did you do now, Nance? I don't know what happened there last night, but they called me this morning to come get you, and said you were being uncooperative."

"Hmm, I'm not sure," I say. "Was I there all night?"

The winding pass back through Pinkham Notch is plowed wide enough for two cars to get through. Steep glacial walls of ice and thick spruce fir trees line the road back home. Bobby and I don't talk. We are both exhausted.

THE next morning I wake up at 3:33. Convinced I can pull myself back together, I shower, get dressed, scrape the ice off my car windshield, and leave for work. I stop at Irving gas station for a coffee on the way. When I pull up in front of the office door, my car clock reads 4:11.

Icy snow spills over my black pumps as I step into the unplowed street pile. Freezing wind blows up my nylon legs and under my wool skirt. My black canvas work bag digs into my right shoulder, and in my left hand the cardboard coffee cup burns hot to my palm.

A windswept pile of snow has blown against the office door in the shape of a frozen wave. I kick some of it to the side with the toe of my shoe and poke my key into the front door lock. It refuses to turn. I take it out and try again. I walk to the back of the building. The back door key slips right in, and the door swings open. I hit the light switch. My desk is gone. The entire room has been rearranged. In the front office I find a cardboard box with my personal things in it. A coffee mug, some makeup, and random desk supplies. I sit down at what looks to now be Glenn's desk in the corner of the front room and begin going through paperwork and plans for upcoming shows.

At seven thirty I telephone Glenn. He sounds groggy and surprised to hear my voice. "Stay there. I'll be right down," he says. By eight o'clock he walks through the front door. Noreen is with him. She looks out of breath. Glenn fumbles for words anxiously as he pulls a chair next to me and attempts to put a sentence together. Noreen sits just behind him. Her back is tall, her hands together in her lap. Her lips are tight.

I have no idea what they are about to tell me. "Glenn, just spit it out. What's going on? Why are you surprised to see me here?"

"Okay, look." He runs his hand up over his balding head, which is now beaded with sweat, even though it can't be much above forty degrees in here. "Nance, you've been relieved as executive director of the company. The board of directors decided against reimbursing the money you put into the business because there was no legal paperwork to show proof. Bobby's telephone call to the lawyer pushed them to their decision in order to protect the company. I was emotional and said you didn't deserve that. They said it was business."

"Glenn, how can you not stand by me?"

His face patches up red. "I tried to, Nance. It wasn't my decision."

"Glenn, everything we've worked so hard for. The huge theater family we have built. That's it?"

"My hands are tied, Nance. I'm sorry."

Every molecule in my body is vibrating cold. I pick up the cardboard box and walk out.

A YEAR would go by before Glenn finishes paying our old debts and is asked for his resignation. But I won't know that until seventeen years later when I see him again.

66

Fear

IN THOSE FIRST few weeks after leaving Arts In Motion, I am inconsolable. I feel like a mother who has walked out on her children. How has Glenn explain my disappearance to more than sixty people of all ages, who I considered family? None of them called after that. The only people I hear from are those wanting to sign up for cancelled ballroom dance classes, and Mumma.

Each time the phone rings, it triggers me into a spell. In search of safety, I drop to my hands and knees and crawl to closets and corners, my blood running fear. Then, choking, dizzy, detached, I listen to phone messages I will never return.

"Nancy? Where the heck are you?" I think Mumma may materialize through the wall and into my kitchen. "Yeah, okay, God." Then just before the phone slams down I hear her voice trail off. "What's the matter with her for God sake? She's some damn kooky, that's for sure."

After that, all that is left of her is a red flashing button on a black box machine and a disembodied voice in my head quoting commandments of moral merit. Honor your father and your mother, it says.

Bull fucking shit.

EVERY evening after the boys are in bed, I sit alone on the screen porch, cigarette ashes smudged into the weave of my tan Icelandic coat, Coors Light poured cold and easy into a body I despise. Trees rustle in dark shadows just beyond the full-length window screens.

Blackness of the still New Hampshire night sky has a way of convincing me it is possible to disappear into the unknown and never be missed, that maybe we are all just banging around aimlessly without purpose, and faith is a useless mechanism. But my heart says my brain lies. I contemplate my toxic life until the sun rises.

At 6:00 A.M., the porch slider whooshes open. Bobby stands with one foot in the living room, one foot on the porch. He crosses his arms over his chest and rubs them. "Were you here all night again? Why don't you come to bed anymore? What's the matter with you?"

I stub out the cigarette and stare at the woods, now lit with morning. "I can't, too scared."

"I don't understand you, Nance. What do you have to be scared of?"

"I don't know, Bobby." I am bound in silent amnesia.

67

Scars

SLEEP IS A daytime drug that wears off just before the boys get home from school. They don't bring friends home anymore because they never know what condition I will be in. I could be making cookies in the kitchen, or scrubbing stains from the knees of a baseball uniform, or I could be dead.

Today I am under a low living room table screaming at someone who isn't there, as daily horror clips run movies though my mind and body.

I hear Josh's voice. "Jason, go to your room. Mom will be all right."

I hear Jason crying. It sounds far away.

"Mom, it's Josh. Can you hear me? It's April 1995. It's almost your birthday. Thirty-nine years old. We're home at Beechwood Drive. You're safe, Mom. It's okay, no one is going to hurt you now. I'm here to take care of you." I see his hand in front of me, then his face. Heavy brown ringlets lie over his brow. His teeth are winter white. He is smiling. I climb out on my hands and knees. Again, today, Joshua hugs me tight until I stop shaking and come back from Mumma's house.

I AM diseased from a lifetime of denial and self-blame. Memories of my father's mauling send physical sensations to places on my body still damp and sooty with his handprints. My throat, still raw from screaming for a mother who chose to stay deaf to the sounds of rape from the other side of her bedroom wall.

Healing the scars of shame seems like an insurmountable task. My fear, addictions, and unhealthy beliefs, born of that shame, have programmed me for destruction. I am the dirty, unworthy, malnourished child, starved for love. Manipulated to believe that I should not question, think, or grow. I keep the world at arm's length. Don't touch me. Stay away from me. Leave me alone.

The residue of every chemical I have ever swallowed, and every abusive touch I have ever received, hangs stagnant in my body. I am below bottom. I want out.

68

Sirens

It is a summer Thursday. Bobby is working, and the boys are in the den watching television. I am standing in the doorway between the den and the living room. My hair is unwashed and I have no makeup on. As I tell the boys I am going to get my prescription refilled, they don't look up. I feel out of body, like I am standing in front of myself. Part of me stays in that doorway calling out to the shell of me walking out the kitchen door. But I go anyway, and drive the ten minutes to Shop 'n Save.

My body sways off balance as I grip for the video display rack behind me and wait for the pharmacist to call my name. With one finger, I push sunglasses back up my nose, take two sloppy steps to the counter, and scratch out a check for the co-pay. Clutching the paper bag to my chest, I zombie walk past the registers at the front of the grocery store and back outside.

In the front seat of my car, I reach for the water bottle. Two small tablets wait on my tongue. The traffic light at the end of the parking lot holds fire red. Home is a left turn. I shake the full bottle of drugs into my hand, cup it to my open mouth, and turn right.

I will have no memory of driving the three-mile stretch of outlet stores and restaurants on Route 16. I will remember standing at the telephone booth just outside Sid's market, next to the North Conway Bank.

I don't think I have ever dialed this number from memory, but as I lean against the booth, my fingers easily find the correct sequence of numbers to push. The metal face of the box presses cold at my fore-head, like the barrel of a gun.

"Good afternoon, North Conway Bank. This is Susan. How may I help you?"

"Dooza?"

She pauses. "Nance? Is that you?"

"Dooza." My words slur. "I just wanted to call and say good-bye."

"What? What do you mean? Where are you going?" Panic grows in her voice. "What's the matter?"

"I just wanted to tell you how much I love you, Dooza, and what a wonderful friend you've been."

"Nance, where are you?"

"Sid's."

"Can you get yourself into the parking lot?" Her voice lightens. "I just want to say good-bye in person. Come to the back of the bank, okay?"

I am now staring at the blankness of the tall wooden privacy fence, my back to the bank, lit cigarette in hand, when the passenger door creaks open.

Dooza bends cautiously to look at me and then slides onto the pas-senger seat. Her smile wrinkles nervously as smoke curls between us. "Hey, Sista. What's goin on?" She lifts the bottle of Klonopin from the center console and looks at the label.

"Nance?" Her voice shakes. My eyes lose focus. "I have to go into the bank and finish something. But I promise I'll be right back. You wait here for me, okay? Don't leave."

Long gray ashes hang to the end of my cigarette, waiting to fall. Minutes tick between inhales. Finally, the passenger door opens and Dooza is beside me. I feel the squeeze of her hand on my arm. I see mascara running black over her rose-blushed cheeks. She is crying, almost breathless as she speaks. "Nance, you know I love you. You are my best friend. I've always told you I would do anything for you. Right? Please, Nance, don't hate me." She hugs me tight. My body is weak against hers. There is no time to hug her back. The door closes and I am alone.

My elbow digs into the D-shaped opening of the steering wheel. I allow it to hold me up. The cigarette filter sticks to the inside dampness of my bottom lip. I watch a dead oak branch hang over the hood of my car. It pumps up and down with the breeze, barely attached to the tree trunk, in spiky dagger claws that wave for my attention.

I hear sirens. They get louder, closer. Something's going on, I think. I take a drag of smoke. It is so loud my ears vibrate, until suddenly it stops. My eyes shift to the rearview mirror, and I see an ambulance T-crossed to my back bumper. Someone in the bank must be ill, I think. Then there is a fast tap on my side window. A police car angles to my left, another to my right. The officer taps again at my left window and asks me to roll it down.

"Nancy?" His voice is deep, yet somehow calming. "Do you need some help?"

I turn my back to him and move to the center of the car. "No, of course not. I'm fine." Another uniformed man appears at my passenger window. Startled, I back to the driver's side. Both doors fly open at the same time. The EMT on the right grabs for my cigarette. Arms scoop under me as the officer swoops me out with one quick yank. Bare feet kick at their blue-covered bodies. Terror screams from my throat. The seven-year-old girl inside me fights restraints. As they pull me into the ambulance, my head winches back to see an upside-down view of Dooza standing beyond the police cruiser, her hands over her face, a co-worker's arms around her.

Once the door to the ambulance closes, it becomes quiet. The face that leans over mine is full. His eyes are blue, like the color of summer sky, and they are smiling. His accent is drawn out like Dooza's. "That's right, hon. Take a good deep breath. It's okay. Don't be scared, you're gonna be just fine. We're gonna take good care of you now." We breathe together, his hand holding mine, my eyes fixed on his until we get to the emergency room.

I am at the end of the gurney table with a sheet gripped tight at my chin when Bobby comes in. "What happened now, Nance?" I don't answer. "You know, they wanted to pump your stomach? But your psychiatrist said you'd never be able to handle it, you would have been crawling under a table somewhere." He pulls a wallet from his back pocket, fingers the insurance card, and turns for the nurses' station.

Dooza sits on a low stool next to me, a big plastic cup in one hand. "I'm here for ya, Sista," she says. "They say you've got to chug this shit, okay?" She lets out a of couple honks, then carefully lifts the container of liquid, activated charcoal to my mouth. It lies gritty between my teeth and blackens my tongue. "Jesus, Nance, it took five men to get you into that ambulance. I guess if we ever meet some asshole creep in a dark alley, you'll be able to protect us."

Dooza wipes one corner of my mouth with a tissue. We both laugh. But that was just on the outside.

69

Jamison

THE TUESDAY AFTER my overdose, Bobby admits me to Jamison Hospital, in Maine, my third psychiatric facility. The road going in is long, like an airport strip, and the building is three stories high. As we say good-bye at the psych ward door, I hug Bobby tight. He lets go first. I watch him walk the length of the hall until he is out of sight. In my gut, I know it will be the last time we do this.

The routine is familiar. Papers to sign, questions to answer, class schedule highlighted. This time it is only my shoes and socks they ask me to remove. Sharps have been left at home. I have no wallet that can be stolen, no belt to hang myself with, no perfume to drink.

In my room I am on a twin bed reading Sally Jessy Raphael's autobiography when my roommate charges in. Without moving my head, I look over the top of my glass frames. With one stocking foot, she kicks the wall, then knots up both fists in front of her salivary mouth and screams out into the hall.

"Fuckin A. Let me the fuck out of here, you bitches." She grabs a metal chair and throws it out the door. I turn the page. She leans down over me. I look up at black, prickly eyebrow growth.

"They're all fuckin crazy here." She makes two fast sniffs, then does it again and rubs her nose. Her yellowed fingernails are different lengths. Small chips of siren red still hang to a few of them.

I sit up and turn the open book to the bed. "Yup, we're all crazy," I say. She snarls and says something I don't catch.

Down the hall, the common room smells like burnt popcorn and floor cleaner. The nurse follows me to a Plexiglas fish bowl off the lounge where people are smoking. It looks like a bus station with passengers bound for nowhere. She flicks the lighter. My jaw shakes as I put the Marlboro to my lips. The end of the cigarette teases across the flame. I draw smoke deep into my lungs, and she closes the door.

The room is stifling hot. I sit down on a gray steel bench. Three men sit beyond me. Through the window we watch other residents wander aimlessly. The man sitting next to me is wearing a black T-shirt that reads JESUS SAVES in white lettering. "Do you believe?" he asks as he takes a drag and hisses smoke between two rotting teeth.

I stare at him. Smoke burns my eyes. "Tell you what. If Jesus shows up and unlocks that ward door, I'll believe anything."

He crosses one boney leg over the other, slumps his spine, and studies me. "You don't look like you belong here. You've got some kind of regal look about you." Ashes fall to my black leggings. He picks at a scab on the back of his hand and forgets he is talking to me.

A woman vomits near the door, then scratches at her neck and backside, like something is crawling under her skin. She shivers like she's not been warm for years. All of their faces look the same, sunken and sad. Their bodies twitch, legs kicking memories of abused groins and pin-holed arms. Minds tangled with experiences that run together like one long, hellish day. Organs soaked rancid with alcohol, veins clogged with poison.

We will all march off to classrooms where shame chases us down in our attempt to process anger, grief, and loss. With each fragmented piece of truth, pictures and body sensations vibrate us in overwhelming terror. We will be asked by therapists to make commitments of better health. They will teach coping skills in sobriety, safety, grounding, and trust. But what they fail to tell us is until we let go of the attachment to belief systems that were never ours to begin with, nothing will change. It is the fear that keeps us sick. The fear of knowing the truth of why we choose to anesthetize ourselves in the first place.

Some of us will follow the discharge plan and go to daily Alcoholics Anonymous meetings. We will stand up and say, "Hello, my name is Nancy and I am an alcoholic," even though we don't believe it. We will suck butts, like they are going out of style and guzzle hot coffee during breaks between testimonials. And some of us will slip out the side door when the step of the week is announced and never go back.

Some of us will find a new addiction in repeated stories of failure, and gravitate to other like energies that will enable us to stay in a familiar depth of despair. We will bitch and blame and play the game of antidepressants and rehab, and wonder why none of it cures us.

We will ask for those who hurt us to love us and say they are sorry, not understanding that perpetrators are incapable of doing so. We will push away those who truly love us, then tell them they are lying, because underneath it all, we don't believe we are worthy of being loved.

Some of us will survive to love ourselves and others, and some of us will die too soon.

70

Detox

I spent eighteen days at Jamison Hospital. That was a month ago. When I called Mumma to tell her I was doing better, she said it was about time I forget about all that stuff and got on with my life. When I told Elizabeth everything, she said she couldn't believe that Jim and Doris would do such a thing, that they were good church people and I should be grateful for all they gave me.

Tonight is Friday. Again, this week, I am too embarrassed to be seen out teaching my dance classes, and with all the meds I am still on, I couldn't do it anyway. With the floors vacuumed and the supper dishes done, I go to the porch for a cigarette and a Coors Light. Josh, Jason, and Bobby are in the den watching a movie. I hear someone walk through the living room. The slider whooshes opens.

"Hey, Sista. We came to see how you're doin." Dooza's wide red lips quiver a bit after she says it. She is dressed in a hunter-orange shirt and a long black flowing skirt that stops a few inches above her tan cow-hide boots. "You've got to get your ass back to class before this country-western shindig ends. I can fill in okay for you in a Texas Two Step, but David says your next six-week session is Latin, and you know my hips just don't move as succulent as yours do." She honks and sits herself across from me at the small table.

David hugs me. He always smells the same, a combination of smoke and old money. "Hey," he says as he sits down and takes out a pad of paper from the pocket of his old gray jacket.

"Okay, Sista. We can do this." Dooza looks determined. David is nodding. "First of all, David and I want a list of all the meds you're on, and we're going to look into how they are reacting with each other. Then we are going to keep checking on you until you get yourself off all this shit. We want you back. We love you, but you're not our Nancy anymore. I don't think those doctors know their asses from their elbows, and Bobby is as lost in all of this as you are."

When I open up to them about my father's incest, Mumma's blind eye, and how tired I am from life, they don't know what to say. Dooza bites her bottom lip, and reaches for my hand as tears pour off her eyelids. David puts one hand to his forehead, looks at the floor, then takes a menthol from his shirt pocket, tapping the end of it on the arm of the chair several times, and groans. Josh and Jason stand on the other side of the slider, looking worn and grateful that Dooza and David are there. So am I.

For the next several months I writhe in bed, like I am plugged into a wall socket as electricity surges throughout my nervous system. Tremors and ticking, kicking and crying, I want to rip my arms and legs off. When I am too spent to walk after thrashing from the physical pain of detox, my seventeen-year-old Joshua picks me up like a baby and carries my forty-year-old twitching body to the bathroom.

On the other side of the door, he waits as I flush filthy toxins out both ends of me. After that, I slide sweaty off the toilet seat and crawl to him on my hands and knees, and again he scoops me up and carries me to my room. Fourteen-year-old Jason sits beside me, reading his old knock-knock jokes and *Garfield* books. It makes me laugh. He does it for hours, grabbing my hand and squeezing tight when my pain comes in electric waves of torture.

One day at a time, one drug at a time, one hour at a time, my body flushes clean. I cry, I sweat, I pray. I think the boys and Bobby do too. And the whole time my heart weeps, hang on, stay alive, you deserve to be happy. And I must believe.

By Christmas I was done with all the antidepressants, narcotics, alcohol, and even the cigarettes. That was our last Christmas together. Four days later, I filed for divorce.

71

Long Trip

TODAY IS SATURDAY, May 4, 1996. Jason's fifteenth birthday. Five weeks before Joshua's high school graduation. Fifteen days before our nineteenth wedding anniversary. Tomorrow Bobby will move out of our Beechwood Drive home.

I have asked that we all go out for breakfast together. Bobby and I are in the kitchen waiting for the boys to get ready when he opens the cabinet. "Do you mind if I take some of these pots and pans?"

I can't breathe. "One more chance, Bobby. Let's try therapy, please?"

He picks his head up and closes the cabinet door. "Too late. I already contacted a lawyer and made a partial payment." It was months ago he told me whoever filed first would have to pay more, and it wasn't going to be him.

I step closer to him. "Were you ever in love with me? Tell me."

"Write me a script, Nancy. You're good at that. Tell me what I'm supposed to say."

"Say that you've always loved me." My hands are trembling. I want to reach out to him.

"I married you, didn't I?" Yes, I think. You did.

Josh and Bobby walk down the kitchen porch steps and get into the car. Jason slides his bare feet into Birkenstock sandals. I pull his sweatshirt up around his shoulders. He turns and looks long into my eyes. "Mom? Why do things always happen on my birthday?"

"I'm sorry, Jason, sorry that I couldn't hang on until you graduated from high school."

He blinks fast, trying to stop the tears. "Mom, why would you want us to be miserable for another three years?" That said it all.

It is a fifteen-minute ride up Route 16 to Friendly's restaurant, longer than usual. Traffic is backed up at the light near the Yield House furniture store. Tourists have arrived for a weekend of hiking and outlet shopping.

Inside Friendly's, we are seated in a center booth, Josh next to his father, Jason next to me. There is a ring of sticky orange juice in front of me on the table. I take a paper napkin from the holder and wipe it clean. Bobby picks up a menu and looks at the laminated page. I watch his eyes. They hold gaze on one spot. Jason is repeatedly flipping the end of a spoon. It leaps from the table and drops with a reverberation that makes my nerves jump. Joshua's six-foot body slumps. With one elbow on the table, he scans the room for anyone he knows, then focuses his bloodshot eyes back to the menu. People talk loudly at full tables around us. The smells of coffee and maple syrup trail past as the waitress walks by with her hands full and promises to be with us in a minute.

Finally, she stands next to us, pulls a pencil from behind her ear and an order pad out of her apron pocket. I notice there is a ketchup stain on one side of it. "Okay, now I'm ready. Crazy here today." None of us respond.

"Wow." She leans back, and takes a good look at us. "You people look exhausted. You at the end of a long trip?"

None of us look up. "Yes," I say softly. "Actually, we are."

72

Cinnamon and Orange Peel

IT HAD BEEN a very long twenty-three years since Bobby and I were pot-smoking kids in his Camaro. I guess we just figured it would all work itself out, even though year after year we repeated the same patterns, oblivious to what was at the root of hurting each other. It was all we knew. We did our best, and we did our worst.

The morning of my divorce I called both my mothers. Elizabeth said Bobby and my father had spoiled me rotten, treated me like a princess, and if things had failed, it was my own fault. Mumma said she hoped the hell the judge wasn't a Jew because if he was, I'd get nothin.

I don't remember what I wore that day and, without looking at the paperwork, I couldn't say what day of the year it was. I do remember that the Ossipee court-house felt like a huge, high-ceilinged cavern, and there were only four of us at the polished wood table, two women lawyers, Bobby, and me. Our voices echoed back words I was terrified to acknowledge. But I never shed a tear. I sat up tall with my best dancer posture and answered all questions with yes and no.

My attorney's gold pen made marks on the top page of a neatly-gathered pile. "Do you understand that you will sign off to Robert both the rental house in Bath, Maine, and the shared home in Conway, New Hampshire, and the total amount owed to him for your expenses on his credit card will be deducted from your settlement amount?"

"Yes." I looked across the table at Bobby. His nose was running. He pulled a white handkerchief out of his front pocket, wiped both sides, and didn't look at me when he did it.

Bobby's attorney continued. "Robert will provide child support only for the younger child, Jason, as the older child, Joshua, will be eighteen years of age. Nancy will have physical custody of Jason, and will be allowed to live in the Beechwood Drive home until June of 1999, when Jason graduates from high school. At that time, it is Nancy's responsibility to make other financial living arrangements. Do you understand?" She looked up at me with no emotion on her face, waiting for my answer.

My heart was beating out of my chest. I could feel it clawing up my throat, knowing once I spoke, I had sealed our fate.

She asks again, "Do you understand?"

"Yes."

I didn't cry until it was over and I was back in my car. I watched Bobby walk down over the granite courthouse steps with a manila folder in hand. His car was parked in front of mine on the edge of the road. He got into the front seat, tapped dirt from his shoes on the side runner, and adjusted the rearview mirror.

In the moment I watched him drive away, a hundred things raced through my mind. The way his knees banged against mine when we danced, the way he made me laugh when he was drunk and spoke with a Spanish accent, how proud he was the day Josh was born, and on that day it was the most I had ever loved him. I remembered how he taught Josh to ride his bike in the backyard of our Bath house, and how he loved to swim with Jason when we went for family splash night at the YMCA. And best of all, our magical six months when we moved to Beechwood Drive, how the four of us cuddled in front of the Christmas tree, watching stars turn on through the huge den windows. I could smell cinnamon and orange peel. I remembered how he hated the spinach casserole I made for him when we were first married, and how much he loved the whoopie pies I made on the first day of school each year. The hikes through the New Hampshire woods, the hours of Monopoly played on the den floor, and how everything changed after I knew my truth.

A year from now Bobby will come to me and say how sorry he is for not being more understanding. We will hug and cry, and he will ask for another chance. But I will have done a lot of healing by then. So we will become friends, something we had never been before.

fire

73

New York, New York

A HALF-ZIPPED BLACK NYLON jacket sculpts his chest. One side of it, embroidered in blue and red, reads HONDA TOP TECH. On the other side, MIKE is spelled out in cursive. Thick, silky black hair hangs slightly over his right eye. He flips it back into place with a nod, then steps through my kitchen door. Our hands meet as I introduce myself. A zing shoots up my spine. I can feel my throat get tight and my face flushing hot. The knowing voice in my soul shouts at me, "This is the man you're going to marry." Oh God, no, I think. I have no interest in marrying, or dating, or anything but pulling myself together. No, I am not marrying anyone.

"Nice to meet you," he says. "I've ridden my bike past your house many times. I had no idea you taught dance classes here." He lets go of my hand.

"Oh yes, I teach here and at the studio up in town. Well, that's at night. During the day I work at Rocky Mountain Chocolate Factory."

He begins to chuckle as his jacket slides down off his shoulders. "A few weeks ago I saw their huge-headed bear mascot dancing on the side of Route 16. Was that you?"

"Yup, that was me. It was grand opening day, and the radio station was there." I take his coat, lay it on the end of the deacon's bench, and lead him to the den as we talk. "Well, anyway, I loved it," I add.

His high Asian cheekbones are pink and slightly freckled, his eyes, the darkest I have ever seen. "I waved to you out my car window," he says.

"Did I wave back?"

"You did." His full bottom lip smiles over his squared chin.

"Mike or Michael? Which do you prefer?"

"Well, my mom always called me Michael, never Mike. Doesn't really matter, I guess."

"Okay, Michael it is."

He listens closely, his six-foot, perfectly postured body standing at attention, arms resting at the sides of his long biker legs. "Ballroom dancing is about proper frame," I begin. "And it is very important for partners to communicate." I step close to him and open my arms. "There are two pressure points. One is in the palm of our hands, my right to your left, and the other is your right hand on my left shoulder blade."

His hand is flat to my back, arm bent parallel to the floor in proper ballroom frame. "New York, New York" plays on the stereo. We step out in a Fox-trot, fitting together like matched puzzle pieces. Tingles race up and down my body. Is it you? I think. My Michael?

It was Wednesday night, June 26, 1996.

ANOTHER Friday-night class has ended at the dance studio, and Dooza is at the door saying good-bye to the last of our students. David is packing up the stereo and lowering it into the cardboard box he carries it in. I am balancing on one foot next to him and pulling off my right dance shoe. "Why hasn't this guy asked me out yet? He has taken private and group classes all summer long, and nothing."

Dooza throws ballroom shoes into her oversized purse. "Well, Jesus, Sista, you intimidate the shit right out of him. Why don't you ask him out? You are forty-one years old, Nance. What the hell are ya waitin for?" She honks and pulls out a cigarette that will be lit as soon as she gets out the door.

Each week, David, Dooza, and I will repeat the same conversation. Until September.

74

Michael

THE NIGHT OF our first date, Michael bashfully admitted he had dialed my number all summer long, and each time before it rang, he'd lost his nerve and hung up. He said a mechanic didn't seem good enough for someone like me. Every date after that there was one red rose waiting on the front seat of his Volvo when he picked me up. And when I got in, country western music would be playing on the radio, even though months later he admitted how much he disliked it. Every weekend after ballroom class, we danced at the Red Jacket lounge and he wore Banana Republic cologne that made my knees buckle when he held me close. And when we walked, my shoulder fit perfectly under his arm.

Michael said his mother grew up in Japan, that his father was stationed there with the air force, and they fell in love without being able to speak each other's language. He said he always wanted a kind of love like that, and someday I would marry him. He would wait years if that's what I wanted.

I told him the best thing I had ever done was give birth to my sons. That Nanny had loved me most for my first twenty-nine years, and that the ocean was like a vein of freedom I must always go back to. And I told him my secrets. The abortion when I was eighteen, how I wished to die driving drunk on back roads, and that I must sleep with covers tight to my chin. Then I told him why. I watched Michael's short nails, holding grease residue, scratch his head, and I knew it would be a long time before he understood how the smell of oil and rubber tires triggered my past.

He said he'd married three times. I said I'd been in three psych wards. He hugged me tight, rocking me back and forth with his breath gentle on my neck, and said, "Never, would I ever send you away, honey. You never have to go through that again. I am here now to love and protect you." And I so wanted to believe that.

When Christmas came he gave me a bracelet with little gold *x*'s and *o*'s and small emerald stones between each one. When I called Mumma and told her about it she seemed surprised. The next day she called me back. Her words sounded pre-planned when she said them. "I think you should marry Michael. He gave you that beautiful brace-let." Her voice was deep and serious. Each word precise. "You know, Nancy, when a man gives you somethin, you owe him."

I wasn't surprised to hear her say it.

75

Bones

It is March 30, 1997, Easter Sunday. At Mumma's house there is no celebration.

From my old bedroom window I watch smoky morning fog hovering ghostly over the river. I slide open the window, then flop down into the small gold-stuffed chair at the end of the bed, a bed that, since I moved out of this room twenty years ago, my parents have slept in. My bare feet are folded under me. Mumma's blue bathrobe is wrapped tight to my body. The smell of her perfume is stale to the collar.

My father lies flat on the mattress he has been anchored to for weeks. I watch breath wheeze in and out of his asbestos-ridden lungs. A black leather-bound Bible rests beside him on the spread. He taps the top of the book with one bony finger, then rolls his head slowly side to side against the pillow. White bands of slime stretch between his thin, parted lips as he speaks. "Have you ever seen anyone suffer more than me?" His eyes blink crusty, and his thoughts break long between words.

"This morning I thought I was dyin," he starts. "I was on a long tobacco road. There were roads that branched off. Ahead was a big platform. Everything was dirty. Old and dingy. Lots of people. All tryin to decide which way to go. Some people I knew. They were lookin pretty gloomy." He stops and holds his breath for just a moment. His eyes are closed. My eyes scan down over him. I can see his kneecaps poking up from under the covers, his body a shell of bones. On top of the blanket, his spindly arms point out from the loose sleeves of a white T-shirt. He moves one hand to his cancerous stomach and groans.

"We were supposed to take things with us. But how should I know what to take if I don't know where I'm goin? I just wandered on instinct. No one seemed to be with me. Just lots of people everywhere. All tryin to decide which road to walk down." He groans again, turning up his top lip like he might throw up. "I didn't feel it was my duty to ask, why are you here? Then I saw a lot of large steel staircases, very worn. Many people have walked up and down. People all on their way to carry out the duty of their last assignment. I was standin at the bottom. I didn't know which way to go. But I knew we were goin on to the next level." He sighs agony. Cancer has eaten him out like a hungry pack of wild dogs.

"Then I was on a bed. Lyin there. It was filled with rocks. I was in a large room. It was a horrible musty cellar. The only light was from a small window at the top of one wall." He takes another breath. "Your mother was there. I asked her if she had made her decision yet. She said she had. But she wouldn't tell me what it was. She was mad at me." His eyes pinch desperate. Then he opens them and lifts his head from the pillow to look at me.

"Nancy, there are people around me all the time now. Lots of people that haven't decided which way to go." His spindly right arm lifts from the soup-stained blanket and points to the window. "A little while ago, that wall disappeared. Now there's a doorway. There is a man in black clothes standin there waitin for me. Can you see him? What do you think's gonna happen to me?" He lays his head back on the pillow, picks up the Bible, and lays it on his chest. "I've been a dedicated servant of the Lord all my life. Surely he'll take pity on me. Do you think?"

I pull Mumma's robe tighter and hug up into a ball. The back teeth on the left side of my face clench so hard, my eye starts to twitch. I answer in quiet anger through my stiff lips, as my father moans in fear, unable to hear me.

I think I will sit here and watch you die, you self-pitying piece of slime, like I have for the last month, since Aunt Lilly called to say Mumma needed me. I have sat here four days a week, unable to cut myself free from our drama, enduring the anxiety of this horror show, just to see you get what you deserve in the end. I will sit here watching you disintegrate before me, as you watch black shadows come upon you. And what do I think? I think death will be no release.

He reaches to the nightstand, picks up a small brass bell, and starts ringing it back and forth, calling for Mumma. I watch him swing it, groaning as it tones. Finally, I hear Mumma stamping up the staircase.

"Look. I'm gettin some damn sick of trampin up and down these stairs. Now what is it that you want this time, Jimmy? I've got things to do." She stands next to the bed, snapping sheet wrinkles from underneath weight so slight, he is pulled along with her quick, forceful tug.

He looks up at her pinched face. His eyes are hollow, his face nothing but a skull draped in thin, pale skin. He doesn't say what he wants. Mumma stands back and jams both fists to her hips. "Now look, someone is comin up after church lets out, with the Easter service bulletin. So let's snap out of this foolishness and be ready."

I go to Tommy's old bedroom to dress, and just as I finish, the front doorbell rings. I hear Mumma sputtering as she stamps back down over the stairs. "Oh for God sake, I'm comin. I don't know why people just don't leave us the hell alone." I watch from the top of the stairs. Mumma greets the young woman with one long, happy, high-pitched syllable. "Hi."

The woman holds a church bulletin and an audio-tape of the Easter service. Mumma takes them from her. "Well, you didn't need to come all the way up here." Then she laughs, like she really didn't mean it. They both come up the stairs.

The woman leans down to kiss my father. He licks his lips and presses his poison mouth against her smooth coral lipstick. Then she and Mumma pull his bony body up on the edge of the bed. The woman lays an afghan over his lap and sits in the gold chair, the only chair.

As Mumma sits on the bed to Daddy's right, I see her foot slowly push the round, white enamel throw-up pan back under the bed. She talks about the weather as she does it. I lower myself to the left of him, my leg muscles tight, like I am squatting over a gas station toilet.

The woman slips her London Fog rain-coat off her shoulders and lets it fall down over her back and into the gold chair. She talks with her hands and giggles as she recounts her five-year-old son's rendition of today's Easter hymn. "It was the funniest thing I ever heard. He was singing along for everyone to hear, and then instead of singing 'resurrection day' he sang, 'It's an erection day.' Isn't that so cute? I had all I could do not to laugh out loud."

My breath stops. My heart pounds in my ears. I feel my father take my hand out of my lap. He traps my fingers in his. Sweat breaks out across me. The woman says it again. "Can you believe that? Erection day."

Daddy's fingers squeeze two quick pulses around mine. His skull turns to me, his smile sick and lecherous. It says, "Remember me." I look past him at Mumma. Her chin twitches nervous and her smile curls phony around a low, awkward chuckle. "Oh yup, that's cute."

My stare fuzzes out at the woman. Why doesn't she see how sick we all are? If my sweat beaded blood and it reeked like a rotting corpse, would she notice me then? I start to go away in my mind, back to what happened in this very spot, in this very bed. The bed that my father killed my innocence in. The bed that he will now suffer in until he dies.

When it's time for the woman to leave, she and Mumma walk downstairs to the front door. I begin to follow, but Daddy calls out to me from the edge of the bed. "Nancy I need to use the toilet. Help me, will you?"

On the quilt closet side of the room, there is a smaller closet where years ago my dance costumes hung. Now there is a toilet in a space so tight, when you sit on the pot, your knees stick out into the bedroom. I see Daddy slowly draw back the afghan from his naked lower half. He coos his words. "Stay here with me, Nancy. I don't mind, if you don't."

I turn my back. "No, wait for Mumma." I sit outside the door against the hallway wall, knees curled to my chest. Icy chills tingle from my tailbone up my neck. It makes my shoulders shiver. I hear him groan as he moves alone across the room, then exhale long when he finally drops to the toilet seat.

My mind wanders back to all of the times I lifted that overhead wooden ceiling panel, with my feet on the coat hooks, one knee on the cross pole, and climbed up into the attic. Of all my hiding spots, it was my least favorite. The pink insulation that lay between the two-hundred-year-old beams made me itch and left dry toxic fibers on my skin. I pretended it was pink cotton candy, but that was tough to do. It smelled like chimney creosote and dead rats.

A thump comes from behind me as my father makes a grunt and hits the floor, like a sack of decomposing fish bait. He cries out for me. Mumma stomps back up the stairs and into the bedroom. "Christ, Jimmy, what the hell did you think you were doin draggin yourself over to that damn flush? Stay in bed for God sake. I'm sick of runnin up and down every time you need somethin." She cusses him back to bed. I stay curled up on the hall floor until she is done, wondering why I can't pull myself away from our drama, and why Tommy is never here to help.

76

Out of Sight

THE NEXT MORNING in the kitchen, Mumma mutters to herself and slams drying dishes onto the counter. From the wall phone, I dial the visiting nurse who comes twice a week to bathe my father. When Mumma hears me ask the woman to bring a portable commode for his bedside, she makes a disgusted snort and slams the silverware drawer so hard, it makes my uncovered ear ring.

Next to me on the low room divider that separates the kitchen and living room is a green doily stuck to the white paint from where Tommy has slopped ginger ale. On top of it is a half-eaten piece of beef jerky and a couple of wheat pennies. Shoved down between the divider and the couch are dusty piles of Daddy's thick newspaper coin periodicals, crumpled church bulletins, and several worn paperback, war novels. It is from here he voyeuristically watched through the gaps of the wooden folding door, and forty years later its ungreased wheels still squeal and slip out of the overhead track. I think every dirty fingerprint that ever touched the wooden knob remains encoded there.

I begin to pull things from around the couch, deciding what I will throw away and what I will dust off and leave there. There are papers, books, and videotapes, two of them. I hold them in my hands and remember how years ago he said he tried to get Mumma to watch them, but she refused. When he passed them to me, he said they would give me something to think about, then he smiled his green-tooth smile, pulling up on the pockets of his work pants and jiggled himself around in them. *When Harry Met Sally* and *A Fish Named*

Wanda. Female orgasm scenes were what they had in common. I wanted to die when I realized it. I drop them into the garbage bag and think how strange that back then I thought I must return them instead of tossing them the hell out.

Mumma is downstairs in the laundry room washing sheets. I am on my knees, reaching under the couch when I hear the front door open. The minister calls out hello and walks into the living room. In one hand he holds a newspaper against his long black coat. He clears his throat. "I thought I would come up to visit with your dad for a little while. How is he doing today?"

My hands grab blindly at two books from under the couch. When I see what they are, I stand and push them out toward the minister. One a Bible, the other a *Playboy* magazine. I take a step closer, turning the front covers to him and watching for a response. It feels rebellious to say it. "I think this pretty much sums up my father's life. Don't you?"

The minister leans in to me. I can smell coffee on his breath. "Don't expect a deathbed confession, Nancy. It never happens." Then he turns and walks up the stairs to the bedroom. I don't move until he is out of my sight.

How odd.

77

How Much Longer

SEAGULLS SCREECH AND swoop in the morning fog outside Tommy's bedroom window. I hear Mumma tramp down the stairs and snap up the green shade in the front door. I pull her old robe tight around me and make the four steps into the bedroom where my father still lies wheezing, again spared from his final breath being sucked out into the darkness of night.

I stand over his decomposing eighty-pound, six-foot body. Boney gray arms lie partially covered in a blue pajama top, his eyes still and fixed on the blank ceiling. Maybe again this morning he wanders lost on a dusty tobacco road or lies weighted to a rank cellar rock pile. His lips are white and dry. Pieces of lifted dead skin hang from them. With slightness of breath he speaks. "I thought last night I would die. But I didn't. I'm still here. How much longer will this sufferin go on? Why can't I just die?"

"I guess you're not done yet," I spit, sick of his martyrdom. Back in Tommy's room, I get dressed, then go downstairs.

In the kitchen Mumma sits at the table. She takes a bite of dry toast, then throws it to the plate. She lets out a disgusted sigh when I sit down next to her, stops chewing, and waits for me to speak.

"He didn't die yet," I say, leaning back in the chair with my arms folded.

She takes a slurp of hot tea, then picks up the toast, bites it, and throws it to the plate again. "Well, I can't do this forever, ya know. I didn't think he'd make it to Easter, and now look, it's five weeks later. I'm some damn tired, that's for sure." As the sound of her half-empty teacup hits the saucer, the front doorbell rings. "Now who the hell is that? We don't need anyone nosin around for God sake."

I walk Michael into the living room and, as I do, his arms feel safe around me. He holds one red rose in his hand. I take a deep, sweet breath of Banana Republic cologne, still on the blue-and-white oxford shirt from the last time we danced at the Red Jacket. I run my fingers up through his thick black hair. He speaks softly in my ear. "I've missed you, honey. You've been here for days. I know you're working hard to take care of things, but don't you think it's time to come home and take care of yourself?"

I let go and push myself back. "No, Michael, not yet. Mumma needs me."

Mumma dries her hands on a dish towel, flips it up over one shoulder, and shakes his hand. "Well, Michael, what are you doin way down here?"

"I didn't call first because I know you're both busy taking care of Jim, but even if I'm here a few minutes, it's worth the trip just to look at her." He puts one arm around me.

Mumma pulls the towel off her shoulder and turns back to the kitchen sink. "Yeah well. It's an awful long way just for that," she mumbles.

Michael slides a pile of newspapers to the end of the couch and sits down in my father's spot. I cringe to see him do it. "Go on with your routine, honey. I'll stay here and watch TV."

I fill a glass with water, drop a straw into it, and head for the stairs.

78

It Was Me

WHEN I GET to the top of the stairs, I stop. One sharp, headless nail pokes into my palm as I grip. The energy has shifted in the thick, stale upstairs air, a vibration that tells me something is about to happen and I have no control over it.

In the bedroom, my father sits balanced on the edge of the bed. His skull hangs to his chest, shoulder blades poking at the back of his pajama shirt. As I get closer, I can see he has pulled the top blanket over his lap and is holding himself up with both hands cupped to the edge of the mattress.

My heart is in my throat. It feels like I am going to pass out or throw up, maybe both. "Daddy? What's the matter?"

He doesn't answer at first, then lifts his head and searches out at the river. "I need to talk to you and your mother. Go get your mother," he demands.

When I come into the living room, Michael stands up, both thumbs stuck in the pockets of his jeans. Mumma bitches all the way from the kitchen up to the bedroom. "Well, I don't know what he's got to talk about, Nancy. I can't imagine why he thinks he needs both of us. Now, I've got things to do so he better make this short."

My father motions for us to sit next to him on the bed. Mumma sits to his right. He lays his bony hand over hers. She fidgets impatiently. "Look, Jimmy, I don't know what it is that you want, but I've got things to do, ya know."

I stand at his left. He reaches his cold hand to mine and pulls me down next to him. I slide a few inches away so our legs are not touching. Oh God, this doesn't feel right. I want to run down the stairs to Michael's arms, but I don't. I wait.

Mumma is trying to shake loose of his grip. "Yeah, okay, Jimmy, well, I've got things to do. Let go of me."

Daddy pauses in thought, his eyes glazed to the river. Then with his hand tight to mine, he says the words that razor slice to my core, through decades of fragmented memories and self-hatred.

"It's time to tell the family secrets."

My body flashes panic. Sweat breaks out across me. My bladder goes weak. My legs are jelly. My bare feet are like cement blocks weighted to the floor. I look at Mumma. Her expression is the same as when she sat down, lips pursed, chin pitted.

"That's enough, Jimmy. Just never mind." She half stands up, then, with his fingers locked to her wrist, sits back. He looks at her anxious face and speaks again. "Doris, you know that I have always loved you."

Her face is pinched in a scowl. Her voice gets louder. "I said never mind, Jimmy, just never mind, that's enough."

His skull turns to me, his eye sockets hollow. His slanted smile leans closer to my face as he coos his evil words. "But, Nancy, you are the one I was truly in love with all these years. We were only together a few times, but it was the best feelin in the world." His fingers pulse at my hand.

My body shuts down as every buried memory, every fear explodes speeding trains of toxins throughout me. Every cell is on fire in a momentary blazing awareness of our truth. I am a long-nailed sewer rat sliding helpless off a shit-slicked river bank, pulled by the tide into the whirlpool of survival amnesia. I am the daughter of denial.

He looks back at Mumma. "Doris, you know I've been with a lot of other women, don't you? I need you to tell me you remember."

Her face is hot. Her chin quivers. "I don't know what you're talkin about for God sake. You're bein foolish. I have no idea what you mean. Now that's enough."

Her hand is still captive in his. "Doris, tell me you remember everything that has happened. I need you to."

Her voice shrieks knowing. "For God sake, Jimmy, that was a long time ago. Now just forget it."

Time has stopped in this horrible, sickening, disgusting moment.

I am in the gold chair, not remembering my move from the bed. All I can hear is my heart banging against my eardrums and a funneling mass of whirring frequency. I see my father still talking and Mumma still trying to shut him up. They look like a faded silent movie.

I am not sure how long it goes on, just that when Daddy is done talking, he asks me to go downstairs and fix him lunch. I think he says it twice before I answer. "I'm kind of hungry now. I feel like I could eat some canned peaches and buttered toast, maybe a little tea."

"Okay," I say. "I'll be right back."

Mumma doesn't get up. She stares mean at him with her lips pressed tight together. Her forehead wrinkling deep lines. As I get up to leave, she doesn't look at me.

Michael stands in the middle of the living room. I won't recall how I start to tell him, just that after a while I realize it will be important to say every word I remember. I don't know what he said, or if he hugged me, but I am pretty sure he must have. After that I think I told him I would be fine and would call him later. Before he went out the front door, I kissed his lips, then carefully walked a tray of hot tea, buttered toast, and a bowl of peaches upstairs to Daddy.

79

Not Done

I have no memory of what happened yesterday after the family secrets were told. But again, this morning, I put my feet on the floor of
my brother's bedroom, wrap Mumma's robe tight to my body, and go
into my old bedroom. Both my father's hands are gripping the Bible
on his chest. "I'm sufferin awful," he groans. "You've never seen anyone suffer like me. Why didn't God take me last night?"

"Evidently you're not done," I say sarcastically.

"No, I guess not. There's more I need to say, and maybe if I tell it,
God will let me die and be rid of this awful cancer. Go get your
mother."

"No. I am not going to listen to you anymore, I can't handle it, and
I am real sure Mumma doesn't want to either. You'll have to talk to
the minister. Isn't confession in his job description?"

In the kitchen Mumma snatches up dishes, then slams them down
on the counter. "What do you mean there's more he needs to talk
about? I think he's said way too much already. This is ridiculous and
I'm not gonna call the minister and bother him again. He's been up
here enough."

"Fine," I say, sitting down at the table. A dirty plate with hamburger grease and ketchup is still there from where Tommy showed
up last night after we fell asleep. "What about Uncle Ike?"

"For Christ sake, Nancy, what is the matter with you? We're not
gettin anyone else involved in this mess, so I guess I'll have to call the
damn minister. God." She stomps to the living room, slams herself
into the chair, and picks up the phone.

Ten minutes later the doorbell rings. Mumma's voice is so defensive and angry when she opens the door, I can feel a wave of ugly heat swell all the way back to the kitchen table where I am still sitting. "Well, he told Nancy he's not done yet. It was her idea to get you back up here and talk to him. I didn't see any need in it, but she insisted."

For two hours Mumma and I sit in the kitchen drinking tea with the television blaring out the weather channel. Finally, the minister appears at the foot of the staircase and makes a hasty exit without saying good-bye. Mumma goes back to slamming dishes on the counter. I quickly gather my things to leave.

I am backing out the front door, pulling two small suitcases, one of which is caught on the expanding arm. I hear my father call out from the bedroom. "Nancy. Nancy, come up here." I don't answer. He calls it again.

Mumma is now standing in front of me at the door. It has been a long time since I have seen the blueness of her eyes, years since I have seen them loving my boys, but in the chaos of this moment I want to believe there is a flicker of that. She takes the door in one hand, pushes it wide open, and watches my face as her exhausted voice calls back up the staircase. "Let her go, Jimmy. Just let her go."

My bags slide out. I stand with them in hand and say good-bye to her. She is still holding the door open with her eyes on me as I drive away from the house. I am going home to Joshua, Jason, and Michael.

80

Dutiful Daughter

AFTER THREE DAYS at home on Beechwood Drive, I go back to Mumma's house. In the bedroom, she leans over Daddy, snapping the sheets tight to the edge of the mattress and punching at the pillow as his skeletal head rolls side to side. He pants quick, shallow, painful breaths as she does it. Mumma knuckles her fists to her hips, her mouth looking like it's ready to spit, and squints her eyes at the corner clutter. The toe of one shoe kicks at a warped cardboard box. A swirl of dust blows up from camera equipment and musty books. My father's hollowness stares up at her. She shakes her head at him, grabs an empty water glass from the side table, and goes back downstairs.

I sit in the gold chair for an hour, watching the big red numbers on Mumma's clock flip one at a time, wondering how much longer it will be before he is gone, and if there is anything else I need to ask before he leaves.

"How do you make clam chowder, Daddy?"

His body is still. I am not sure if he has heard me. His dry lips part and press together several times before words slip between them. "Cream," he says, with his eyes closed. "And diced potatoes. Small pieces." Long, breathless pauses stretch between ingredients.

When he has finished, I stand and look down at him. He is a powerless pile of bones. His volatile, narcissistic manipulation of me is over. I am no longer his emotional captive. The chosen one, whose purpose was to satisfy needs of a fraudulent church and community leader in a world he described as miserable. We were a father-daughter lie.

I lean over his bald head. "I'm leaving," I say.

His nearly translucent eyelids open halfway. In the yellowed eye-balls of a criminal, I see nothing but pity for himself. "Are you coming back?" he groans.

"Probably. I don't know when."

His lids lower shut as he speaks his last words to me. "Nancy, nothing you could do would ever surprise me."

My hand pauses on the top curve of the weak wooden, hallway banister, still holding on through years of shaken turmoil. As the headless nail pulls at the wrist of my sweater, I turn back for one last look at him. "Good-bye, Dad."

At the front door, I pick up the bags that have waited but a few hours this time and leave.

81

Mother's Day

Four days have gone by. It is Sunday evening, May 11, 1997, Mother's Day.

When I answer my kitchen phone, Mumma's voice is frantic and frustrated on the other end. "I'm tryin to get your father to swallow his pills and he's just starin at me. What a mess we had here a little while ago. I was downstairs, and all of a sudden, I heard a bang. I went upstairs and he'd tried to get from the bed to the pot chair and fell down between the two. His bowels let loose and messed all over the carpet and down the side of the bed, and ya know, that mattress was pretty expensive. I'll never get that stain out. I had to get your brother up here to help me lift him. I was some damn mad, now let me tell you."

From the crackling on the line, I can tell she is on the upstairs phone next to Daddy. "Mumma, at any time while you were trying to shove the pills down his throat, did he say anything to you?"

"No, he didn't. He's just layin here starin at me and still won't take the damn pills."

"Mumma," I say firmly. "He's gone into a coma. Don't try to give him any pills or water. He can't swallow it. The fact that his bowels went means it won't be long. I am leaving right now. I'm on my way." I am driving two hours back to Bath. Mumma needs me.

It is eleven that evening, when I jump the stairs two at a time to get to her. In the dim light from an antique glass lamp, Mumma sits atop the covered pot chair, her rough fingers pulling impatiently back and forth across the knee of her polyester pants. At the end of the bed, in the gold chair, sits the minister. His tall frame is a tight fit to it. His fingers woven over a Bible in his lap. He says hello as I reach past him and awkwardly hug Mumma.

Other than my father's slight, infrequent breath, the room is eerily still. Thick, yellowed mucous eyes stare dull from muscles gone limp. Gray, sooty, whisker pricks have grown for the last time around his green-tooth smile. Dry, callused hands, still stained from years of grease, lay motionless. My father's essence is gone.

I sit next to him on the bed. Scenes of us flash past me. How he threaded worms on my fishhook at Sebago Lake, how he sliced tomatoes paper thin for the best Italian sandwiches, how one Easter he hid jelly beans all over the house for the boys to hunt for, and how it confused me when he did nice things for us. In one fast, fearful moment of doubt, I want to believe I made the whole abuse thing up, that I must have done something to invite it, that it was my entire fault all along. Tears drop to the ghoulish face I now press my wet cheek to. "Please forgive me, Daddy, for everything I did to hurt you, and I will forgive you for everything you did to hurt me."

When I look up, the minister's brow is tense. He stands and puts one hand on Mumma's shoulder, then looks deep at her. "It's going to be a long night, Doris. I'll check back in the morning." He nods at me as he leaves the room.

For an hour, we watch Daddy's chest slowly rise and fall, breath barely passing over slightly parted lips of parched chalky white. We say little to each other. Mumma makes disgusted sighs, rubs her forehead with two fingers, then rolls her nylon knee-highs down her leg and into donut shapes at the top of her shoes. Finally, she stands up and slats her robe off the inside closet hook.

"Well, this is stupid. I'm not gonna sit here all night. I'm goin to bed and get some sleep."

"What? You're going to sleep? Mumma, he's about to die."

"Well, I'm tired, Nancy. It's been a long day for me, ya know."

Even in the moments of his death, she has abandoned me. I lean forward and put my hands on the bed, feeling somewhat sorry that he will die in a dark room with no one to say a final good-bye. "Do you realize that when you wake up, he'll be dead?"

She pushes the closet door shut and stamps one foot to the floor. "Look, I can't stay up waitin for him to die for God sake. This could go on all night."

After washing her face in the downstairs bathroom, Mumma comes back, climbs into bed next to Daddy's bones, and reaches for the lamp switch. She speaks quick at me. "Go to bed, Nancy." The room goes dark.

82

Stillness

I HAVE NOT SLEPT more than five minutes at a time. At the foot of my brother's bed is a black-and-white television, and on top of it a stuffed doll with a Beatles hair-cut and a ball and chain around one leg. Even though I have taken the dirty ashtray downstairs, the bed pillow smells like butts and beer. I sit up, lay my head into my hands, then look over at the clock. 3:20 A.M., it reads, in blaring red. There is a gurgling death rattle coming from my old bedroom, gasping for breath, breaths without rhythm. As the clock turns 3:23, all is quiet.

In the hallway I switch on the light and call into their dark bedroom. "Daddy? Mumma?" I can just see their outlines. Mumma lies facing the wall, snoring in a muffled wheeze. Daddy lies on his back, stone-like, beside her. I walk around the end of the bed and lower myself to the top of the pot chair, keeping my eyes on my father's stillness. I am sickened and I am relieved. I wait and watch for ten minutes. It is strangely peaceful. Finally, I reach across his lifeless body and push at Mumma's shoulder. I do it again and call to her. She turns over and pulls herself up on one elbow.

"He's gone now," I say.

Looking at him, she puts her fingers to her lips, pauses, then takes them away. "Yup. Well. Okay," she says as she stands up, turns on the light, buttons her robe around her nightgown, and sits back down on the edge of the bed. "Well, there's no sense in callin the funeral home and wakin them up too. I guess we should wait a while." She sighs sick and belches gas from low in her gut.

Mumma and I don't cry. We don't talk. For three hours we watch death morph my father's face as foggy, yellow eyes tick shut and his jaw releases like over-stretched elastic, his mouth hanging open, a dead tongue silenced under a snot-colored fake front tooth.

In the kitchen, morning sun streams bright from across the river. It feels warm on my back and shoulders as I sit down at the table. The minister sits across from me, leaning with my shadow to avoid the blinding rays. On the stove, the tea-kettle whistles. The wall clock above it reads 6:10. Mumma spoons freeze-dried coffee into three mugs and pours boiling water on top. The smell of melting crystals flips my stomach. The minister's spoon tings bold to the rim. A trail of brown foam circles behind it. He looks at me for a moment, then goes back to watching his coffee swirl.

Finally, he speaks. "Nancy, are you going to say the eulogy at the service? I think it would be a good idea, and let me say this, no one has ever told me they regretted it after it was over."

I don't answer him. I press both hands tight around my hot coffee cup and hold them there until the burning is the only thing I feel. From the kitchen table I can see Daddy's body being carried down over the stairs in a zipped black bag and out the front door. The minister takes a sip from his cup, then sets it back on the flowered plastic tablecloth. Mumma stands beside him. She carefully folds a paper napkin in half and lays it at his elbow. She doesn't look at Daddy.

83

Funeral

THE METHODIST CHURCH is packed with more people than I have ever seen here at a church service. We sit in the left front pew, my stomach in a knot and Mumma nervously running her rough fingers over the knee of her cream-colored skirt. With the other hand she plays with her gold-and-pearl necklace, then adjusts it between the lapels of her lilac jacket. I reach for Jason's hand. Joshua, Bobby, and Tommy all sit beyond him. I have asked Michael not to come to my father's funeral. I don't want him to see me lie.

As the minister gets closer to the introduction of my eulogy, Mumma shifts anxiously beside me. Her whispered words are quick. "Well, I'm goin to the bathroom."

I grab her arm. "Mumma, it's almost over. Can't you wait?"

"Well, that's too bad, Nancy. No I can't." She stands, steadies herself on the arm of the pew, then hurries down the side aisle of the sanctuary.

The microphone squeals as the minister adjusts the neck of it and speaks. "I would now like to invite Jimmy's daughter, Nancy, to take the pulpit."

Shit.

At the lectern, my notes lie on top, my fingers hooked under the wooden frame of it. The closed casket holding my father's remains sits center stage off to my left, surrounded by oversized arrangements of gladiolas and chrysanthemums. I stand square to the back of the church, my eyes searching more than two hundred sets of eyes looking back at me, silent and waiting for me to say something. In the row behind my boys are Daddy's brothers and their families, behind them a group of his high school class of 1937, and throughout the sanctuary and balcony, church and community members I have known my whole life. I quickly scan the crowd for my friends, including the girl my father insisted on driving home alone from our house one dark winter night when we were eight. That was the night I blocked our front door with my body, shouting she was afraid of him, and when he came back from her house, he bent over me, laughed through his beer breath, and said I was right.

Seconds feel like minutes as I scan faces, wondering how many know more than I do about who my father really was. I am an actress playing the part of a believable daughter, whose run will end after this final performance. My mouth tacks dry, like words will stick to the back of my teeth.

"My father loved this church. He spent his seventy-eight years here, often reading scripture from this very spot I stand. As you know, he operated his own business for fifty years, served as board chairman for the city of Bath and this church. He was president of the elementary school PTA, president of the Little League organization, and in the 1960s a Boy Scout leader. I would say he touched a lot of people along the way, wouldn't you agree?" I lift my eyes up for just a moment, then continue.

"Many years ago, my father told me a story he wanted shared at his funeral, and how he also wished to be cremated. It was during a time that good custodial help was hard to find. He said, 'Nancy, I want you to go to the balcony of the church, open the jar of ashes, and sprinkle it down over the sanctuary carpet. That way I know I'll always be there." A slight ripple of laughter waves through the pews.

"I recently found a letter that my father wrote, talking about the loves in his life. I would like to quote from that now." I take a breath and adjust my glasses. "'The three great loves in my life have been my religion, my family, and my work. I believe the reason they have been so rewarding to me is that I have been willing to listen and follow my Christian beliefs. My religion needs my prayers, my attendance, my stewardship, and my financial support. I have listened to the needs of my wife and children and they have filled my need for companionship. In my work I have had great satisfaction in treating my customers as I would like to be treated myself. I have never regretted anything I have done to try to deserve and preserve these loves of mine.'"

I look out at the congregation, remove my glasses, and finish. "My family and I would like to thank you for your prayers. I ask that you remember my father for his involvement in the city of Bath and for his sense of humor. Thank you."

What a bunch of crap. Every kindness was a setup for his manipulation in the practice of his own perverse satisfaction. And how the hell does that play out in a community without anyone knowing? People knew. I'm just not sure who. Part of me still wants to believe it didn't happen. But it did. My body reminds me of it every day, and that is how I know it is true.

It is easy to not have him in my life now. I have no emotional attachment and no need for him to love me. But with Mumma, that is different.

A YEAR later, in the spring of 1998, I find a note from Mumma in my mailbox. It reads that the Bath Methodist church has created an annual award in my father's name. A plaque honoring his dedication and commitment to the church will hang in the entryway. Each year, one name of a deserving Christian member who exhibits the devotion as he did will be added.

From the mailbox, I am stamping hard down over the driveway, granite gravel spearing into the soles of my bedroom slippers. My body is shaking so hard, I sit on the porch step and fold my knees to my chest in order to get control. Tall pine trees sway and whisper overhead in the mountain spring wind. From inside the envelope, I pull out the enclosed church bulletin Mumma has sent with her short note.

THE JIM STEEN MEMORIAL AWARD

Presented by the members of the Methodist Men to a person who has demonstrated exemplary acts of charity and service in the spirit of Christian goodwill in their church and community.

The annual award will be presented on Easter morning
during the service.

My back teeth clench. I want to dial up someone at that church,
scream into his unconscious brain and ask him, "According to rever-
ent Christian belief, how many scriptures does one preach and how
much financial support does one donate to be forgiven the crime of
pedophilia?" Then, I will drive to Bath, rip the fucking thing off the
church wall, run with it down onto Mumma's boat dock, light that lie
on fire, and throw its ashes into the river.

But instead, I tuck both notes into the envelope and seal it back up.

84

Knowing

IT WAS THE first week in December, 1997. I was in my kitchen cleaning up from a family dinner. Michael and the boys were in the den. Bobby took my hand, looked at the diamond ring, and said I deserved to be happy.

"We're still family," I told him. "And I appreciate that when we stand at the sidelines of Jason's football games we do it as a team, me, you, Joshua, and Michael. The boys are watching us, always watching the example we set. There is nothing more important than that." Bobby agreed.

Now it is four months later and again tonight we have all finished dinner together. The boys have gone to the den, Michael has gone back to his apartment, and before he leaves to go to his, Bobby says we need to talk. At the kitchen sink, I push my hands down into the hot soapy water, laying them flat on the bottom of the pan. Water covers my wrists and rides up my bare arms. A white plastic serving spoon floats to the top. The edges of it are beaten and chewed from the times it has slipped into the teeth of the garbage disposal.

Bobby leans both arms on the counter. "I have a proposition," he says firmly.

I pull my hands out and grab for the dish towel. "I know what you're going to say, Bobby, and I won't leave the boys. Under no cir-cumstances am I leaving my babies."

"Come on, Nance, they're not babies. It has been two years since I left, and I just want a chance to spend more time with them. That would free you to marry Michael."

"I don't need to be freed, and I can't leave the boys. I'm their mother. They need me."

With our voices escalating, the boys come into the kitchen. Tears are welling up in Jason's eyes. I take both his hands in mine. "You need me here, don't you? You need your mother."

Jason lets go of one hand and wipes his face with the sleeve of his sweatshirt. "Mom, I need Dad too. I only have one more year before I go to college. Come on, Mom, give Dad a chance."

I put my hands up over my face and start to cry. Joshua reaches for my shoulders. "Look at me, Mom. Why don't you let Dad move in, and you and Michael can get your own place and get married. It's not that we don't love you or want you here, it's just that Dad loves us too. Jason and I want a chance to spend time with him. It's okay, Mom. It's okay."

It felt like I had been hit in the gut with the end of an uprooted railroad tie. That night after Bobby had left and the boys were in bed, I cried myself to sleep, wishing I could go back in time and make it all better, knowing that was not possible, and knowing now what I had to do.

TODAY is the first day of May 1998, three days before Jason's seventeenth birthday.

The baskets and dried flowers have been taken down from the living room beams, and empty spaces have been left throughout the house where Nanny's antique furniture used to sit. I have packed the good china, the silver tea service, and a few kitchen things we had duplicates of. It has all been delivered to a condo two miles away, in a development off the Route 16 outlet strip.

There is a pile of Bobby's things on the living room floor. A duffle bag of clothes that will be hung back in the bedroom closet we once shared, and the antique trunk he moved out with two years ago, which will go back in its original place next to the porch slider.

We have finished dinner, Bobby, the boys, Michael, and me. I walk back and forth through the house, memorizing the wall stencil patterns, and the whooshing sound of the slider between the living room and screen porch. In the den I take a last look in the family game closet with floor-to-ceiling games we played almost every night. The broken Nerf basketball hoop is still stuck to the top of the doorframe. I stand in Joshua's doorway, remembering how grown-up he felt being the only one with a first-floor bedroom when we moved here nine and a half years ago. In the hall, I pull my nails down through the long gouge in the wide railing from where Jason slid the cat. At the bottom of the stairs I open the closet and run my hand over the three packed shelves of photo albums, numbered and indexed with twenty years of hiking, picnics, and vacations.

I feel Michael's hands on my arms. He speaks softly in my ear. "Honey, it's time to go. You can do it. I'm here." I close the closet door and walk with him to the kitchen, where the boys are waiting.

"Okay, well. I guess I'm going now. You guys be good. You know where I am if you need anything." The words seem empty, and when I hug them, "I love you" is not nearly enough to say, but in the moment it is the only thing that comes out.

With all that I will walk through in life, nothing will be more difficult than walking out that kitchen door.

The sun has set. It is already dark, after eight o'clock, when Michael helps me into the front seat of his car. The idling engine vibrates every nerve in my body. I ask him to wait. Sitting in the dark driveway and looking into the kitchen, I watch my family hugging and laughing. Everything about me feels turned inside out.

Michael reaches for my hand. "Okay, honey? We ready? It will be just fine. I know it's hard for you to leave. It will take a while for you to adjust, but it will be fine, you'll see."

I want to fall into his arms for comfort and tell him to shut up at the same time. I do neither. As we pull out of the driveway, through my tears, I watch the house lights blur into long, fingery branches of gold.

For the next two weeks I will cry day and night, doubting and hoping that I have done the right thing, yet knowing in my heart I did.

85

Lemon Cake and Strawberries

It's been eight weeks since I left Beechwood Drive, two years to the day that Michael walked through that kitchen doorway for his first dance lesson. It is Friday, June 26, our wedding day.

From the front porch of Dooza's log home, large, white paper bells sway in the summer morning breeze. On the front lawn there is a white tent and two tables underneath it shaped in a *T*. They wait to be spread with white tablecloths and seven full picnic baskets, one for each of the six couples who will celebrate our happiness.

Our golf carts, rented from Allen Mountain Golf Course just up the road from Dooza's, have carried Michael, Dooza, David, and nine of our closest friends to the top of the mountain, where Dooza will officiate. The day I asked her, I pulled my car right into the same bank parking spot I had overdosed in three years ago. It felt good. I smiled when I spied Dooza eating lunch at a picnic table just beyond it. She said marrying Michael and me was the next best thing to marrying me herself. Then she honked and hugged me tight.

Joshua drives our golf cart up the loose gravel to the top of the mountain road. As we get closer I can see Michael waiting for me, Dooza waiting beside him with papers in hand. When the cart stops, Jason is there at my end of a white-paper aisle that has been spread over the moist, green carpet of the fifth tee. Early storm clouds have now parted. The sun is shining bright overhead. Birds tweet so loudly, it feels like I am the star in a princess movie. Jason takes my arm and helps me off the golf cart. I pull the skirts of my wedding gown along with me and drop the lacy hems gently to the ground. Joshua takes my other arm. He leans into me just as we start the walk to Michael. "Be happy, Mom. You so deserve it." Jason kisses my cheek. "I love you, Mom. You deserve the best."

Michael is gorgeous standing on a large, flat rock at the end of the paper runner. He looks so tall in black slacks and a white jacket. He reaches for my hand and, as he does, one tear rolls down each cheek. He tips his head down and wipes both eyes with one finger. I know our friends are standing there with us, but my eyes are on Michael. He is so good, I think, such a good man, and the boys love him. I love him too.

After our vows, we dance right there on top of the mountain, and he softly sings, "Have I Told You Lately That I Love You" with his cheek pressed against mine. "I love you, my beautiful bride," he says as we finish. Bubble orbs blown from tiny soapy wands float around us. Golfers waiting to play through raise their clubs and cheer congratulations. Time has stopped in this beautiful moment. And I am grateful.

Back in Dooza's yard, I step out of my white satin shoes and twirl in circles until my gown spins out like a hoop dress. Everyone dances and laughs, and we eat the most beautiful huge fresh strawberries we have ever seen, picked by Dooza that morning. When the lemon cake has been eaten and the presents have been opened, Michael and I get into his car and drive away, blue ribbons waving from the wipers and antenna.

"Fifty years," he says. "In fifty years we have a date. Our golden anniversary."

I wave back at everyone in the driveway, then look at him. "Honey, do you know how old I'll be in fifty years?"

"Yes," he says, his eyes still glowing misty. "And on that day you will be even more beautiful than you are today. You will always be my beautiful bride."

June 26, 1998. Every moment was perfect in every loving way.

86

Truth

IT WAS AFTER five months of marriage that I began therapy with my psychologist, Ridley. A year has passed since then. When I am on the dance floor teaching with David, I look confident, polished, and happy. No one would guess what I keep hidden, except for Michael. He is the only one who knows the truth.

In our bedroom, morning sun will soon peek in the window. The television volume is low. It has been on all night, running repetitive infomercials for skin creams and exercise equipment. At 5:30 A.M., Michael carefully slides away from me and out of bed. He never shuts the television off. He knows that will startle me. Then, just before he leaves for work, he delivers my hot cup of coffee. I hear a slight *ting* as he sets the mug onto the glass coaster on my nightstand, and again, today, I wake crying and dissociating from places in my past, where colors and conversations run together. Blankets clutch at my chin, my fingers tingle numb, my knees pull tight to my chest. I scream at the man who stands beside me. I can smell his hot nicotine breath, see pig-bristle hair sprouting from waxy, yellow ears, hear his throat rumble. "Get away from me," I scream. "Don't touch me. Leave me alone." We do it every day.

His voice is patient and loving. "It's okay, honey. It's Michael. You are forty-four-years old, we are at the condo, and you are safe in your own bed. No one is going to hurt you. You are my beautiful bride, and I will protect you."

When I am able to move out of my locked position, the sun is over the trees, Michael has left for work, and my coffee has long gone cold. At 10:00, I shower and dress. Today I will see the psychologist.

THE sound of my black Z28 Camaro is like a race car when I get beyond the Route 16 outlet strip, with Mount Washington ahead of me, on the road to Jackson. Even though it is December, my feet are bare, the convertible top is down. Heater on. Latin music is blaring from the CD player. As I pull into Ridley's driveway, a woman walks by, looks at my vanity plate, and smiles. "RUMBA" rolls off her tongue.

Two fingers make hard pressing circles at my temples, then at the base of my skull, where for a year it has banded tight like a torture device from the whiplash injury. The day I got rear-ended at that red light, I was more concerned about the crunched back end of my new car, but driving away I heard my knowing voice come loud in my head. It said," Your life has just changed." Some nights my eyes feel like they will explode right out of my face. During class I get so dizzy, I fall sideways off my ballroom shoes and David has to hold me up, and several times I have had to ask Dooza to fill in for me.

In Ridley's office, I am jammed at the end of the couch, my feet curled under me, pillows piled to my chest. Some days when I am here, I travel so far back in time, it feels near impossible to come home before the hour is up. Some days I ask Ridley to talk so I can just listen, but today he holds an open book out to me and points to the page. His face is tan for this time of year. Deep wrinkles make smiley lines from the corners of his blue eyes, and his hair is streaked blond like a California surf boy from back in the day. He watches my face as I look at the book where he holds his finger, then asks me, "How do you relate to this word, Nancy? Can you tell me?"

Shame. It jumped right off that page and grabbed my breasts. I could feel its fingers knead into me, and I could smell cigarette smoke and whiskey. "Don't tell Mumma. Don't make Mumma mad," I heard it say, and between my legs I got all tingled and locked up. I hated Ridley in that moment. I cried until my stomach hurt, then pounded my chest to make myself stop. It sounded hollow. He never said anything, he just let me do it, and when I was done I felt embarrassed.

Then I asked him why in all these months he had not prescribed antidepressants like the other doctors had. His eyes never left mine when he said it. "You don't need them this time. You are stronger now."

I was silent for a while, then blew my nose and said, "You know what? You're right, I am." We both smiled. It was a good healing day.

87

Balance

My truth is crippling. I want to sleep it away, board a train and run from it. But I will never travel fast enough to leave myself behind. Day by day, different areas of my body remind me of things it never forgot. Vaginal pain like I've been kicked inside, wrists sore from pushing away the weight of rape. My body is processing and presenting information. I am a circuit board of cell memory, a storehouse of emotions and beliefs I have amassed about myself and how I have interpreted the world around me.

Today in my condo, Joshua balances on the edge of the white tuxedo couch. He wrings his hands between his knees. He looks scared to hear what I will say. "Mom, you don't have to talk about it. Jason and I have always known what happened to you. How could we not know? Remember, we've been the ones taking care of you all these years."

It makes my heart sick to hear it. I want a do-over. Go back in time and be a better me, not the drugged and frightened mother. "Josh, I am so sorry you and Jason had to live like that."

He leans forward to where I am sitting in the desk chair and hooks one finger around mine. "Mom, I know I don't see you much, even though we're just a couple of miles apart. But I am always thinking about you. You tell me how proud of me you are, but you should be proud of yourself. Everything I've gained in my life is because of your teaching and support. On the days that I'm down and things are really tough, I think about how much you have been through and how strong you are and I feel better. Mom, I'm so proud of you."

I have to keep going, I think. I have to do it for the boys.

SOME days healing is just so hard, I get into my bed and stay there. I want go home to Beechwood Drive and back to the days when we shared daily precious family moments, eating tacos, helping with homework, and saying "I love you" before I snapped the lights out at bedtime. Two years from now when Jason is in college and Joshua is living with friends, Bobby will sell that house. Twelve years from now I will drive by it, see a FOR SALE sign out front, and pull into that driveway again. The trees that once surrounded it will have been cut down, and the earthy, brown salt box shingles will have been painted a putrid swamp green. I will get out of the car and peer through the windows into an empty house that will look so much smaller than I remember. The wallpaper in the kitchen will have peeled, and the living room stenciling will be painted over. For a moment I will believe that I can have it all back again. But my children will be grown men by then, with lives of their own, and this will never again be our home. But forever I will cherish those years we had in the woods of Beechwood Drive, before my body and mind overflowed illness. Before I was ready to know my truth.

88

Sick of You

WHEN I BROUGHT the white tuxedo couch home to our condo, I loved how perfectly it fit in the loft across from my desk. But again, today, I am curled at one end of that couch with the blue homemade afghan Mumma bought at the church fair. My fingers are bent, hooked through the crocheted loops, and sore from holding them like that for an hour. The frayed yarn is knotted tight, dampened with tears, and against my mouth. I am staring at the desk phone. It has rung three times this morning. All three times Mumma has left a nasty message, each one more impatient than the one before it. The fourth time I answer just to make her stop. My stomach clenches, like diarrhea is about to burst from me with the sound of her voice.

"Nancy? Well, it's about time you answered. What's the matter with you?"

I look across the room and into the bathroom. A pile of towels pulled from the rack are heaped on the floor. It's where I hid early this morning when the front doorbell rang, where I cried and dissociated and thought I was eight. "I'm sorry, Mumma. I was in the bathroom."

"Yeah well. I just called to see how you're doin."

My bare feet slide down between the two couch cushions. I bury them under the nearly weightless upholstered foam. I pull a stack of books from the coffee table and onto the cushion. I can hear Mumma cranking the kitchen window open, and the sound of the old tin measuring cup scoop into the bucket of sunflower seeds. In my mind, I see her leaning out to fill the window feeder as I've seen her do a thousand times. Mumma loves her birds.

I hug the afghan tight to my chest. "I'm not doing well, Mumma."

"Are you still havin those God-awful headaches?" She doesn't wait for me to answer. "Well, you better have surgery or somethin so you can be rid of this mess. You certainly aren't gettin any better, that's for damn sure."

"Mumma, it's not just my headache. I'm having bad dreams and memories, and every night I wake up screaming and kicking at Michael. I did the same thing to Bobby for years."

"Well, why the heck would you do that? That's just foolish." I hear the birdseed cup ring against the old tin Humpty Dumpty Potato Chip bucket and the lid slam down over it.

"Because I am remembering things, things I don't want to remember. I want to believe the abuse never happened, but it did. We both know that."

Her exhale is like hot steam through a sewer grate. "No, Nancy, I don't know that."

My body is shaking, shoulders to my ears. The receiver is hard to my head, so hard there is no other pain than at one temple.

She says it again. "What is the matter with you? I think it's time for a new therapist. He hasn't done a damn thing to help you. Makin you remember way back is not makin you better. Why can't you just get over it like other people do?"

My tongue is dry. It makes my voice sound thick. "How do you know I'm not getting better?"

"Well, look at you for God sake, you're a mess."

I can hear the suction of sweat cupping my ear, smell my morning breath on the mouthpiece. I fill my lungs and yell out at her. "Do you think I will heal like a broken leg? I am broken all over. If you unzipped me, I am black-and-blue from head to toe."

"Yeah, okay, Nancy. You know it all." In my mind I can see her sitting at the kitchen table, crossed leg swinging with the toe of her shoe locked up to the ceiling.

I pinch my eyes tight together and fill my lungs again. "The reality is that your husband molested me and where the hell were you?"

Her words are immediate. "I don't know, Nancy. I must have been there. I guess I was just a rotten mother, or so you tell me. So, if you say it happened, it must have, cause you know everything, don't you?"

My feet are now flat under my butt, ready to fight, ready to run. I press the afghan heavy to my breasts. My voice is like a projectile aimed to slash her throat and drop her fast to the floor in a whirlpool of anger.

"Mumma, how do I process that my father, someone who was supposed to protect me, raped me night after night for years while my mother looked the other way?"

Her scream is loud and staggered like a spray of bullets. "I didn't look the other way. I didn't know anything about it for God sake."

"I tried to tell you. Why didn't you listen to me, Mumma? You were supposed to love and protect me, and you didn't."

"Okay, Nancy, that's enough. You've been telling me that since you were a little girl and I'm sick ta death of hearin it. Don't you think I would have known what my own husband was doin for God sake? I was married to him for fifty years."

"Mumma, you just said you didn't even know what he was doing in your own house."

For a moment there is silence, then her words run thin over hypocritical lips. "No, I guess I didn't. God, this has just ruined my life. I didn't know any of this. I didn't know what he was doing. It was after I was asleep. I stayed on my side of the bed, way over on the edge. How was I supposed to know where he went when he got up?"

"Mumma, you knew. Before he died, he asked you to tell him you remembered it all, about me and the other women."

"No, he didn't, Nancy. You were the one that said there were other women. I didn't hear your father say anything like that."

"Of course you heard him. The day he told what he called the family secrets, you tried to shut him up. If you were totally unaware, you wouldn't have done that." My chest is on fire. "I can't imagine what it's like to be you, Mumma. Even with all I have been through, I would still rather be me. You are a mean, self-absorbed woman, and your only concern is saving yourself."

She slams down the phone. It feels like she slapped my face, as enraged heat vibrates every cell in my body, reminding me that I was purchased for a self-serving, immoral purpose, dressed like a doll and paraded into church on the hand of a false father. My knotted fingers are flaming with anger, wanting to grab at her and shake her until she is broken down and wailing with regret for not saving me. One number after the other, I punch the face of the phone. It rings nine times before she picks up and yells hello. When she hears my voice she hangs up. Again, I call her back. This time she answers on the first ring. I don't give her time to speak.

"From now on, Mumma, when you call and ask how I am, expect to hear the truth. As much as you want to blame me, it is not my fault. It never was. And here's a question. What about the way he treated you? There were so many inappropriate things done in front of me. Like when he put his hands down your blouse and grabbed your breasts at the dinner table, and when he put his hand up under your dress and complained to me that your girdle was too tight for him to get at you. He watched me. He did it in front of me. How sick is that?"

"Oh for God sake, Nancy, he didn't do that all the time."

"What about some of the time, isn't that enough?"

"Yeah, okay, Nancy, you know it all."

I am scared to say the word, but my voice is daring and removed from the child I am growing out of. "I know the way you feel about sex, that it's only done after you are married, is that right, Mumma?"

She answers sternly and high-pitched. "Yes, if you're married and a man takes care of you, then sex is expected."

My throat clenches like the words may stick. "Is that what you did, you exchanged sex for a place to live?"

Her answer comes easy and abrupt. "I guess you could say I did, but I didn't like it."

Sour acid boils up behind my tongue. "Well, was it expected from me, Mumma, in order to live there?" I fear her answer.

"Yes, I guess it was. He didn't get what he wanted from me, so he went to you. And don't you think I know there were other women? He had plenty. I don't know why for God sake. He had it anytime he wanted it from me."

My heart pounds like it will dislodge from my chest and gush up my throat. "Mumma, do you remember how I begged you not to leave me alone with him and you would say, oh for God sake, Nancy, don't be so foolish, your father would never hurt you."

The fight is leaving her tone. "Yes, I remember that."

I lower my voice and speak slowly. "Do you know that is why I never wanted to go to school, Mumma?"

"Yes, I know that now. You never wanted to get up in the morning and you never wanted to go to bed at night. I can see that now."

I am holding back tears, waiting for her apology. "Then why the hell didn't you see it then?"

"When you were a teenager, Nancy, you and your father would fight bad." She makes a long sigh, remembering, then continues. "He would chase you up the stairs and into your room, and you would scream for me to come help you."

"And, Mumma. Why didn't you?"

There is no remorse in her response. "I guess I figured your father would take care of it."

"Well, you guessed right, Mumma. He did." My body is sweaty and exhausted from degrading myself in verbal vacillation between me as the child and me as the adult. Demanding that she heal my pain and tell me there is still a chance that she will love me.

Her words slide meaningless with bitter breath. "I wish there was somethin I could do, Nancy, but I guess there isn't, so you betta just forget it."

I have little strength left to beg her love. I curl into a ball in the corner of the white tuxedo couch and pull the blue afghan back to my face. "Forget it? Do you have any idea what a ridiculous statement that is, Mumma? I was a child. It wasn't my fault. You were the adult. Tommy and I just wanted you to love us. We needed you to save us."

Like our conversation never happened, Mumma's voice lightens. "I called the minister this morning. I told him I felt terrible that you went through all that, and it happened right here in my own house, and I never even knew about it." She pauses, then says quietly, "I love you, Nancy."

I wait. Then respond low. "I love you too, Mumma."

"Yeah," she shouts through gargled spit and slams down the receiver.

I hold the phone in my hand for a long time until silence turns to repetitive blasts of disconnection. When my eyes come to focus, I am looking through the bedroom doorway to my nightstand. I hear the phone receiver click onto the box rest, then feel my knees burn through black leggings and my fingernails dig into the dull beige carpet.

"I hate you, you selfish, lying bitch."

Gulping for breath, I drag myself across the room like an injured cat. I pull open the nightstand drawer and quickly pop the top off a prescription bottle of painkillers. Three shake into my hand. Maybe it's four. Fat tears flood my eyes and glue colored capsules of numbness to my wet palm. I am screaming for help at a blank ceiling, hoping it will open up, praying someone will appear with loving arms, lift me out, and tell me I am worth saving. I hear nothing but my own fear pounding at my eardrums and snot sucking up my nostrils. I look down at my hand, shaking, once again filled with toxins that will temporarily take me somewhere else. My teeth scrape across my palm and bite the drugs off my skin like sticky, rancid, carnival candy. They wash into my stomach with a swallow of cold coffee. On the floor of my bedroom, under the crisp white cotton dust ruffle of my bed, I curl into a ball and wait for sleep.

As long as I am living to please, rebel against, or be validated by my mother, I cannot be a complete adult. The grown-up part of me knows that. But the chosen child holds resentful to the painful truth, that Mumma failed me, turned her back to a screaming child, a drunken teenager, a shamed woman. I am on a quest to make her aware of that until she loves me, or dies.

89

Priorities

IN THE CORNER of Ridley's couch I have built a fort of pillows. He sits at his desk beyond me, wearing a tan winter sweater. Above it, summer-sun hair is spread long and windblown in all directions. We talk about our convertible cars, how we both love the free feeling of the open sky over our heads, and how the Fourth of July is our favorite holiday. He asks me why. "Freedom," I say.

He reaches both arms up, then folds his hands behind his head. It's what he does when he is about to say something I might not want to hear. "Nancy, would you be open to contacting your family's minister? He has known your parents a long time, and he could be of help to you. Would you be willing to do that?"

"I am willing to try, but I don't think he is interested in helping or hearing from me. My father gave a lot of money and time to that church. How would it look if the parishioners knew the truth about the minister's right-hand man? The church is a business, Ridley, always a business first. "

January 2000

Dear Reverend,

I am writing in hopes that you are willing to speak with me. I realize this puts you in an uncomfortable situation and you would normally not assist parishioners from your prior church now that you've been transferred out of the Bath area. However, I am asking for your help and that you share with me what was said to you when my father admitted our family secrets.

For all of my life, I have fought to hold the door shut on my memories. I now know that in order for me to be a healthy adult I must process my childhood trauma. For more than a year I have been in therapy in regard to the incest issue. I am working to heal forward. I am asking if you would you please help me.

Sincerely,
Nancy

Dear Nancy,

Because I hold you in such high esteem, I am concerned you might be hurt by what I am about to say. After much soul searching, it is clear to me that I cannot reveal to you anything your father shared with me when I was called to his bedside on the occasion you recalled. At my ordination, I made a vow to hold all things shared with me in a confessional setting in strict confidence.

Since your request seemed to me to offer the potential of offering you great help, I decided to discuss with my district superintendent the possibility of breaking my vow. She and I agreed that your request represents a clash of two good things. Opening a possibility of healing for you and keeping confidential whatever your father might have said to me on his deathbed. Such clashes comprise the toughest ethical binds, but our discussion led me to reaffirm my vow of confessional confidentiality.

The fact that your father revealed to you and your mother, as you have written, the family secrets, seems to me to be a sign that he was confessing to you, and at the same time validating what you had been saying to him and your mother for years before his death. From a woman's perspective, my district superintendent believes that your father's admission contained implicitly, if not explicitly, the acknowledgment of regret you are seeking.

The courage you have mustered to open doors of memory you have for so long kept tightly shut is truly remarkable. Your bravery combined with God's grace will bring you the healing you seek. Though I have not shared with you all that you were hoping to read, I am praying that the little I have offered will contribute in a small way to the bright future you want so much, and that God so much wants to give you.

Grace and peace,
Reverend

Dear Reverend,

I am questioning your priorities. In your last letter you made the point that you could potentially offer me great help. However, your choice was to remain silent. In doing that, you hold some of the secrets of my life. I am confused. Why would you protect a dead man and ignore the help that you could offer me?

The resulting dissociative disorder from my abuse is an amazing thing. It has kept the shade pulled down over glimpses of muted memories until I was strong enough to begin a conscious healing process. Somewhere behind locked doors are the answers to all my questions, a fill-in to all the blanks. It will be a long journey, I know, but I am ready to begin.

A conversation with you would be greatly appreciated. Please reconsider.

Sincerely,
Nancy

Dear Nancy,

Your recent letter and renewed request to discuss in person whatever your father might have said to me prior to his death surprised me. I did not expect to hear from you again because I thought you understood my decision.

To state things as clearly as I can, your father's conversation with me prior to his death was confessional in nature, largely because you made it so. You were the one who wanted your father to confess to his pastor. You were the one who called me to hear what he had to say. And you were the one who left the two of us alone because you understood that the conversation that was about to take place was a confessional one. Finally, I am the one who vowed when I was ordained to hold all confessional conversation in strict confidence.

Now I must ask you to understand that I cannot correspond with you any more about this situation. I am unable to remember writing anything to you that even remotely suggested that I could potentially offer you great help. I have decided firmly to be faithful to my ordination vows.

Sincerely,
Reverend

In this moment, as I read the minister's final words, I fall backward into a hellish pit of shame and guilt, off the edge of reason and below where I have ever been before. My heart throbs wild with fear. Numbness rides hard down my arms and legs. I am catapulting, body and mind, back to every age, every rage of attack of Daddy's touch, Mumma's words. It's all the same. In the end, the fires of hell will consume what is left of me in retribution for conscious truth-telling to a man of God.

The letter falls to the floor. The minister's handwriting stares heartless up at me. Hands hot and blindly searching for safety, I crawl from corner to corner, rooms that change at will like I am worm-holing through time and dimensions. I am ten in Mumma's living room, Daddy's hands squeezing tight to my waist. I smell whiskey and cigarettes. I am nineteen, running up the staircase to my bedroom, Daddy grabbing at the back of my bell-bottomed pants. The banister creaks as I death grip it and kick at his chest, a dark blue work shirt with JIM written over the left breast pocket. I am fourteen, curled to the headboard of my bed. His words come loud in my fear. "Daddy loves you. Daddy would never hurt you. I picked you out special. Who else do you know that gets dance lessons and pretty clothes like you do?"

Festered shame oozes out like toxins from a pus-filled zit. I live again, what never left me, like everything is happening at once on a time loop of residual haunting. I am jammed in the corner of the hall, screaming at my father, from every decade of delusion. "You are nothing but a piece of fucking low-life shit. I hope you spend eternity scuffing up and down cold metal stairs searching for something you never find, crawling frozen on your belly through wet, filthy cellars. How stupid was I for not seeing our truth sooner. I hate you. I said I forgave you, but I lied."

One stair at a time. Minutes. Maybe hours until I can get to my bed, a little girl with perfect banana curls and a petticoat dress bangs her fists to mine, a forty-four-year old woman with running mascara and rug-burned leggings, a wall of shattering glass between us. Begging to be known and released from the unconsciousness she was groomed to hide in, I fight to get her out and love her up. Climbing stairs on our hands and knees will be the last partial coherent moment I will have for the next fifty-two hours.

From two thirty on Tuesday afternoon, when I opened the minister's letter, until I came out of my dissociative spell at dinner-time on Thursday, I was locked in a horror movie. It played full-screen, living-color scenes of my life, just as real as when they were stored in my cellular memory years ago. Each one marched forward, daring me to deny what I always knew as truth. I saw tiny blue flowers on a woven stretchy undershirt, heard my father's work pants, heavy with coins and keys, hit my bedroom floor. Felt rough, hang-nailed fingers against my private skin. Year after fear it went on, until my body and mind had showed me enough to never doubt my truth again.

When Michael came home from work that first night I did not know he was there. While I trudged forty years of hidden memories, Michael missed two days of work, meals, and sleep. He never left my side. But I wouldn't know that until it was over.

My body aches now from the fight. It is dark out. I am not sure what day it is, not sure if the sun is about to rise, or if it has already set. I look at my sweetheart slowly inching to me on the bed, discolored circles round under his eyes, whiskers grown long on his normally clean-shaven face.

"Oh my God, Michael, I am so sorry. How can you still love me, with all I have put you through?"

He drops his head. Then looks back up at me. I think he will cry. "Honey, you have to stop saying you're sorry and start believing you are worth being loved. You won't fully heal until you do." He leans toward me from his side of the bed. Thick, shiny black hair hangs over one gentle brown eye. He wipes my sweaty bangs back off my forehead and kisses me where salty fear beaded minutes before.

Michael lies down next to me and sighs with exhaustion, grateful that I have finally come back to him. He reaches for my hand, holds it in both of his, kisses it, and lays it to his heart. "Honey, anyone can love you on your good days. I will love you on your worst."

That was soon to come.

Hiking wooded trails. Picnics. Pure happiness.

Cup a tea. In Nanny's kitchen. It smelled like date and coconut squares hot from the oven.

River view of my childhood home.

Popham Beach, Maine. Winter 1984. The ocean was the vein of freedom I always went back to.

My favorite photo of the boys. Kancamagus Scenic Byway. New Hampshire.

Our happy place. 1986.

Pickpocket pigmy goats. It was the best laugh Mumma and I ever had.

Space Mountain. Her hair was blown crazy to the sides and she didn't even mind that it wouldn't go back into place.

Goodbye Bath, Maine.

Hello Conway, New Hampshire. 1988.

Beechwood Drive. I will never have a best life moment more loved than this.

Home.

A wooded storybook dream.

When the water is racing. And the tide pulls at your feet. Remember, I love you oceans.

David and I teaching in North Conway.
Dooza graduating from a six-week ballroom session.

David and I. Ready for an evening
performance.

With David and Dooza. Red Jacket Inn. Best friends and dance
buddies.

One day at a
time. One hour
at a time.

Leaving. 1998.
Wishing I could go
back in time and
make it all better.

Every weekend
Michael and I danced
at the Red Jacket.

Wedding day. June 1998.

Be happy, Mom.

One tear rolled down his cheek. Dooza officiated.

Golfers, waiting to play through, raised their clubs and cheered congratulations.

Lemon cake and strawberries. Every moment was perfect in every loving way.

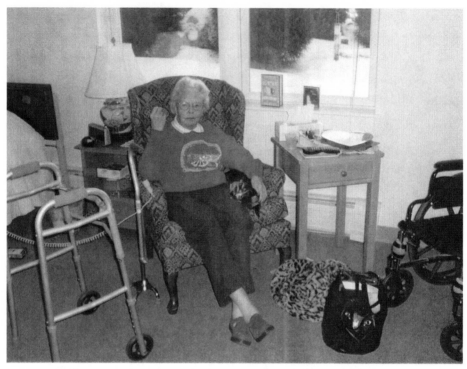

Nursing home. 2008. Mumma waved her red-polished nails, bit into a chocolate, and said she'd rather die.

I am free. A ceremonial
birthday purging.

Popham. 2010. It was my own voice in the tide that saved me.

earth

90

Witch City

Aᴛᴇʀ ᴛʜᴇ Vᴏʟᴠᴏ dealership closed in the Mount Washington Valley, Michael said he could get a job anywhere. It was April 2000 when we moved three hours south of North Conway. The day we interviewed with the owner of the brick federal home, Michael sat with his hands folded politely in his lap while he and the woman talked Volvos. Her words were polished and educated as she looked us over and said she wanted a young healthy couple who would stay long-term, that we would have half the second and third floors and the door between our kitchen and her back stairway would remain unlocked for safety purposes. Then she asked if I would be teaching ballroom dance classes locally, I said I hoped to, but I knew I wouldn't.

Morning sun is pouring in the front living room windows of our second-floor apartment and reflecting off the dark-stained floorboards. On the window seat I have laid Nanny's one-hundred-year-old quilt, and over the yellow Italian marble fireplace are tall crystal candlesticks that Mumma received on her wedding day, much too fancy, she said, to ever be used. I hear the *ching ching* of the trolley bell as it rolls slowly by. The driver's voice comes loud over a speaker. "Chestnut Street is said to be the most beautiful one-way street in the county. These sea captain mansions were built in the early 1800s during the China trade. Today it is still where the rich people live." I laugh every time I hear him say it. Again, today, I lean out the window and wave at them. People on the right side of the trolley look up and wave back. A police car follows. On the door is a silhouette of a witch on a broom. Around it reads, SALEM, MASSACHUSETTS, THE WITCH CITY, 1626.

At 10:30, the skirts of my long white cotton dress sweep behind me down our winding wooden side stairwell. Sandals wait on black-and-white, checker-board flooring. I drop my work bag off my thumb and let it hang heavy over one shoulder. In our narrow door yard, under a tall, sprawling elm, the hinges of the old black doweled gate creak as I pull it shut and begin my daily mile walk down cobblestone paths, through Pilgrim graveyards, and to the mystical, maritime shops of Pickering Wharf.

At 11:00, I flip the OPEN sign in the store-front window and wedge the door open. The sandwich board that I unfold to the sidewalk reads, METAPHYSICAL TEACHER – INTUITIVE ADVISOR. Just beyond it, boats bob high on the Salem Harbor tide. Back inside the shop, I light two sticks of incense and dig them into sprawling plants on either side of the large angel-themed white wicker room. Sweet, swirling smoke and New Age music calls to passing tourists who wander curiously by waiting for a glimpse of a real Salem witch.

A few minutes later, Lucrecia stops just inside the doorway, sun shining through the skirt of her long amethyst chiffon dress. She pulls the hem up over one knee and strikes a pose. "Good morning, baby. Time to rise and shine and greet the day." She waves one arm up over her black silky hair, then strides long like a model across the room to my desk. Her patchouli perfume is strong as she leans over and air kisses both sides of my face. Then she sits down at her desk, crosses her bronzed legs, and with long red nails, combs her sleek shoulder-length hair across the top of her head. Taking a tissue from her oversized jeweled purse, she daintily dabs both corners of her lined ruby lips. In her younger years she could have passed for Elizabeth Taylor. Even now, in her mid-sixties, she outlines her eyes in thick black pencil. One black spot dots her upper right cheek. Soothing Italian-inflected words slide beautifully over her pouted lips. "How are you feeling today, my bella donna? Come here and let me work on that nasty headache." I pull a chair to her desk and let her lay warm fingertips to my temples.

It has been over a year since the Camaro rear-ender whiplash, months of radiating headaches that travel the back of my neck and band my head in torturous pulsing pain that wobbles my vision and flips my stomach. Now far from Jackson, New Hampshire, and the safety of Ridley's office, I have just finished reading *I Can't Get Over It: A Handbook for Trauma Survivors*, written by Aphrodite Matsakis, Ph. D., almost four hundred textbook-type pages that I have highlighted in bright yellow marker over words too painful to say out loud. Pages of facts and statistics, tear-stained and nail-torn. Pen-gouged margins of things I have never told anyone, scribbled just before I dissociated far away from the living room couch. A friend waiting patiently for me to begin again, saying, "Take all the time you need, there is no rush, you are not alone, you are not crazy, and somewhere inside you have always known the truth." Lucrecia understands that.

Her fingers smell of lavender oil as she massages the sides of my head. My shoulders drop and relax. The telephone rings at my desk. "Let the machine get it, honey." Her voice remains at peace as she reaches to her past. "Nancy, you must listen to me. It is not possible to be healthy in body if we allow fear to control us. Fear leaks into places and screams for attention in the most mysterious ways. Fear of past, fear of future. It's all the same, and it's what destroys us. After I was raped in a day-lit parking lot, I suffered two consecutive heart attacks. I lived in terror every day for years. I shopped and filled my house with things I didn't need, pulled down the shades, and buried myself inside." Lucrecia brings both her hands together in a praying position under her chin and leans back in the chair. Her eyes are focused on mine. She doesn't blink. "So now I ask you the question that someone finally asked me. How long do you want to be the victim?"

I feel a flush of embarrassment wave down my body. Is she blaming me for my own pain, the woman who has become my mentor, a friend I told my secrets to?

"How long?" she asks again. "How long are you planning on hanging onto the emotional pain your physical body is asking to let go of?"

My throat is constricted. I swallow hard around it and stand up. The room feels smaller. I don't know the answer, and I won't, until months later when I drop to such a low tide still point I will be forced to fight for life, or let go forever.

91

Drugged and Dazed

It is the last week of July. I am in Dr. Gray's examination room with both legs folded under me on the medical table, paper crinkling under my bare, clenched toes. On the edge of the sink cabinet is a *Reader's Digest* magazine lying open to an article titled, "Brandon's Fight for Life." I close my eyes, press my fingers into my temples, and make hard circles, stretching my scalp as far as it will go.

There is a tap on the door. Dr. Gray says hello and sits on the stool at the end of the table. Her smile is slight as she adjusts glasses up over her rounded cheeks. Her voice sounds tired. "No luck with this last medication, Nancy?"

I flatten my hands to the table and press until my back is tall. One knee taps in rhythm. My chest is tight. "No luck," I say.

She holds her pen close to my medical chart and doesn't look at me as she speaks. "On a scale of one to ten, ten being the worst pain you have experienced, where would you say you are on the scale today?"

I let my back slump. Pulling my fingers up through my hair, I shake my head. "I don't know. I hate that number scale. It makes no sense to me." My nose is tingling, and I can feel my upper lip start to quiver.

There is silence as she reads my chart, then looks up and speaks again. "I'd like to ask you to reconsider a narcotic choice. We have run out of things to try. I am going to suggest that you take a new drug that is being found very helpful for acute pain."

Tears flood off my eyelids. My voice is resistant, remembering how grueling it was to detox from narcotics five years ago. "No, I really do not feel good about taking a narcotic. I can't go through that detox again."

Her tone is short. Mumma's face flashes in front of me. "Look, Nancy, we have tried several other medications that didn't touch the pain. As far as medication goes, this is what's left."

I watch her write across a script pad. My insides feel cold. My underarms are sweating. "Well, how long would I take it, and what happens when I need to stop?"

She is abrupt. "Don't worry about that now. When it's time, you will simply cut back and stop, that's all." She rips the page off the pad and holds it out to me. It reads, Oxycontin.

My gut says no. My pain says yes. I am desperate for relief.

SINCE I was a teenager, taking a handful of pills has been routine as putting on my makeup. Pills for panic, anti-seizure, anti-depression. Valium, Thorazine, Prozac, Klonopin, Ativan, trazadone, Xanax. Amitriptyline, desipramine, Tegretol. And worst of all, the opiods. Darvon, Demerol, Tylox, morphine. Capsules of calm. Microscopic Band-Aids temporarily adhering to my pain, prescribed to me by medical professionals I believed knew more than I did about how to heal my body and mind. Doctors briefed by pharmaceutical representatives who wine, dine, and deliver drug samples of the latest top seller.

It has now been eighteen months since I put that first small white Oxycontin tablet on my tongue, the day my body began shutting down. Everything has slowed. My reflexes, my bowels, my breath. I am in a battle between living with the drugs and dying without them. As my headaches increase, so does the Oxy, Dr. Gray upping the dosage five milligrams at a time by having me cut the ten milligram tablets in half. In addition to the 110 milligrams of Oxycontin per day, a dose equivalent to what dying cancer patients are prescribed, Dr. Gray has added 2,700 milligrams of the anti-seizure drug Neurontin. I am lethargic, confused, unable to put a full sentence together. My words are slurred and I forget what I am trying to say. My balance is gone, there is no sign I was ever a dancer, and when Michael and I go to the grocery store, I hold on to the cart like a child as he pushes it. I look drunk.

At work I sit at my desk watching the clock for my next dose time, when I bite the pill in half. Sometimes I just sit and stare at the ledger book and don't know I'm doing it until Lucrecia says, "Go home, baby." Then I zombie scuff the mile back past the Witch Village Museum, shortcut through the three-hundred-year old cemetery, and by the time I get to the end of Chestnut Street, I am worn down in tears. On my hands and knees, I crawl back up the wooden winding stairwell, stagger through the dining room, and the kitchen into the bedroom, where I drop to the bed and wash down another Oxy. Thirty minutes, timed. No pain. Pure bliss for three minutes. When Michael gets home from work, I am crying or sleeping. How did I get so far into this? It started out as a fender bender, and now my whole ghostly past is pounding at me from behind my eyeballs.

92

To My Knees

TODAY IS THE same as yesterday. Only the date has changed. Wednesday, January 16, 2002. On my nightstand are two bottles of pills, hot coffee, and a packaged chocolate-frosted Rice Krispie Treat. In one half hour there will be three minutes of bliss.

Now it is noontime, and Michael has come home from work to take me for a checkup. I am still in bed, body wired and mind panicked, when he walks into our bedroom, but it's too soon for my next Oxy dose. He takes my wrist and pushes it into the sleeve of my heavy Peruvian sweater. "Breathe, honey, breathe. You're not breathing." I sit back at the edge of the bed and stare at the white closet door. He slides boots onto my feet, then leads me downstairs and out to the car.

Dr. Gray walks Michael and me down her office hallway to an exam room. I tip from side to side, a pinball between them. Michael grabs for my arm and pulls me to him. My knees buckle. Dr. Gray watches, looking puzzled. "Why are you limping, Nancy? Do you have a bad knee?"

Michael holds the weight of my vibrating body in both his arms. "She's not limping. It's the drugs doing this to her."

Dr. Gray stops in front of her office door and looks at Michael. "Oh? I don't think so. The drugs shouldn't do that."

In her office, Dr. Gray sits down, rolls her stool to the wall, and points to a scale chart of happy to sad faces. She asks which one I relate to today. I am feeling shit crazy, think I'm going to die. But I don't see a matching face for that.

93

Listen to Me

A MONTH HAS GONE by. I am not sure what I have done other than twitch, cry, and watch the clock for my next dose of Oxy.

It was a week ago Michael and I met with a physical medicine and rehabilitation physiatrist and she scheduled a pain-management cervical nerve block, saying it should end my headache pain, but before the procedure I must lower my drug dosage. I cried in her office when she said I never should have been prescribed all that medication, and each time I broke the seal on the Oxycontin tablet, it was like shooting heroin directly into my blood-stream. When we came home, the elm tree on the bedroom side of the house was full of black crows, like something out of an Alfred Hitchcock movie. Michael and I stood at the gate and watched overhead as they hopped from branch to branch in eerie quiet.

Michael stayed home for a week after that appointment to keep close watch on what I took, decreasing ten milligrams of Oxy a day. I screamed and begged for him to let me take more. My nerves ran like fire through my arms and legs. Two or three times a day, I sat in a tub of water, hot as I could stand. In bed I pulled at the roots of my hair and thrashed my body back and forth on sweaty sheets. I wrapped into a fetal position and held to my impacted gut. I hadn't had a full bowel movement since October. I cried chemical tears.

TODAY is a Thursday, February 14, Valentine's Day. Michael and I are sitting in the waiting room at Boston Hospital. I am freezing cold, vibrating on the seat with a clipboard on my lap. I watch my hand scrawl a signature onto the release form. My fingers spasm and slip from the pen. Michael takes it from me. I clench his arm and lay my head on his shoulder. A nurse walks toward us. Her form is fuzzy. "Nancy? We're ready to take you back for your procedure."

Michael helps me to stand. He feels warm against me. I don't want to let go. He kisses my lips good-bye. "It's okay, honey. You're going to be just fine. I will be here waiting for you."

The nurse and I start down the hallway. I know she is asking me questions, but my answers don't make sense. My brain feels off-line. I am drunk with toxins. Another nurse steps quickly up to my left side and scoops under my arm. "Are you limping?" he asks.

In the procedure room they ask me to lie on my stomach. I am looking at the floor through an open-face cradle, listening to the doctor review what will happen. "We will numb the injection area on the back of your neck. Then there will be three other injections, which will go between the vertebrae, but you won't feel it. Your job is to remain perfectly still. Do you understand?"

My fingernails dig into the cloth-covered headrest. I take a half breath. "I understand."

From my right, I feel the doctor's hand flat against the back of my head. "First injection. Here we go." The needle pricks under the skin. The fluid stings. I hear the man's voice from my left. "Okay. You did well, Nancy. Now we wait." I am shaking bad. Everything is moving. Why didn't they put me to sleep? It's better to be unconscious. That way you don't feel the pain.

Needle number two slides between the bones of my neck. My body flinches. "No, stop. I can feel it," I yell to the floor.

The doctor is startled. "You can feel that? How is that possible? We numbed the area. All of the drugs in your system must have shut down your natural pain endorphins. Don't move."

Two hands weight heavy on my shoulders. I scream again. "I can feel it. Wait. Listen to me." Injection three. Toes webbed. Hips locked. Mmmmmm. Science class. Frogs. Live dissection. Tweezers. Oh, God. Oh, God. Mmmmmmm. Get out. Get out. Mumma, save me.

94

Going Home

W<small>HEN</small> <small>WE</small> <small>GOT</small> home from Boston Hospital that evening, Michael heated chicken soup for dinner. It felt good going down my throat. So did the extra Oxy. I slept well that night. But for the next five days my body screamed louder than ever for the opiate, and detoxing felt so absolutely impossible, I went back to my old dosage.

I<small>T</small> is five days later, Tuesday evening. My body and soul connection is beginning a two-week journey of final separation.

In the darkness of my bedroom, with Michael sleeping beside me, I find myself standing up outside my body and stepping into the back-yard at Mumma's house.

I am standing in the center of a beautiful swirl of blue. It looks like gallons of paint are blending to form a work of art. There are too many shades to count, colors of blue I have never seen on Earth. The faster they swirl at my feet, the wider the circle gets, like an upside-down cyclone. It lifts me from its center. I am warm and happy, so happy, and there is no pain. I hear Jason's panicked voice. He is standing outside the circle reaching for me. "Mom, don't go. You can't leave yet, you're not done." I am a balloon floating free just beyond his grasp, floating high in the center of blue. "Mom, come back," I hear him cry.

It is the evening of Tuesday, February 19. My last sleep for fifteen days.

95

Between the Tide and Clouds

JASON AND THE blue backyard vortex are not in my sight. I am now suspended over the water at Mumma's house, dressed in a long gown of deep burgundy velvet, reclined on top of a tremendous luminescent hand. I feel it supporting me. I am joyous, my arms open to the side, my palms turned up. A bright, comforting light illuminates through me. I can hear my thoughts. I feel so peaceful. I didn't need my body after all.

Sparkling diamonds of sunlight ripple on the Kennebec high tide and under the dock of my childhood home. Four children sit perched on the edge of the weathered structure, all clutching fishing poles, lines lowered to the water below. Tommy is at one end impatiently pulling the line and flipping the hooked raw hot dog up into the air. One of the neighbor boys watches an eel loop close to the surface as the other boy grabs for a tin bucket. The girl who sits between them laughs, throwing back her head and swinging bare feet in rhythm with the waves. It feels so good to be her again on the river I love.

And then I am back, dropped hard like Dorothy in a spinning house, crash-landing into Michael's arms. He didn't even know I was gone. One of his arms is under the pillow. I lie still, watching his eyes blink and his nose inhale one huge breath, then he smiles. "Good morning, my beautiful bride."

I can see the clock behind him. 6:15 A.M., Wednesday, February 20. I nestle closer. "Honey, I have to tell you something you won't want to hear," I tell him. "I don't want to scare you, but I really need you to listen." He pulls me tighter against him. "Michael, my body is getting ready to die."

He presses his lips solid to my forehead, then with one hand tucks my head to his chest. "Honey, you are not going to die. I won't let you. I can't imagine my life without you."

"But I am dying, Michael. I know I am. I feel like we need to prepare, but I'm not sure how. Promise me you will be strong when I can't be." He doesn't answer. He just rocks me in his arms and sighs.

I don't remember much of what happens today. Like every other day, Michael put a coffee and a Rice Krispie square on my nightstand and tells me to eat it before I take the Oxy. Unlike every week except this last one, through the bedroom window I watch crows hop in the tree. I try to walk to the front of our apartment, but only get to the refrigerator in the next room before falling sideways. In bed, I rub my hard stomach. My legs are on fire. I kick and cry. I take a hot bath.

It is still Wednesday, almost 10:00 P.M. I am propped up in bed with a photo album on my lap. Michael snores beside me. He has been asleep for a while. I am not sure how long I have been turning pages of my children. They look blurry, and I don't remember taking these pictures. There is writing, but the words don't make sense, like I wrote them backward in a foreign language. I think somewhere in my brain I must know what they mean, but it's locked in a file I am unable to open. I try to read out loud. My throat makes sounds, but all I hear myself say is, "I don't know. I don't know the words." Over and over I try, then put the album on the floor and shut off the light.

There is a high-pitched humming in my ears and pinching pains in my gut, like I am about to give birth. My body trembles so hard I can hardly walk. I am bent over with one hand around my stomach, grabbing for the bedroom doorframe with the other. I pull my nightgown up over my butt and fall to the toilet seat. Shit blasts from me with such force, I fear organs have come with it. Sweat pours from my chest and drops puddles onto my bare legs from under the cotton gown. I pull the nightgown over my head and throw it to the bathroom floor. In front of me is the half-opened door. I grab both sides of the knob and lay my head against the thinnest part of the wood. The seam of it digs a line into my scalp. Long groans vibrate behind my pursed mouth. The toilet fills. I reach behind and flush several times. Then I am freezing again. I struggle the nightgown back over my head and crawl on my hands and knees to bed. Vomit rolls up my throat and strangles me. Sweating hot. Unable to breathe. I crawl to the window, pull up on the sliding frame, and push my face against the screen. I suck cold February air, as much as I can hold, into my lungs. Then back to the toilet. For seven hours I blast months of backed-up waste into the sewer, crawling between the bed and bathroom, freezing, sweating, crapping, and remembering how, that was the end of Daddy. He died shitting his brains out between the bed and the pot chair, leaving brown stains down the side of Mumma's nice expensive mattress.

In the bedroom, Michael is on one elbow, watching me from his side of the bed, my fingers shaking, snatching up the Oxycontin bottle and seizing at the cap. "Michael, I have to take more meds now. I can't wait."

He is impatient. "Honey, lie down. It's only five o'clock. You have to wait, it's too soon."

Finally, the cap pops off. White tablets spill out over the bedspread and onto the floor. I fist some off the spread, I don't know how many, grab the bedside water, and swallow.

Michael jumps to his feet. "Honey. Honey, stop."

My body is shaking so hard, it feels like someone has both shoulders. I grab for the Neurontin bottle. Yellow capsules fly out of the bottle and onto the bed. I am not sure how many I put in my mouth before I gulp them down. My throat tightens. I need more. They won't go down, not even water. I can't swallow.

Panicked on the other side of the bed, Michael jumps to his feet. "Honey, what's wrong?"

"Shutting down," I squeeze out.

Michael grabs his jeans and pulls them on. "What do you want me to do? What am I supposed to do? Do you want to go to the ER?"

"No, they'll send me away. Yes, I can't breathe." I am pacing, dragging my body and falling into things.

Michael is calling Lucrecia as he pulls on socks and shoes. "Okay, we'll meet you there," I hear him say. He runs through the apartment, down the end of the block to the garage. Then gets me out of the house and into the car. By the time we drive four minutes up Highland Avenue to the hospital, the drugs have kicked in.

96

You Promised

My body is screaming from the inside. Every molecule has been altered. I am shutting down and dying. My mind is all I have to save me.

In the emergency room, the doctor takes my vitals. "I tried to reach your primary care physician, Dr. Gray," he says. "But she is on vacation and won't be available until Monday." Then he is gone and a young woman is standing beside me. She says she is the on-duty crisis worker and that Dr. Gray's partner has been contacted, but refuses to treat me.

I am leaned back on the gurney with a thin white blanket clutched in my fists under my chin. My mouth is dry. Everything feels slow.

The crisis woman stands beside me with a clipboard. "Nancy, I have some questions that will determine where we will send you. First of all, do you have a history of drug abuse?"

"No," I say. I hear her pen scratch the paper.

"Do you have a history of alcohol abuse?"

"No."

"Have you ever seen a therapist for any reason?"

"No, I never have."

"Have you ever attempted suicide?"

"No."

"Does anyone in your family have a history of mental illness?"

"I'm adopted."

She looks up at me. "So you don't know anyone in your biological family?"

"That's right."

She adjusts her glasses and looks back to the clipboard. "Would you say that you have ever been depressed?"

"I would say I have never been depressed."

In thought, she taps the pen on the board. "Well, Nancy. I'm going to do my best to find a place that will take you and get you some help. I have to say, it is very difficult to find a place for someone like you. If you had a mental health history we would have several choices. But for you and normal people like you, it's a challenge to find an appropriate place." Michael and Lucrecia say nothing. The woman continues. "I have two options. There is an outpatient hospital in Boston that you could drive to each day for the next couple of weeks. What they would do is administer a drug that would help you to withdraw. The other choice is for you to be admitted to a drug rehab facility in this area." She looks over at Michael. "It's a beautiful place out in the country. It's like a retreat. In fact, they call it the country club. I'll let you talk about it, and I'll be back in a bit."

When she leaves the room, I grab Michael's arm and pull him down to me. My whispered breath feels hot between our faces. "Michael, please don't send me away. You promised you never would. Please take me to Boston. Don't send me to that place. I swear to God it's no country club."

His voice is scared and exhausted. "Honey, I can't do this alone. You have to help me. She said it's a very nice place. They'll take good care of you. I don't want to lose you, honey. You have to listen to them."

"No, Michael, you have to listen to me. Remember, I've done this before. They'll treat me like I'm crazy. Don't do it. I won't survive."

Michael lifts my chin so we are eye to eye and wipes hair off my forehead. "Honey, you won't survive if you don't go. And you're not crazy, you're sick."

After we left the emergency room, Michael took me home. I packed a bag for three days. I took off my wedding ring and put it in my jewelry box. Then I took the framed photo of Joshua, Jason, and me off my dresser, kissed them both, and put it back. Michael helped me downstairs and sat me on the front porch while he went for the car. Overhead in the huge elm tree, black crows hopped from branch to branch, and I watched them, wondering if I would ever return.

97

Vermilion

A SMALL WHITE CRAFTED wooden sign hangs off the side of a tree. Its black letters spell VERMILION. It might lead one to assume that on this wooded land beyond the trees that hide it is a grand summer estate. What appears at the end of the hillock drive is a barn-red, 1700s-style New England inn, with haunting gabled dormers jutting from its third story. Beyond it and up another hill sits a barn with no visible windows. What it feels like is a 1930s movie set of a run-down resort. Months from now, I will learn it was the inspiration for a 1913 mystery thriller Broadway play.

Michael parks the Camaro at the kitchen entrance, and as he pulls at the handle of that locked door, three men stand on the other side watching us trying to get in. One of them opens the door and asks what we want. He tells us to follow him to the second-floor office. There is no indication if he is staff or resident. We weave a maze of hallways so narrow, I stand with my back flat to the peeling wallpaper as someone passes. Bright blue paint chips have loosened from the woodwork and fallen to the floor. The smell is foul, like decades of illness have passed without open windows. Then, like we have stepped from back-stage wings, we are on a wide-elbowed main staircase. I run one hand along the wall to keep my balance. The other tightly grips to Michael's free hand. My shoulders twitch, my stomach rolls, my butt squeezes back diarrhea.

In the office, I write what looks like someone else's signature on several forms. Michael stands beside me combing my hair through his fingers and talking to a wide-hipped nurse. I can't understand much of what they're saying, just that she is hurrying him out. "She'll be fine. You can see her in two days during weekend visiting hours," she tells him.

I clench my fists around the front of Michael's open coat. "No, don't leave me here. I can't make it until the weekend. Please, Michael, you said you'd never do it." Swaying with the pull of his hands firm to my upper arms, all I hear him say is, "I love you." He kisses my lips, turns his back, and leaves.

The wide-hipped nurse steps toward me. "Let's get settled," she says. "First we need to search you."

I back toward the office door. "No you won't. I'm not staying. My husband will come for me tonight."

She chuckles. "He just left. He's not coming back. You will have to learn to follow some rules, Nancy. There are two different groups in this facility, those with drug or alcohol issues, and those with just mental health issues. Different rules for different groups. After we are done in the bathroom, you will meet with the staff to determine which group you fit into."

She stands facing me. A large set of keys rattle in her folded hands. She nods at the toilet. "Sit down and take off your shoes and socks. Then I need you to stand up and stretch your arms to the side, parallel with the floor." She pats me down. The search ends.

Next I am taken to a stark room with a pitched ceiling. One long table sits surrounded by empty chairs. I am there for a long time. People come and go with paperwork, most of them repeating the same questions. My answer choice, lie and deny. If they know nothing, there is nothing to defend. A tall, thin, masculine-looking woman is standing at the end of the table with her legs apart, her arms folded militantly across a navy blue blazer. Her eyes never leave me as she fires.

"Do you have an addiction to drugs?"

"No."

"Have you ever had a problem with alcohol?"

"No."

"Do you know why you are here?"

"No."

"When did you last take Oxycontin?"

"I don't remember."

"How long have you been taking it?"

"A while."

"How much are you taking per day?"

"I'm not sure."

"How did you get your drugs?"

"I didn't get my drugs. I have a doctor."

"Have you ever seen a therapist?"

"Never."

"Has anyone in your family ever been depressed?"

"No."

"Have you ever been suicidal?"

"No."

"How far did you go in school?"

"College graduate."

"Have you ever been sexually abused?"

I don't answer. Her hands slap flat on the table. She leans into me. Her voice is loud. "Nancy, you need to tell us how much Oxycontin you have been taking, and where you got it."

My body is jerking. I am an electrical conductor, fighting to stay on the cold metal seat. "Don't you understand? I have been taking this drug for headaches with a prescription from my doctor. I had no idea what I was taking until I started hearing about it in the news. You are treating me like a criminal. I am not a drug addict.

"You are now."

"Please, I am so sick. It's time to take my Oxycontin. I brought it with me."

Her arms scissor back to her chest. She laughs sarcastically. "Oh, you're done with that. They're gone. It's illegal to have Oxycontin in this facility. From the time you came in this morning, you've gone cold turkey."

Today is Thursday, February 21, 2002. That is all I know for sure. The next four days will run snapshot frames of horror, each floating separate from the other. Mind chatter, linear configurations of past and future are non-existent. Huge blocks of being will disappear, leaving me in the present moment of survival.

My body is a storm of the worst flu, food poisoning, and hang-over gnarled together beyond imagination. Below my ribs is a baseball-sized rock slashing and chafing the inside of my stomach raw. My mind, a loss for words, with pictures dim and vision blurred. My skin simultaneously burns hot and ice cold. I am going to die here by my-self, shaking with electric current charging through my body, like I am a 1950s corn popper with shorted wires. I am going to die, and Mumma will have to bury me.

The hallway is narrow. It bends to the left. In the shadowed room, faded red fireplace bricks have fallen into a cold abandoned hearth. There are two dormer windows with tattered green shades, and two twin beds. A thin, young woman lies motionless, flat on her back, with large dark-rimmed glasses perched halfway down her nose. Maybe she is dead. On the other bed is my canvas L. L. Bean bag. Things are turned upside down in it, from the nurses rooting through it, looking for sharps. I curl into a ball and lay my head on top of it. I let myself cry for a long time. When I lift my head, the thin woman has gotten off her bed and is standing beside me, staring at a small plastic cup of bloody red liquid. She holds it close to her face. "Urine," she says. "I think something is wrong."

My legs are electric rubber. My back skims against the wall, one ago-nizing side step at a time, to the office. The sound of my nails hitting the sliding glass window feels like straight pins in my eardrums. A bald black man watches my arms and legs jerk uncontrolled. The nurse puts a pill in my hand. I am spinning. The black man has me in his arms on the floor. The nurse is yelling for him to let go. Then it is her face over mine. "Why do you keep passing out? You do it again and we are sending you up the hill. You're too high-maintenance. We can't watch you and we won't."

FROM a different room and bed, I am looking across the hall at the office window. Then a man with a mustache bends close to my face. Both his eyes make one. He holds out a pill. "Take this. If you don't, you'll be even sicker."

"I want to call my husband. I need to go to a real hospital."

"What you need is an AA meeting. You think you're better than everyone else, don't you? You're an addict. How else will you learn to stop using if you don't go to meetings? Where do you think you're going to learn the skills to stay away from the stuff on the streets? What will you do then? You'll be right back out there looking for more. How much extra were you using?"

My eyes are hot. They squint and blink. "I only took what I needed for my headache."

"Oh, so you did take extra. That makes you an addict. You should have been responsible. It's your own fault."

IN the hallway, I stumble and bang from one wall to the other, lost and listening for the voices. Someone behind me shouts, "Keep going, the meeting has already started." Falling to my hands and knees at the top of the stairs, I butt-slide down the staircase one step at a time, watching my filthy, twisted yellow socks lead the way. I drunk-stagger into a room filled with occupied chairs. My legs move without knowing where. Random hands press to my body as I tip and fall into them. I am in a metal chair in front of the Alcoholics Anonymous speaker. My arms and legs reflex, like they are not part of me. My head is dead weight. Then a woman is talking at my side. I stand. All is black. I hear someone yell, "The meeting will continue." I am in a different room now, lying on a couch. The woman is looking down over me. I can't breathe. I am gulping air. Heartbeats hammer my throat. The woman's white blouse is gripped in my fists. "Don't send me up the hill. Please don't send me away." Two men fumble with an oxygen tank. Through the swish of blood in my ears I hear one say, "Anyone know how this works?" The tank is rolled away.

HOURS. Days. I don't know how long I have been here, how I got to this ripped-up living room chair, or how to get back to my room. People walk by socializing. Somewhere inside, where I am still alive, it makes me happy to see them. A tall heavy Hispanic man speaks in soft broken English. "You better be careful. They planning to send you up the hill. That's where the hard-core go. You no want to go there. You never last. I was there. I no last. It's one small room, plastic chairs and a table. They watch you. This place here, much nicer. The girl in with you when you came in, she go there. No one see her again. We all thought you on heroin, but they say Oxycontin. Man, you die from that shit. I see it. Worse than heroin or cocaine. I know not easy for you. We here. We all look after you." His mouth smiles.

MY stomach burns. Diarrhea blasts into every filthy toilet I find myself on. Every inch of skin crawls. Drugs seep rancid out of every pore. Lightning bolts crack where my nerves used to run. I am out of my mind crazy with pain. It grows worse as time ticks. I rock and kick and gulp for breath. I do not drink. I do not eat. I do not sleep.

AT the back door on the first floor is a small empty closet. On the wall is a pay phone. A light bulb hangs from the ceiling. It is brighter here than anywhere else, except for the office across from my room. My brain scans files for our home number. The operator rings a collect call. I am standing outside myself, moving between two dimensions. I am fragile, I am mighty. "Michael, I'm begging you to come get me.

You don't understand how sick I am. If you do not come, I will die." I hold tight to the receiver. I don't want to miss a word. I hear the clicking of the computer and the solitaire game shuffle. His words are lazy. "Honey, you've got to try. I don't know what else to do. Okay? Just hang up and let me get some sleep. I'm tired." I am violently shaking, puke rising up my throat. I slide down the wall and crumble to where stale cigarette butts have been stomped on. Nauseating smoke and February cold blow in from the open door. Someone calls, "You okay?"

There is nothing lower than lying on the cold dirty floor of a mental ward with your privates smeared in feces, and begging someone you love to save you.

98

To the Moon and Back

I AM SITTING CROSSED-LEGGED on the bed, frying from the inside, limbs jumping. There is no stillness in the body I am separating from. In the hallway, someone stands with his back to me. His hair is long to his shoulders, dark and curly. He turns and walks to me. His face smiles, but even through my dead eyes I see fear in his. He sits next to me on the bed and speaks softly. "Mom." I cry in his arms. "Jason, I knew you would come. Get me out of here." Again and again I say it. After all the time he spent with me, all the things he must have said that slipped lost between my broken sentences and fragmented thoughts, there is only one thing that downloads to my survival file. "Mom, they won't let me take you. Pretend you're in a play and act your way out."

THE petite blonde woman with the untweezed dark eyebrows is leading me to the closet. Her hand feels cool in mine. She passes me the telephone. "Mom, can you hear me? It's Josh." My ears are ringing. He is far away.

"Josh, get me out of here. They aren't listening. No one believes me. To hell with Michael. If he really loved me, he would get me help." My arm is wrapped to the top of the phone box. My legs are poison jelly. "I know, Mom. I believe you, and Michael is doing his best. Don't fight them, Mom, just play the game and you can get yourself out.

Maybe tomorrow, I don't know. But every hour is one hour closer to home."

In the dining hall nothing stands still. Residents I know by size and voice, and people who have come to visit them, vibrate past me. My clothes are twisted and disheveled from three days of thrashing. A chunk of hair hangs in my eyes. I am an unmanned drone, step-kicking my way to somewhere else. I don't see Michael until he stands, reaches for my hand, and pulls me to the padded window seat. He holds me close, gingerly at first, then tighter. I reach under his coat and curl around his warm body. My groan is guttural. Words slur. "Please, Michael, take me for help."

He puts a water bottle in my hand and tells me to drink. "Honey, I can't promise anything. Tomorrow morning I will go to work and think about it. When Dr. Gray's office opens, I will call and see what she wants to do." It hurt so much when he said it. It brought back the memory of when I was a kid and swinging so high on the swing set, I fell off, landing hard on my back, breathless. It was an empty panicked alone feeling, watching the seat wave back and forth over my face, not knowing if I would live or die.

Night arrives. In bed, Michael's water bottle lies loosely in my hand, an unconscious extension of my arm, a blending of molecules with no boundaries. I am gasping for breath, melting into the weakness of my body, wondering if I should give in and welcome death. My stomach burns. Down the hall in the bathroom, I fall against the walls, trying to pull my black leggings down over my hips. It takes all my strength to stay balanced on the toilet seat. Next to me, flung over the top of the curtain rod, is a dried-out dirty washcloth and on the floor, a piece of shit-stained toilet paper that has been here as many days as I have. Yellow-green fluid is still pouring out of me. I am so inebriated, it is impossible to wipe myself clean. In the hours of a fearful death, somehow that doesn't matter.

A FACELESS nurse shouts up the hall to me as I press sideways along the wall toward her. "You won't be taking the clonidine any longer. I think that's what made you black out. The Oxycontin raised your blood pressure, and the clonidine lowered it. Every time you stood up, you passed out." She slides the office window shut and disappears. When I reach the wooden shelf, I lay my head down over my folded arms and rap my knuckles on it. The window slides heavy in the metal track. She sarcastically spits like Mumma. "Now what?"

My legs spasm and kick. My knees buckle. "Please let me call my husband. I'm going to die."

"Oh no, you're not going to wake him up. It's the middle of the night. He's sleeping." Her words are singsong. "And you're not going to die. Maybe you'll think about that next time you want to take an Oxycontin. Think about how sick you are now. When you get out, you'll have to find an AA sponsor and go to meetings every day. Addicts have a one-in-fifty chance after leaving rehab. They go back to the drugs, or they die."

"But if you could just give me something for the pain in my stomach . . ."

She cuts me short. "Now look. I've given you Mylanta and a hot corn pack for your stomach, which you couldn't tolerate the smell of, cold packs for your headache, and Neurontin for your jitters. There is nothing else I can give you. You can't keep coming to the window to bother me. I've got things to do. Now go lie down and relax."

My head bobs over my hands. "Please. I am so sick."

She makes a disgusted sigh, reaches down under the counter, then stands back up with her closed hand out to me. "Are you Catholic?" She drops a wooden cross and rosary beads into my open hand. "Know any prayers?" she asks. "It doesn't matter which one. Just say something for each bead as you hold it." Her lips purse in an awkward smile.

I leave my door open a crack so I will see the office from bed. I turn off the lamp and lie down. My body temperature is still burning up hot and freezing cold to the bone. I pull the sheet and thin blanket over me, and my large Peruvian knit sweater over that. I shake feverishly, breathing in rhythm of my slowing heartbeat. The beads are smooth between my fingers. Prayers in rhyme and mantras past are gone from my database. One bead at a time, over and over, I hear my inner voice chant. Joshua, Jason, Michael. Joshua, Jason, Michael.

ALL is quiet now except for the buzzing in my ears. The night noises of Vermilion are gone. It is so still, I think I may slip out of the world unnoticed, almost like I was never here. Fear is dissolving. Peace is filling all the cold spaces of my being. There is a gratefulness that comes with death. When you realize that always, always love has been with you. That each person you have smiled at, been angry with, or held in your arms was part of who you were. And your fears were the root of what strangled and sickened you. And without fear there was only truth. Truth, what you had been running from all along.

The room is dark. It feels so good to lie flat on my stomach with my legs stretched out. I am no longer shaking. There is no pain. There is only warm bliss, like I am being hugged by everyone I have ever known all at once. Beside me, the brightness of the moon beams under the tattered shade. It lights my face and tones a sound I recognize and follow. My entanglement of earthly worries has now become silky strands of light, connecting all that was and all that will be. The vastness of the universe sparkles a partial web of blue and white crystals before me. I am smiling as I reach out for the window frame. The coolness of the air comes to me, and I go to it through the seams of the storm pane. I exist outside my body, gracefully melting into the energetic cosmic flow. A black, wavy, silk fabric stretches from me to the golden orb. All night, I dance like liquid on the gleaming pathway between here and the moon.

And then, it was dawn.

99

Kicking Out

I WON'T LIVE ANOTHER night. Today I get out of Vermilion, or I die here.

I am sitting on the edge of my bed, shaking, my knees hugged to my chest. I can see a wall clock over the office window slider. 6:30 A.M. I rock front to back. Hot skin, cold bones, stabbing stomach pain. I am rattling down a train track, heading back to Michael and the boys. One hour closer to home. Five minutes at a time. In my mind, I hear Bobby's words from years ago. "I won't tell the boys that their mother gave up."

I have talked the wide-hipped nurse into letting me call Michael. She takes me to a small room adjacent to the office. Michael's voice is groggy. "Honey, what's the matter?"

I can see the nurse in the other room, doing busy things. I stand out of her sight. "Well, good news. I am calling to tell you I can come home today."

"What do you mean you can come home? Did the doctor tell you that?"

I cup my hand to the side of my mouth and talk close to the mouthpiece. "Not yet. But he will. The nurse thinks I'm doing much better. I'm not taking any meds and I'm not passing out."

He sounds annoyed. "Honey, you're confusing me. I can't take you out until you are well enough to leave."

I step toward the office. "Here, I'll put the nurse on. She'll tell you." I muffle the receiver into my chest. "My husband wants to talk to you." She makes a confused face, squinting up her fat cheeks, and takes the phone from me. She digs one hand into her waist as she says hello. Quietly, she listens to Michael, then defensively rumbles at him.

"No. I didn't tell your wife that she could leave. I don't have that authority. Only the doctor can release her." She passes the phone back to me.

"No, Michael, of course she didn't say I could leave. It's not her job. The doctor is coming in at nine o'clock. Call me at nine-fifteen. I have to go."

The doctor's office desk is covered with Monday-morning paperwork. He opens up my file and doesn't look at me when he speaks. "So, it appears you are doing better, Nancy. Not passing out, and you have been to AA meetings. Good." His pen scratches fast across the paper. "Support system at home?"

I sit up tall in the chair, my arms wrapped tightly to my stomach, which is clenching in pain, my bowels about to explode. Bile is flooding up my throat. I swallow it back. "Oh, yes, two mothers, birth and adopted. They are amazing, very supportive. They call every day to check on me. Blessed, that's what I am. So blessed to have them."

"Wonderful. That's what we like to hear. You're all set, then. You can leave as soon as your husband gets here." He passes me an AA meeting schedule for Salem. I say thank you, smiling inside at my performance, and head for the toilet.

In my room, on the twin bed next to mine, is a pile of dirty bedding and someone else's discarded clothes. I have no idea whose. I have not washed or changed my clothes since I came in on Wednesday. It never entered my mind. On the floor is my L. L. Bean canvas bag with all my things left undisturbed. I take the Peruvian sweater off my bed and hold it to my nose. A poison chemical smell burns up my nostrils. I sneeze repeatedly and drop it onto the pile of sheets and clothes. On the wall is a sink. I don't remember seeing that either, but there lined up on the edge of it, are a dozen small paper medicine cups half full of water. I lean into the mirror over the sink. My face looks ashen gray, my cheeks dry and sunken. Even with my vision severely blurred, I can see the blood-red rims of my eyelids. I run my tongue over my top teeth. My gums are sore and my teeth are fuzzy. It hurts to touch my hair. There is a smell seeping out every pore on my body. It smells like I have fallen facedown in a musty swamp of chemical runoff. My stomach flips. My heart flutters fast, then slow. I start down the hall to the cafeteria. If I show up for breakfast today, maybe they will believe I am well enough to leave this hellhole. I can't trust they won't change their minds and keep me here.

In the dining room, staff is watching. I get in line for breakfast, then find an empty spot at a long table. In the cold metal chair, my feet tap to the floor. They don't stop. Two men across from me watch me struggle to open the small box of Rice Krispies. I ask if they will help with the cereal pouch. When neither one can do it, the bald black man passes it back to me and smiles. "You look better today. You were toasted when you got here. Staff was really pissed the day you passed out at the med counter and I caught you. But if I hadn't, you would have split your head open on the floor. We didn't think you'd make it through the withdrawal. We prayed for you in meetings and watched over you. I don't think you knew that though. You were messed up bad." A plastic cup of orange juice shakes as he holds it in both hands and puts it to his lips.

I am poking at the cereal pouch with a plastic fork. "Yeah, I don't remember much, but thank you."

He puts the cup on the table. "Hey, it's important to have someone there for you. I'm still learning that." He leans back in the chair and raises a pointed finger up over one ear. "I tried to kill myself. Put a gun to my head and pulled the trigger. Nothing happened. I tried again. Nothing happened. I pulled it a third time. Again, nothing. On the fourth shot I pointed the gun away from me. It went off. I figured the Lord was trying to tell me something, so I decided to get help."

I sprinkle some cereal into the Styrofoam bowl and pour milk over it. My stomach clenches as I put a spoonful into my mouth. I can't do it. At the trash barrel I spit it out and drop the bowl in. A man wearing a tight gray sweat suit approaches me, his dark hair standing up in cowlicks, his body wired. He laughs as he speaks. "Hi, Sue."

I stop in front of him. "No, Nancy."

He pulls at his hair. "Oh, I thought your name was Sue."

My legs march in place. "Well, you've probably been calling me that all along and I just never realized it."

"Hey, but you're lookin good today. Drugs kickin in, huh?" He laughs harder.

My arms and legs tic. "No, they're kicking out."

100

Forgotten

THE HIGHWAY HOME to Salem feels endless. The Camaro's leather passenger seat is slippery underneath me. In it my body painfully twists and folds. Trees and cars pass in blurry vibrating swishes. I crack open the window and let the freezing February air blow against the dullness of my face. My bare feet press to the cool relief of the windshield. My stomach is on fire. My heart pounds in skipped beats. My lungs have forgotten the rhythm of breath. Joshua, Jason. Joshua, Jason.

From the driver's seat Michael reaches for my leg. His hand sears hot through my leggings. "Oh, honey, it will be so good to have you home again." He veers to exit 45 and watches the rearview mirror traffic fall behind us down Route 95. "Your mother called last night. Mumma, not Elizabeth. I told her you'd been in the hospital. I don't think she understood. Finally, she said she couldn't hear me and hung up."

I comb into his black hair and let it brush thick through my fingers. If this is the last Earth moment I have, at least it will be with him and not in the filth of Vermilion. My words pant out in labored gulps. "Michael, I need you to take me for help."

His eyes dart between the road and me. "Honey, what's wrong? Breathe. I knew I shouldn't have taken you out so soon. Calm down, honey, you're scaring me."

I close my eyes and feel the miles pass. When the car stops we are parked outside the gate at our Chestnut Street house. Overhead in the sprawling elm, the crows wait. Michael scoops me into his arms and carries me inside to the second floor. On the post at the top of the stairway hangs Nanny's gold-braided cord with the three brass bells. It chimes sweetly as we bump against it. I am limp in his arms as he carries me through the dining room, past the antique pitcher collection, through the kitchen past the counter where my date book lies open. They all feel like distant belongings of a previous life.

In the bathroom, I peel off my clothes and let them fall to the floor. My stomach is deflated. I reek of death and chemicals. I step onto the scale. Michael reads the numbers. Thirteen pounds lost in five days. His hand is tight to my wrist as I step into the claw-foot tub. Morning brightness blares through the white shower curtain from the window behind it. The underside of my acrylic nail extensions are shit-stained yellow from what has been pouring out my butt for the last week. Michael turns on the faucet. My back arches to the brutal spray of a million tiny pin-pricks on my raw, naked skin. I moan in agony. My muscles twitch. I smear a handful of jasmine shampoo into my hair. Bile bubbles up my throat. Fluid feces pinch my bowels. Unable to stand any longer, I partially wash the soap out of my hair and let Michael wrap me in a robe. He lays me down on the bed.

The part of my brain that tells me what things are is off-line. I am thinking in pictures now. Thoughts without words. Again, I am moving beyond the attachment of my body that anchors me here. There is a warm tingling washing over me. Happiness curls the corners of my chapped, pale lips. I am so happy. On the dresser beside me, golden sunrays beam against my favorite photo of the boys and me, taken on the day I married Michael. Such peace. Beyond it, a box flashes moving color pictures. Michael waves something in front of it. The volume lowers. I am fascinated.

"Yes, I can bring her right up," I hear him say.

I DON'T remember Michael carrying me out to the car, or the ride up Highland Avenue, just a vague memory of sitting in Dr. Gray's office, Michael holding my shoulders back in a chair, and hearing bits and pieces of him trying to explain what happened these last five days while the doctor was on vacation. I don't remember much else, just that she told him I should drink fluids.

So, on Dr. Gray's advice, Michael took me back home.

101

Crows

I DRINK GATORADE AND water all through the night. "Drink as if your life depends on it, because it does," Michael says. But as fast as I drink, it comes back out. All night I trudge back and forth from the bed to the toilet until I can no longer pull to my feet.

It is 8:30 in the morning when Michael wakes to find me lying on my side, staring at the photo of the boys. My skin is ashen, my eyes dilated. I am unable to talk or move. With no response, I am barely breathing. But I can hear his panicked voice. "Look, either you see her now, or I am taking her to the emergency room. Either way, I am leaving as soon as possible, or she won't make it."

I lie in stillness as my physical body shuts down. I am not afraid. Inside I am smiling. There is a high-pitched humming that fills the room, and at the end of the bed, a gray fog of a woman with her hand out. And music, a parade of every beautiful instrument ever created on its way to me.

I hear Michael's voice again. "Lucrecia, I need your help. Come fast, I'm losing her. I'm losing my bride." And then he is gone, through the apartment, and down the block for the car.

I feel my spirit lift and surrender. All is peaceful. And then a noise, pulling me back and weighting me to the bed again.

Crows. It is the crows that save me. For the last two weeks they have sat in the tree outside my bedroom window hopping from one branch to the other, dozens of them, waiting, I thought, to usher me away. But it was this very moment they had been waiting for. Screeching loudly, they spread their wings, lifting and landing on the one branch that hangs across my window. Screaming wildly, they pack side by side, heads jutting forward, beaks cawing for me to come back.

Pictures of Joshua and Jason scan across my inner vision, thousands of them all at once. I hear Michael crying, "I can't lose her." I feel him take me from the bed. Lucrecia is wrapping me in my long winter coat. I am now conscious enough to flash my eyes at the boys' photo on top of the dresser. She grabs the frame and drops it into her bag, and again I am carried out to the car.

On the sidewalk in front of Dr. Gray's office, a nurse waits with a wheelchair. She opens my door. I can smell the driving rain as it blows sideways in the winter wind. I feel the tug on my weighted body as she and Michael struggle to get me out of the bucket seat. Then she is racing me down unfamiliar back hallways. I hear her say, "We had no idea she was this bad." My head flops forward like a rag doll. She pulls it back against her stomach, pressing her hand firm to my forehead as she runs. In the room, set up with emergency equipment, there is an inclined padded chair draped with white sheets. Several nurses rush in to hoist me up onto it. For forty-five minutes, nurses arrive from surrounding offices. They all take frantic turns trying to insert the slender IV needle into my collapsed veins. The young nurse who wheeled me in is crying. Lucrecia is in the outer hallway screaming at Dr. Gray to get in and help, but she doesn't. Michael is pacing near them.

The humming frequency around me grows louder, higher. I am funnel-spinning out the top of my head, then pulling my expanded self back into the confines of my small Earth container. I do it over and over, fighting to stay, preparing to leave. Lucrecia is at my side now. Her beautiful olive complexion is pale, her rouged cheeks wet with running black mascara. I feel her fingers vibrate on the place between my eyebrows, and hear her voice quiver demands from miles away. "I'm here, Nancy. Look at me. Don't you leave."

"Boys," I squeeze across parched lips.

Lucrecia grabs the large-framed photo from her bag. With both hands she holds it in front of my face. "Look at them, Nancy. You can do it. Do it for the boys."

Brown-eyed children. Smiling young men. Brothers, best friends. Locked on their faces as I fade into the frequency of my journey. "My babies," I hear my heart say. "Take care of each other. I love you forever." I feel my essence pulling to where they are. I cannot stay any longer. I hear one last huge breath of air go down into my lungs, and one final exhausted exhale. I can't feel my body.

"I've got her," I hear a woman shout. The needle has effortlessly slid into my arm.

102

Fluid

FOR THE NEXT three days, from eight o'clock until five, I lie on the padded table in Dr. Gray's back exam room, an IV drip in the bend of my arm. I feel like a withered, dying plant coming back to life.

In the hallway, a pharmaceutical representative walks by with two big trays of deli sandwiches. A nurse follows him with a box of clinking Snapple ice tea bottles. I hear her laugh and say, "You are so good to us. We love to see you reps coming."

It takes three days of office IV, three nights at home of constant water and Gatorade, and one panicked midnight trip to the hospital emergency room before I am hydrated enough to do it alone. Joshua, Jason, and Michael never leave my side.

At home I rock and thrash in bed as my nervous system overloads in excruciating power surges. Jason gets on the bed and holds my hand tight. I scream into the pillow. I hyperventilate. He puts cold washcloths on my face. He plays a surfing video and puts shells from Hampton Beach on my bedside table. "Mom, you can't get to the ocean, so I brought it to you. You always say how healing it is."

I sneeze again and again, smelling something that no one else can, an overpowering odor of pond scum and decomposing meat. Joshua fills the room with lit candles until the smell disappears. While I soak in a tub as hot as I can stand, Josh fills a hot water bottle to lay under the backs of my legs in bed. He holds a straw and Gatorade to my lips. I drink gallons of it. Both boys help me to the toilet, close the door, and sit on the floor outside. They ask me to talk, so they know I'm still conscious. My stomach is still knotted hard as a rock. My bowels, still firing toxic yellow bile.

My skin, too sensitive to touch, has broken out in a red bumpy rash that covers my body. Michael gives me Zantac to help control the stomach acid. He feeds me cut-up bananas, raisin toast with butter, and squash with brown sugar. It is the best food I have ever eaten.

I HAVE gone fifteen nights now without sleep. Fifteen dark nighttimes of shaking, painful spasms, and constant trips to the toilet. Fifteen days of tortured pain for me, Joshua, Jason, and Michael. Tonight will be different. I have given in to taking three-hundred milligrams of my prior seizure medication, Neurontin, just enough to calm my twitching limbs and allow my body to sleep and begin to heal.

Joshua has gone home to North Conway. Jason is back at UNH. The house is still. In the bedroom a street-lamp shines softly under the half-pulled window shade. Michael and I lie between the cool crispness of clean white sheets. He curls beside me and laces his fingers through mine. His eyes are wet. "I'm sorry, honey. I didn't know. I did my best, but it wasn't good enough. I should have listened to you. I always say, I trust your gut more than other people's facts. But this time I didn't. I thought the doctors knew what was best for you. Honey, please forgive me." Our salty tears blend together with our kiss. I don't tell him it's okay, because it isn't just yet. That will take some time.

The photo of the boys is back on the dresser. Michael snores beside me. My body is beginning to calm. Tonight I will sleep. My eyes are heavy. Between slow blinks at the white ceiling of our bedroom, a light begins to manifest above me and spreads like an open window to the heavens. The fluid vastness of the universe sparkles a web of blue and white crystals, so close I reach my hand up into it. It is a reminder that I am, and always have been, part of its pure, blissful love.

I slept well, grateful for another chance to live. And the crows? After that, we only saw them fly by on their way to somewhere else. They never stopped to perch in our elm again.

103

Moving On

MORE THAN A year and a half of daily walking and physical therapy has passed. Gratefully, the headaches are gone and so are the drugs. Today in the bathroom I lower myself into the hot water of the claw-foot tub. Lavender-scented waves wash against the top lip of it. November-morning snow blows icy through the screen of the open window and across my face. Steam rises off my glistening skin. On the sill is a full wine goblet of cold ginger ale. Next to it is a packet of relocation brochures. "Welcome to Gulfport, Florida, 2003," it reads across the front. On the inside, below a pink-and-green tropical border, it reads, "Bohemian hideaway of free-spirited artists. Key West-style beach community. Your little piece of paradise." When the ginger ale is empty and the bath water has gone cool, I pull the drain plug and watch it spiral away. Then I get dressed. Elizabeth will be here soon.

IN the high-ceilinged dining room, my mother's voice sounds small. She sits across from me with one elbow weighted to the edge of the table. In her hand she holds a triangled half sandwich. It waves side to side as she speaks. A chunk of chicken falls from between the bread. "What does your mother think about you running away to Florida?" She takes a bite.

My stomach squirms. "I'm not running away. I'm moving forward." Elizabeth stops chewing and holds her breath for a few seconds. She looks at the wall. Her eyes squint the way they do when I know she disagrees with me. I start talking, hoping that she won't. "Mumma already thinks Salem, Massachusetts, is at the end of the world. I guess it doesn't matter if I go another thousand miles south. She says she figures she'll never see me again anyway, or by the time I do decide to come back, she'll be dead. At least she's hoping to be."

Elizabeth throws the sandwich onto the plate. The two half pieces of bread fall to different sides. Lettuce and chicken salad spill onto the table. Her eyes are fire. Her words shake. "Your parents have done everything for you, Nancy. You should be grateful. Dance lessons, money, cars, college. And your mother loves you desperately." As she draws out the last word, she closes her eyes and tilts her chin up like a dramatic Golden Age movie star. "Remember when the three of us had lunch at your house and I met her for the first time? I knew she was scared to go against her husband's wishes, but in secret she did it anyway. She kept referring to you as her daughter, and that you were. She seemed so proud when she showed me the photograph albums of you as a child. She said she always knew one day she would be sitting with me and sharing those memories. She knew one day you would find me, because you are just that determined." With two fingers, she rubs the gold locket that hangs from a chain on her neck. Inside are two photos of me, one as a baby, one as a woman.

Under the table I re-cross my legs. I finger the chips on my plate and slide my lips hard over each other. Elizabeth lays both arms on the table. Her chin begins to quiver and her voice goes soft. "The other night I lay awake thinking back on the day you were born. You were so tiny lying there in my arms. You hung on to my finger with such strength, it was as though you knew we would soon have to let go. I can still feel that tiny hand clinging, and my heart still breaking. When I gave you up, the social worker told me that your parents were faithful church-goers and your father was a well-respected business-man. She said you would have a good life. I just don't understand." She lays her napkin over her food and leans back in the chair.

I can feel my heart pounding up my throat. "You still don't believe me, do you? You want to believe I made the abuse up." I watch her eyebrows lift and make lines across her forehead. "I wanted to believe that too. But I always knew. When we met, I told you my father was a good man. Then years later I told you the truth."

My mother pushes herself away from the table. "If you hadn't been born, you wouldn't have gone through all that." She hangs her head in both hands. "You must hate me for giving you up to a family that abused you. I hate myself for it. This has been the worst thing in my life, you being born. But I learned a long time ago, whatever pain happens in our past should be forgotten, because nobody cares anyway."

She bolts from the dining room table and into the bathroom. She falls to her knees with her head over the toilet, gagging and dry heaving, leaving perspiration on her upper lip. Then she sits to the floor and cries. "Why can't you just forget about it, Nancy? You have let it ruin your life. Admit it, you failed at everything you ever did. How long have you ever stuck with anything? Go to Florida, find a job, and stay there for at least fifteen years. When you are sixty-five, then you can think about coming home. You owe it to Michael for all you've put him through." She tears off a wad of toilet paper and wipes her nose. "And I'm sorry I could never be the mother you wanted me to be."

I kneel down and take both her shoulders. Part of me wants to shake her and scream, Never, do I ever want to be like you. I sit down next to her on the bathroom floor. "No, Mom, you weren't the mother I dreamed of when I was a little girl, that's true. What you are is a woman who is angry at herself for still living in the wish that you had been the woman that you wanted to be and never were."

She levels her face in front of mine. Her eyes go crazy. "Hit me. Go ahead, hit me. I deserve it." My mother's cry for private fears and things lost is far beyond the day I was born. We have both stuffed secret lives into our emotional pain bodies, waiting for the truth to be beaten out of us.

I watch tears drop off her chin. My voice is calm. "Any woman who asks to be hit has absolutely no self-respect. Do you understand where you are taking yourself? I love you, Mom, but this is the last time we are ever going to have a confrontation like this. I am moving on, and I am going to surround myself with positive people, and enjoy my life. That's what I deserve."

Before Michael and I leave for Florida, Elizabeth mails a shoebox-sized gift. I peel off the brown paper wrapping and inside find one flat piece of four-by-five tissue paper, a rock base larger than my fist, and several big chunks of sharp broken glass. Two days later she calls. Her voice is nonchalant. "Did you get the candle I sent you? Did it arrive okay?"

"No," I say mechanically. "The globe was broken."

"Oh? That's strange. I wrapped it. Maybe you can fix it."

"No. I don't think so."

Her vowels drag. "Too bad."

It made me feel kind of sad for that woman.

104

That's Not It

IT TOOK TWO months to find a home.

After looking at dozens of brand-new buildings of white-walled rooms and perfectly landscaped yards, it was the 1940s money-pit house, a block up from Gulfport Beach, I fell in love with. The wooden steps were rotted, a rope handle hung in place of a doorknob, and the only way to get to the second floor was up a ladder through a hole in the ceiling. In the corner of the living room sat an antique drawing board. Delicate pencil sketches covered large white sheets of paper. An abandoned coffee cup with BELIEVE written in gold sat next to it. One dead fly floated on top of its inside darkness. I could hear the walls cry a sweet sadness, begging me to stay. But it was the pink house a few blocks up that we bought. Its 1950s linoleum flooring with thin green lines and wide black slashes running the full length of our nine-hundred square feet, reminded me of the Bath Memorial Hospital. The day the sewer backed up and flooded that floor, I stood in the shower, crying and hugging myself until the hot water went cold. The next week I painted each of the five rooms a different tropical color. Blue, green, yellow, pink, and purple. Cockroaches ran across those walls, dropped to the floor, and crunched under my $3.99 flip-flops.

Down the narrow streets from our house to the beach, I rode my bike under thick foliage canopies, past trees heavy with mango and fruit I could not identify. Bungalow homes painted in multiple colors hid amongst tangled vines of draping fragrant flowers. Big green Quaker parrots screeched from the tops of palm trees. Swishy-tailed geckos scurried across my path. A sign in the middle of a small puddle pond read, 'DO NOT FEED OR MOLEST THE ALIGATOR'. Gulfport, Florida, our little piece of pink-flamingo paradise.

Each weekday morning, I drove Michael to the Clearwater Volvo dealership. Then, with a sheet of notebook paper pasted with tiny cut-out newspaper want ads, in order of the St. Petersburg grid, I applied for jobs all the way back home. I took three that didn't work out, none of which I was qualified for, a waitress, a bartender, and an after-school group leader-/-night time bus driver for a black teen program in the crime-ridden neighborhoods of South St. Petersburg.

The last and longest-running job was as a teacher at a Baptist church school. The day they hired me they offered two positions. The head teacher for fifth grade and assistant for the pre-school class. Since I figured I probably couldn't even pass fifth grade, I took the latter. In the office, against my own principles, I signed a contract stating I would follow the Baptist protocol to be a faithful weekly Christian church attendee, and I would have no contact with people of alternative sexual lifestyles. I had no intention of following either. When they asked at what age I had been saved, never ever was my thought, unless I count the time I was pulled by the hair out of a re-stroom toilet during a 1972 J Geils concert. I answered, twelve. I kept my personal history brief. What I wanted to say was, I am a Jewish convert, I teach Dirty Dancing with my gay ballroom partner, and I read tarot cards, but I really needed that job. For eight months they called me the free-spirited one, and paid me seven dollars an hour to change diapers and care for precious two-and three-year-old children, who I loved. In October, I started coughing. In January, I collapsed.

It is Wednesday, January 5, 2005, a year since we arrived in Florida. The clock over the school cafeteria lunch window reads 12:35. I am pushing chicken and stuffing around my plate with a fork. My chest is fighting for air. I turn my head and make one loud crackle cough into the bend of my arm. Again, today, it explodes from the bottom of my lungs with such force, my ears pop. Sudden numbness tingles down both arms. There is thumb-sized pain pressing deep under the left side of my collar-bone. Sweat beads my face and trickles down the middle of my back. I watch my lunch drop into the trash barrel, and I start down the hallway for help. To my right in the school kitchen there is a wall of commercial appliances. A teacher stands at the sink. I take a few steps toward her. My words wheeze out between two blasts of coughing. "I think I need to call my husband. I'm not feeling well." Then my back is sliding down the door of the stainless steel refrigerator and everything goes black.

My clothes are soaked with cold sweat. Everything feels far away. I hear a man's voice. "Nancy? Can you talk to me, dear? What happened?" Inside the ambulance he pumps a blood pressure cuff tight around my arm. A needle pricks into my vein. The EMT adjusts a bag of fluid over my head. Then he is close to my face. "Same thing happened to me last year. Classic heart attack symptoms."

I close my eyes. "No, that's not it," I say.

In a wash of sweat and flashing lights, I speed for help.

105

The Truth of It

I SPENT THE NEXT week in Clearwater Hospital running tests and blood-work. Pneumonia was the first diagnosis. Cancer was suspected. During a total-body PET scan, four areas of my body lit up. Lungs, liver, spleen, and lymph nodes. I was put under anesthesia and two biopsy samples were taken from my spleen. Then they sent me home. The next day the doctor called to say she was still waiting on the results, but she was pretty sure it was lymphoma.

"No," I said. "That's not it."

IT's Saturday morning, two days later. In one moment I am sitting quietly at my desk. In the next it feels like a dagger has sliced under my left rib. With one hand to the fireball of pain that has split open my spleen and the other clawed to the couch, I roll to my back, curl both arms behind me to the wide-mounded arm of the white tuxedo fabric, and dig my fingernails into the weave, like hanging on to it will save my life. My arm muscles lock. My fingertips go numb. Michael's words are panicked. "Honey, is it your spleen?" I don't speak. I don't open my eyes. All I can do is control my breath in rhythm. I think, this time, he will know what to do.

Soon I hear sirens, then Michael arguing with the EMTs. "I need you to take my wife to Clearwater, where her doctors are."

A man speaks in my left ear. "Is it your spleen?" I nod yes. A needle slides into the bend of my arm. I hear his voice again from across the room. "If she is bleeding internally, we are ordered to take her to the closest hospital."

Heart monitor, sirens screaming, Gulf Hospital emergency room. Catheter, CT scan, morphine, intensive care unit. For the next two hours I lie dazed in bed. Michael paces beside me, watching for the ER doctor to reappear. A nurse walks toward us with a clipboard in hand. She looks confused. "Now, what are you folks actually waiting for? I believe you can leave now."

Michael takes a step toward her. His words are impatient. "Her spleen burst. What do you mean, we can leave? The ER doctor is contacting a specialist for emergency surgery."

The nurse looks down at her clipboard. "He is? No, I don't think so. There is nothing here about emergency surgery." She looks up at me. "Your CT scan showed you are hemorrhaging. But the doctor who saw you in the ER has gone home, and he didn't leave any instructions."

I see pink flush up Michael's neck. He taps one finger to the chart. It makes a dull sound. He looks like he may explode, but his voice is calm as he stands square to the nurse. "I want you to make arrangements for an ambulance to take my wife out of here and transport her to the Clearwater Hospital. Do you understand me?"

For one week I lie on my back in the Clearwater Hospital waiting for the hemorrhaged blood to re-absorb. The day of my discharge, the doctor pulled a chair against my bed, sat down in it, let out one big sigh, then smiled. "We have a diagnosis for you, Nancy. You have sarcoidosis. It is a chronic inflammatory auto-immune disease that spreads throughout the body, leaving deeply imbedded sand-type granulomas and scar tissue. Some people heal in the first year. Others become very ill, with joint and nervous system problems that remain indefinitely. The most serious stages include restricted breathing. You are a stage three, and your lungs look pretty full. Sarcoidosis is not curable, but it is treatable with steroids that may halt its growth. At some point we will need to talk about chemotherapy." He stands up and shakes my hand. "I wish you the best. It is a very odd disease. No one knows what causes it."

I take my hand out of his and say thank you. What I wanted to say was, oh, I can tell you what caused it. My lungs held in the hot, rancid breath of a child molester. Each grain of scar tissue is from the hundreds of times I screamed for my mother to save me. My liver has been flooded with the anesthesia of alcohol and drugs, my spleen, pounded against by the body of an unconscious narcissist. And because of the fear he implanted in me, the filtering system of my lymph nodes has been clogged with his crippling belief in regard to my worth. On the outside I may have looked fine, but on the inside, there has been a slow-growing saturation of disease and dysfunctional breakdown of my ability to fight off and protect. And the truth of it is, it's my own chronic fear of those memories and fictitious beliefs that have kept me ill. That will end now. I am sick of being sick.

106

Disconnecting

MONDAY, APRIL 11, 2005. It is my last day of work at the Baptist church school. The cafeteria clock reads 6:15 P.M. Eleven female teachers balance dinner plates of food on their laps and take turns saying good-bye to me. The principal with the blond bob starts. "We are praying when you get back to New England, you will find good Boston doctors who will heal you."

The kindergarten teacher wipes her lips with a paper napkin. "I appreciated your soft countenance and constant smile."

Betty, the lead teacher in my pre-school room, goes next. "Each morning when you came in, the children couldn't run to you fast enough. They loved Miss Nancy."

The first grade teacher, who had been in the kitchen when I passed out, laughed and agreed. "I have to say, your mysterious free spirit has certainly intrigued us."

The teacher's aide with the shiny black hair lays one hand to her heart. "We are happy to have known you."

When all had finished, I smiled graciously and said I appreciated their kind words. What I thought about saying was, if you had really known me, would you still have hired me? Would my life experiences have changed your minds? When I was a teenager, I stole a bag of liquor out of the backseat of someone's car and drank it with a bunch of stoned girls. I don't remember the first time I had sex because I was shit-faced, unless you count being raped by my father from age five through twenty-one. I don't remember much of that either. I aborted a baby and never told anyone other than the man I guilted into marrying me. Some of the best friends I've ever had are gay. And I still don't understand why it's a sin to dance and worship the Earth.

But instead I leaned in, shook their hands, hugged some of them, and said I enjoyed working there. They said they loved me and they would be praying for my good health. I walked out with a gift bag of cards, candles, and dish towels. All the way back home I smiled.

THE Florida morning sun is so hot at the end of our driveway, I can see waves of heat rising off the tar. I drop into the shaded lounge chair and place my mug of coffee on the small table next to me. A long-legged crane strides by. A half-dozen green Quaker parrots screech from atop a palm tree at the edge of the lawn. I hold the cell phone tight to my ear and wait for Mumma to answer on the other end. Before she says hello, I hear Tommy's dachshund barking and Mumma yelling.

"Tom. Get that damn dog away from the door for God sake." Then she lets out one long-forced stream of aggravation and yells hello into the receiver.

"Mumma. It's me."

"Nancy? Well, for Christ sake, I told your brother to shut that stupid dog up before I got to the phone. God."

"I'm coming home to New Hampshire, Mumma. We've sold the house."

"Yeah well, I think you're better off to stay right where you are."

"Don't you miss me at all, Mumma?"

"Well, I guess so, Nancy, but when you decided to move away, I figured I'd never see you again." She tilts the receiver from her mouth and yells again to the front of the house. "Tom, did you hear me? I said shut that damn dog up."

"My doctors here in Florida want to put me on big steroids and chemotherapy to fight this auto-immune disease. But I refused. I have to get home first, then decide." Her disgust is hot in my ear. I hear her living room television crank full volume. "We will be an hour north of Boston and two hours from Bath. I'll be able to visit you, Mumma."

"Ahuh. Look, Nancy, you left Bath a long time ago. Tom and I have done fine without you. You don't need to come nosin around here.

Tom's not doin so good, and you probably shouldn't see him like that anyway."

Tommy is yelling for her to get off the phone. "Jeepas, Mom, hang up."

"What do you mean he's not doing good?"

"Well, the damn police won't leave him alone. You think they'd give him a break, but soon as he gets out of jail for one DUI, he's back in trouble, and they haul him off again. I don't think I'll ever live long enough to see him grow up."

"Mumma, you can't keep letting him live there. It's toxic for both of you."

"Well, where else is he supposed to go? He hasn't had a job for years. After he left your father's shop, all he could do was pack sardines and wash cars, and they fired him from both, for drinkin. If he'd only gotten married like the other kids, he wouldn't be in all this mess."

"Mumma, he has a house right down the street. As long as you are letting him drink and drug in his old bedroom, why would he leave? He's got a good deal. You feed him. You do his laundry. You and Daddy bailed him out every time he got arrested, paid his fines and lawyer fees. Can't you see how you're enabling him?"

"Well, someone's got to enable him, Nancy. No one else gives a crap about him. I'm all he's got."

"Mumma, he is forty-eight years old."

"Yeah well. I'm not hearin good today. I'm gonna have to let you go." She steams one long disgusted sigh.

I hear Tommy screaming. "Jeepas, Mom. Was that Nancy? That bitch."

Her receiver slams to the wall rest. My end goes dead.

107

Toxic

In May 2005, Michael and I move to the old farmhouse in Epping, New Hampshire, and transform what used to be a small barn into a dance studio.

For the next two years I teach. I dance until I no longer can. By August 2007, my lungs are painful, my breath draws hard, my body slows, and once again I begin dumping pills down my throat. Chasing the sarcoidosis now spreading like cancer, methotrexate and prednisone soak into every cell of my body, with Boston doctors urging me to make a drug therapy commitment of one full year. Against my own inner wisdom, I agree.

Every day for one year, I wash a yellow chemo tablet down my throat, then lie to myself and call it sunshine. It settles in with the other unknown diseased things buried deep in the cellular memory of my body. For one year I watch my tall-postured dancer frame slump and age, my face blow up fat and gray, and my hair go dry and brittle. I spend half my day sleeping and shitting, the rest painting. With my stomach clenching, and limbs twitching electric charges up and down the nerves of my legs, I go on a year mission to paint every room in the house, fourteen of them. Each brush stroke is like a choreographed dance step. Thick passe's of beautiful color cover the walls like melted chocolate. Sea Foam. Caribbean Walk. Ocean Blue.

Now it is mid-summer 2008, 6:00 P.M. on a Friday. I hear Michael's Volvo pull into the driveway. I am in the front living room on the top rung of a step-stool. Moon Tide green arches in one peaceful wave over the bay window. Andrea Bocelli's sweet Italian tenor rises from the boom box on the floor. "Time to Say Good-bye." I lean over and dip my brush into the paint tray. Chemical sweat trails from both temples and drips off the end of my nose. I straighten up and make one more stroke across the wall. My body sways. Both knees buckle, one, then the other. My head shakes, like it may axis off its stem. Sweat makes sticky tracks down my chest, leaving salty puddles in my cleavage. Michael comes into the room, takes my hand, and helps me down. At first he says nothing, he just holds me tight in his arms. My tears roll down his neck.

"Honey. You need to rest. Go to bed now. Tomorrow you can start again, or you don't have to. You can do whatever you want, whatever feels healing for you."

He walks me to the staircase. I drag one hand across the smooth yellow wall. It feels cool on my skin. Halfway up, I stop and sit down. My heart pounds in my ears. My lungs sting with every inhale. "It's called Morning Sun. I chose all of the paints because of their names. Did I tell you that?" He nods yes and sits down next to me. His eyes are sad.

"Michael, how can you still love me? I don't look like the dancer you fell in love with. I'm a mess. I look like an old woman."

He takes my chin gently in his callused fingers and kisses my lips once. His wide eyes hold tears at their edge. His words catch and pause briefly between sentences. "I love you more today than the day I married you on that mountain. You're sad, you're scared, but you're still my beautiful bride. To me, you are more beautiful on your worst day than other women are on their best. No, honey, I don't see an old woman at all. I only see my bride." Then pulling me from the step, he helps me to bed.

It is August 27, the last time I sit in the doctor's office at Massachusetts General Hospital. I have kept my word. It has been exactly one year to the week that I have been swallowing a daily dose of poison, waiting to feel better. I never did.

The doctor scrolls the computer screen and mumbles the results of my last CT scan, the fifteenth one. "All right, Nancy, I think we will try another round of steroids and maybe a new drug in place of the methotrexate, something a little stronger."

Both my feet are flat on the floor. My back is straight. "No, I don't think so. I'm done with tests and drugs. Every time you check my progress with a CT injection, my body is again flushed with chemicals. I have done what I said I would, one full year, and I am now sicker than when I began, so sick I have almost forgotten about the auto-immune disease. There has got to be a better way to heal."

He leans back in his desk chair. It makes a crunching noise as it rolls over some floor grit. "I can tell you, Nancy, people who have been through trauma always have a harder time with diagnosis and treatment. We have never talked about what your specific issues are, but it is obvious to me when patients have had trauma."

I don't blink when I say it. "And do you think all this drug therapy was not traumatic for my body and mind?"

His response comes quick. "I think there are other things going on with you, Nancy. It's not just the drugs."

I stand. My brown leather purse bounces off one leg. "You know what? You are absolutely right. Toxic is toxic. Whether it's drugs, drink, people, action, or thoughts."

"That's it?" he says. "You're leaving? You are going to abandon your progress?"

"Not my progress, for now, just drugs and doctors. As of today, I am cancelling the rest of my tests and appointments."

He sticks one hand in the pocket of his white lab coat and laughs in a mocking kind of way. "Well, then, who do you think is going to manage your health care now?"

"I am."

Down the hallway and through the double glass doors of the office, my flip-flops clap out an applauding two-count beat. I am not sure how, but I will dump out the poison, all of it. It is not me and I am not it. I will not allow myself to take ownership of what is not healing for my body or spirit. It will take a while before I really understand that.

Sometimes it takes screaming yourself into a drooling nose-blowing mess and shitting your brains out before you really see what toxic crap you have ingested over a lifetime. But I will do it. As Mumma says, I am some damn determined.

108

Booze and Bird Watching

IT IS JUST after ten in the morning, the day after my Boston appointment.

All the way to Bath I have thought about what I told the doctor yesterday. I am. I say it out loud. I am the creator of my own life, and every choice I make has the power to heal me or make me sick, body and mind.

At Mumma's house, I pull my car next to the rock wall and lilac bushes, then reach for the cooler in the backseat, clam chowder and broccoli quiche for lunch. The dark green shade in the front-door window is pulled tight and the door is shut. Fifty years later it still smells like dump smoke and melted crayons. Before I can ring the bell, I hear Mumma and Tommy yelling and the old dachshund barking.

"I told you to get that damn dog upstairs and do it now before Nancy gets here."

"Jeepas, Mom, Daisy Mae needs to go out." I hear the swish of her hand swipe against his nylon jacket. "Mom, don't hit me. She's gotta piss bad."

"I don't care what she's gotta do. You and that dog get upstairs now."

The front door flies open. My brother's emaciated six-foot body does a drunken stumble backward. The dog leash makes a wild loop through the air and spins out of his hand. He slurs through missing teeth. "Oh jeepas, Mom, she's here."

Just as fast as he slams the door in my face, she opens it back up. "I told Tom to get that damn dog upstairs before you got here. He thinks he's real funny. God."

I step inside, shutting the door behind me. Mumma's gray hair, which used to be coiffed with every strand in place, looks windblown and ratted. She has on the same faded yellow jersey that she has worn since the boys were little, thirty years ago. There is a ketchup stain where her cleavage used to be. I can hear Tommy's muffled cursing coming from his room at the top of the stairs. The dog is still barking, jumping at me like it will attack.

"Well, I'm some sick of this," Mumma says, then reaches down, takes the two short front legs of the elderly, overweight dachshund, yanks her off the floor, swings her out over the steep cellar staircase, and lets go. The dog rolls and clunks down the last couple of steps, then yelps and whimpers as she lies in a heap on the bottom. She flips back over to all four feet, shakes from head to tail, and limps back up the staircase, like it's just another day.

"Want a cup a tea, Nance?" Mumma says lightly. Then leaving me standing shocked in the front hall, she gaits toward the kitchen and snaps on the stove burner. After a couple of minutes I follow her into the kitchen and sit down at the table.

"Mumma, you just threw that dog down over the stairs. I can't believe you did that. Why did you do that?"

She bangs two empty mugs onto the table. "Well, I told your brother to take that dog upstairs and he didn't, that's why. I don't know what's the matter with him."

I take off my glasses and rub my forehead with one hand. "He's trashed and delusional, that's part of it."

She pours hot water over my teabag. "Yeah well, you have no idea what it's like to have the cops comin round all the time and accusing him of stuff. Then I have to drag him off to court and spend months and years here all by myself. And when he is here, he doesn't do a damn thing to help. He's up in his room all the time drinkin and God knows what else."

The mug is hot to my fingertips. "How is he getting the alcohol if he's always in his room?"

"Well, I take him to the store and give him money for cigarettes. It's not my fault he comes out with booze."

"It is your fault. You're giving him money for drugs and alcohol, and then you're taking him to pick it up. He needs to live in his own house. As long as you make it convenient for him to be sick, he will never get any better. The more you do it, the sicker he gets. You've done it his whole life. Mumma, he's fifty-one years old."

She stops stirring the milk in her tea and slams the spoon on the table. "Look, Nancy, I'm his mother, ya know."

With the mug in both hands, I suck hot tea into my mouth. It scorches the inside of my upper lip. We are silent.

From the kitchen table, I can see every room on this floor. Two living rooms, bathroom, and front hall. Residual emotional clutter haunts every corner, like eleven years of piled-up decaying trash has been left untouched since the man I referred to as Daddy died here.

The carpets are stained with dog urine and feces, and in front of the couch is a sour pool of wetness from spilled alcohol and tomato juice. A grimy pair of Tommy's sneakers from the 1980s sits next to the room divider, where our father's police scanner, church bulletins, and old tide chart remain. Tommy's cigarette papers and a bag of loose tobacco sit on the bottom shelf next to the family Bible and *The History of Bath*. This is his domain now. It's where he slams his body into the broken springs of the sagging couch, flicks ashes onto the floor, scatters pages of the *Bath Daily Times*, and yells out his breakfast order.

When Tommy reappears, his nylon jacket and old Miller High Life T-shirt have been replaced with a dingy white dress shirt. The collar is stained with a thick yellow ring, and the cuffs are just below his elbow. It is unbuttoned all the way to his waist, exposing his graying chest hair, and tucked into jeans several sizes too big and cinched in a creepy high rise with a worn leather belt.

Leaning to the floor, he gathers the dog up in his arms, plops her on the table, laughs, and pushes her toward Mumma. "Kiss Mom, Daisy Mae." Then he brings up a loud belch and blows it in my face.

Mumma snatches her tea. "Oh for God sake, Tom, get that damn dog off the table." Then lowering her voice, she picks up the plate of Pepperidge Farm short-breads and holds it out to me. "Want a cookie with your tea, Nance?"

I swallow hard. A memory of being clothes-lined while playing tag pulls fast from my database.

"No, thank you." I move to the blue chair next to the bathroom. Mumma takes the mugs to the sink, then sits in the rocker at the end of the couch.

Tommy dead-weight plummets into the couch sag. From underneath it he pulls out a bottle of rum. He takes a long swig, then chugs from an open liter bottle of ginger ale. He belches again and sets it on the forty-year-old carpet covered with circles of big black cigarette burns. He takes a lone toothpick off the book divider and picks at a back tooth, then sets it on the shelf again. With two fingers, he takes up a cigarette, lights it, blows out smoke, and watches the end burn. Then he looks at me for a long time, laughing and throwing his head back. His voice is soggy. One eyebrow twitches. "Jeepas, Nance, you're fuckin beautiful. I wish you were my wife."

I am cold and frozen in the chair. The disgusting chair, next to the disgusting bathroom door. Mumma and I look at each other. There is a slight squint of her eyes. She continues rocking, never moving her hands from the arms of the chair.

My brother stands up from the couch, walks three drunken steps, and falls heavy down over me. He smells like burnt doobie roaches and vomit. His lips pucker at my face. "I want you. There, I said it, Nancy, I want you."

With both hands and one foot, I push him away. Stumbling back up the stairs, he calls out from his wired body. "Oh, jeepas, now I have to go to my room and calm down."

I am beyond horrified. "Mumma, did you hear that? My God. I never, ever would have thought that could happen. Where the hell did that come from?"

She rocks and blinks like smoke has swirled up at her. "Yup, well, he's actin more like himself today. I guess he's feelin better."

I sit out to the edge of the chair, pull my open sweatshirt tight over my chest, and hang on. "Mumma, he just said he wanted to have sex with me."

"Yup, well. I didn't hear him say anything like that, Nancy." She rocks harder. One foot is off the floor with the toe of her shoe pointed to the ceiling. She looks out the window. "Did you notice my birds today? They are just all over those bird feeders. I wish the damn squirrels would leave them alone. They're eatin all the seeds. Poor little birds."

My bowels feel like they will let go right here. My arms and legs are electric Jell-o. Before I can stand, Tommy is back in the living room, his body looking like it will break as he slams into the vortex of the couch. I pull to my feet. My adrenaline is rushing. "How dare you speak to me like that? You know what happened in this house. You know what Daddy did to both of us. Why would you do this to me?"

He hangs his head between his knees and covers his ears. "I know. Jeepas, Nance, I'm sorry." Then grabbing the bottle of rum, takes a long chug. Spit strings down one corner of his mouth. "You think I like livin like this?" He lights a cigarette, takes a hit, and for a few seconds holds his breath. "You think this is what I wanted to be when we were little?" He twitches and laughs like he will cry and rolls his yellowed eyes. Smoke comes out his nose as he rubs the baldness of his head. "I hate this." Then he ashes his cigarette and lays his head to the back of the couch, staring shell-shocked past me. His pasty skin is rutted with red craters. One big zit boils on the side of his nose.

Before I rushed out of the house, I said good-bye to Mumma. I remember her chin was pitted in exasperation and I could hear the sound of her amethyst ring rhythmically hitting the wooden arm of the chair as she rocked. But I don't think she heard me. She was bird watching.

109

Mundane to Insane

Tommy has spent the summer of 2008 in his childhood bedroom, living and dying on alcohol, ginger ale, cigarettes, and pot. Mumma says he's not coming downstairs to eat anymore and doesn't get out of bed to urinate. She says she's some mad that the house reeks, and tells me to stay away. The only person allowed inside is the handyman child molester who comes for coffee and steals old tools and things from the shed and boathouse. Mumma says, "It wasn't his fault he was fired from the school system, the girl asked for it." I told her when a fifty-year-old man touches a fifteen-year-old girl in that way, he ought to be shot. Mumma says he brings donuts and runs her to the bank anytime she needs to go and I should stay out of it, it's none of my business.

The day I went to that slime ball's house to ask him where my grandfather's antique tools were, he was tutoring a kid in his garage. I asked him how it is he's allowed to teach children after what happened. Then I asked him if he had any idea what being sexually molested does to a kid's head. His greasy gray hair fell into his eyes. He brushed it to one side, looked at me like it was no big deal, and said, "No." I said, "Take a long look at my fifty-two-year old brother, drunk and pissing himself in his childhood bed. That's what."

The night before the accident, I call to check on things at Mumma's house.

"I don't think Tommy is going to make it through the week, Mumma. He's going to die right there in that filthy room. You're going to go in some morning and find him dead, unless he burns the house down first."

"Yeah well, he better stop drinking because he's got a court date tomorrow and they may be taking him from there, right to jail. He's some upset. He thinks they'll keep him for two to three years this time." She lets out a long, disgusted sigh.

That next afternoon, I wait until two thirty before I call Mumma. When she answers, she sounds worn and short-tempered.

"How did it go in court?" I ask. "Did they take Tommy to jail?"

"No, they didn't take him to jail. They continued it to another date. He's back home with me, and we've got one hell of a mess here."

"What mess?"

"Well, I got up this mornin and got ready to take Tom out to the courthouse. It got to be eight o'clock and he still wasn't up, so I bellowed up the stairs and told him to get movin. He didn't answer so I went up to his room. When I pushed the door open he was standin there naked, covered in blood."

"What do you mean he was covered in blood?"

"Well, I don't know, Nancy. He must have fallen in that junked-up room of his, tryin to get to the bathroom."

"Well, what did he fall on?"

"He thought he fell on deer antlers in the bottom of his closet. I guess they stabbed him in the back."

"In the back?"

"Then he said his testicles were comin out his rectum."

"What? Well, which is it?"

"Then he said he sat down on a broken piece of metal stickin up from his bed frame. His testicles are split wide open."

"How do you know that?"

"Well, I saw them, Nancy, that's how. He bent over and showed me. I was some damn mad, now let me tell you. What a mess he made. Looks like a murder scene up there. Blood everywhere. There's a big puddle of it right at the bedroom door. I guess as he was fallin he musta grabbed a bunch of shirts from his closet and hauled them down with him, cause all those shirts were soaked in blood and layin on the floor. I had to go get a big bath towel to sop up the carpet." She blows long out her mouth and into the phone.

"And after that?"

"I was so damn disgusted, I got in the car, went to church, and folded newsletters."

"But you said he went to court."

"Well, yes, Nancy, he had to go to court. He called his lawyer, told him that he couldn't make it, and the lawyer said that Tom had to go anyway. So he put on two pairs of underpants and I took him out for God sake. I don't know what's the matter with that lawyer."

"Okay. I am trying to understand this. You say his testicles are split open, he bled all over his room, you took him to court, and then you brought him back? And he fell some time during last night? It's now ten to twelve hours later and he hasn't had help? At any time did you think you should call an ambulance?"

"Well, no, Nancy, I didn't want anyone in this mess nosin around."

"Mumma, you are in crisis. Call 911 now. Do you understand me?"

"Yeah. Okay, Nancy. We'll see."

Five minutes passed before I called her back. During that time she had called the fire department. They were confused and called the police. Tommy was taken by ambulance to the hospital. More than twelve hours had gone by since the accident had happened. The doctors told Mumma it was too late to repair the injuries. His urethra was severed, his bladder severely damaged. Some time in the dark, drunken hours of the previous night, he had impaled himself on the four-inch spike of broken metal bed frame. The area between his rectum and scrotum was slashed open, and Mumma was some damn mad.

110

Gone

THE NEXT MORNING when I arrive at Mumma's house, she is sitting at the kitchen table. One foot is tapping wildly midair. "Now why the hell do you think you need to be here, Nancy? Are you happy now? Tom's gone."

I fall into the kitchen chair beside her. "He's gone?"

"Well, not gone, but he may as well be."

In the hall, the thin wooden banister shakes in my hand. All the way to the top, the gumminess of it makes a sticky noise as I grab and release it. The hallway outside Tommy's bedroom seems darker than it should be on a late-summer morning. With one finger, I slowly push the door open. Splatters of blood are everywhere. It looks like a gunshot crime scene. The ceiling is speckled red, and a cardboard box on the top shelf of his open closet is bulleted from where he must have grabbed for his groin and franticly shaken the blood from his hands. On the closet floor is a piece of polished wood with small deer antlers attached. The tips are blood red. Between the bed and the window are three pot plants growing on top of our old toy box. On the floor next to it is a full jug of vodka, and a large canvas suitcase with a broken zipper, filled with pornographic magazines. Scattered across the floor are odd socks, thirty-year-old high school math and English papers, Matchbox cars, eight-track tapes, empty alcohol bottles, and over-flowing ashtrays. Layers of Tommy's life soaked in his own blood.

The bare pink-flowered bed mattress is soiled with large circles of body fluids and cigarette burns, too many to count. A full-length imprint of my brother's bloody body is stained to the quilted top in varying shades of red. Two bloody handprints smear down one side of the white woodwork and the back of the door. On the floor is a wide, dark puddle, still moist from where he must have lain and bled throughout the night, calling for our mother to save him.

It takes two and a half weeks of arguing before I am able to convince Mumma she must allow someone in to clean out the room.

I have arrived at her house, just ahead of the ServiceMaster and the bio-hazard trucks. When I go upstairs, I find that Mumma has climbed across the bacteria-infested bloody mess and pulled out the suitcase of porno magazines. When I ask her why, she says she might need that old bag some time and doesn't remember what she's done with what was in it. As the men go up and down the stairs with sacks of bloody things, the nightstand, squares of contaminated carpet, and the gruesome mattress, Mumma paces back and forth between the kitchen and the front hall, cussing at them. It is like the front window shades have been snapped up for all the world to see into our family secrets.

After that, Tommy spent two months in the hospital and then another six weeks in a nursing facility. Despite my pleas to his doctor, lawyer, and case-worker not to release him to my mother's house, back he came by way of taxi after making a stop at the bank and liquor store. By nine o'clock that evening he was shitfaced and banging on the outside of her locked front door, screaming for the dog to let him in. He was arrested and sent to the Maine Correctional Center with a sentence of two and a half years.

Mumma was mad that she had to spend another winter alone, and claimed no compassion for Tommy, who was locked up, again detoxing from drugs and alcohol, this time with a catheter bag hanging off his body.

spirit

111

Christmas

MUMMA WENT DOWNHILL fast after Tommy left that October. From then until Christmas, my phone rang often with reports from the neighbors. Several times they found her lying outside in the cold snow, one day, up the street at the edge of an embankment on her back with a dead gray squirrel next to her. She said she was kicking it out of the road when she lost her balance. While shoveling snow at her front door, she slipped on the ice and slid right under the car. Someone walking by heard her cussing and pulled her out. Another time she was found in the tangled bottom branches of the lilac bushes. She said she'd been there for hours and didn't know "why the hell someone didn't find her sooner."

The day I took her to the doctor's office, she bitched and moaned the whole way there, about how it's nobody's business what she does. When he saw the black-and-purple splotches on her arms and legs, she had to admit she had been falling indoors too. He became insistent when I told him that several weeks ago she'd hit a tree with her car after coming back from visiting Tommy at the nursing home.

The doctor rolls his desk chair close to Mumma and kindly takes her hands. "What could your son possibly need from you, Doris, that the nursing staff can't provide?"

She pulls her hands out of his and makes four sharp air slashes as she talks. "Well, Tom drove me crazy until I took him a disposable camera. Now he's telling me I have to get it developed so he can send pictures of his groin to the damn lawyer that made him go to court the day he fell in his bedroom." Then she wrinkles up her nose and shakes her fist. "That stupid lawyer."

My eyes zip back and forth between the doctor and Mumma as she does it. He never breaks eye contact with her. He smiles softly and says, "Doris, I care about you and I want to know you are safe. You are eighty-seven years old and in good health, other than you are continually falling. We have tried everything there is to help you. You won't allow anyone in your home, and you refuse to use the life-alert button around your neck. You have two steep sets of stairs. That, and the situation with your son, are detrimental. You just can't do this anymore. I am forbidding you to drive, and as we have talked about for a long time, now I must stress that you move to an assisted living facility within the next few weeks."

Mumma's chin drops to her chest. Her eyebrows pinch in an angry *M* at her nose. "Locked up in a nursing home? No way. That's my worst nightmare." Then she sits up taller and quickly snaps one pointed finger toward the doctor's face. "Can't you just give me a shot and put me to sleep? I've lived too long. I'd rather die."

I LEAVE her home alone that day. It is Christmas Eve. Before I walk out, I check the fridge for food and clear a path for her to walk through. She sits in the hollow of the couch, watching me. "Are you going to be okay, Mumma? I'll be back Friday morning. That's less than two days from now." I lean down and kiss her cheek. It's chilled.

Her voice is weak. One hand brushes the front of her face like she's swatting flies. "Oh, yes. I'll be fine. I've been here by myself all these years. Today's no different."

Then I drive back home to Epping. I am not giving up Christmas with Michael and the boys.

112

For the Last Time

It is late morning, the day after Christmas, when I arrive back at Mumma's house and find her sitting in the same place I left her, the hollow of the couch.

"Mumma? Aren't those the same clothes you had on two days ago? Have you been up around at all?"

She is lethargic. "No, not really."

"Have you eaten?"

She looks past me. "I wasn't hungry."

I move closer to her. "Did you go up to bed?"

"I tried, but my legs were too weak, so I slept here." She drops her head into one hand. Her chin begins to twitch.

I sit next to her on the couch. "I stopped at Hill House on the way here this morning. They have a beautiful room on the first floor. There is a private kitchenette, a bathroom, and two birdfeeders right next to the sitting area window. We can get more if you want."

"Yeah well. I'm not feelin good, Nancy. I don't think I can go."

"It won't be today, Mumma. They need four days to get it ready for you." My stomach is rolling. It makes one long growl. "You can see Whiskeag Creek from your window. It's where you learned to ice-skate, remember? I know it's not home, Mumma, but it's only a mile and a half through the woods. Not too far away, and you already know so many of the staff and residents."

She shakes her head as it rests in one hand. "Now this is some damn kind of mess I'm in."

By eight o'clock that evening we are both exhausted and ready for sleep. I reach both hands out and pull her from the couch. "Do you want to sleep upstairs in your bed tonight, Mumma? I'll help you."

At the bottom of the staircase, I stand to Mumma's left side. My left hand is in hers. I brace her back with my right arm and grip at the old banister. "Here we go. One step. Both feet, then rest. Lead with your good leg, Mumma." A third of the way up, I feel her begin to weaken. With my left arm snuggly around her waist and my front pressing against her back, I pull us up, gripping the loose, gummy wooden banister. "One more. You can do it. I've got you."

Her body goes limp. She loses consciousness, her sudden weight heavy in my arms. My leg muscles tense. I lower us to the worn carpet. Within a minute she comes back, blinking her eyes, and stares across toward the front door. She is between my arms. My hands are death-gripped to the rungs of the railing.

She sounds defeated. "Well, Nancy, I guess you're right. I do need help."

I hug her tightly, snuggling my head between her neck and shoulder. It takes me by surprise when I hear my body releasing long, sobbing wails. She stares ahead without moving or speaking.

After a few minutes, I wipe my face down the sleeve of my sweatshirt and take a huge breath. "Okay, Mumma, we're a team now. We are going to slide down on our rear ends, one step at a time, until we reach the bottom of the staircase. Then we are going to stand up and get you back to the couch. Can we do it?"

She turns her head and smiles at me. For now the lines of anger have smoothed on her face. This time her words are determined. "Well, of course we can do it." I feel a flutter inside me, like I did the day Joshua was born and she said I'd done a good job, he was the most beautiful baby she'd ever seen.

In the bathroom I wash her face with a warm cloth, down the sides of her nose and across her chin. I pull her nightgown down over her gray hair, then smooth her front curls back from her forehead. In the living room, two air mattresses I have brought from home roll out across the filthy floor in front of the couch. After I blow them up, and cover them with sheets, blankets, and pillows from upstairs, I lower Mumma down onto one. She settles into the puffiness of it and lets out one long sigh. I pull up the blankets and kiss her cheek. "I love you, Mumma."

"I love you too, Nancy. Thank you." It feels so good to hear her say it.

With the beds in an *L* shape and our heads together, I reach out and lay my hand over hers. Within a few minutes, she is asleep. I listen to her breathe. It has been a long time since I have seen our house from this angle. Fifty years since I lay under our Christmas tree watching the big colored bulbs and rolling bubble sticks of red, green, and yellow. I remember how they reflected off the hundreds of strands of tinsel Mumma and Nanny had patiently placed one by one on each perfect branch. I remember the clean balsam smell, and how Nanny and I loved to sing "I'm dreaming of a white Christmas," along with Bing Crosby. All the furniture was dusted spotless, and dozens of Christmas cards were taped around each painted wood-work door-frame. In the kitchen, the good china and silver, used only at Easter, Thanksgiving, and Christmas, were laid out on the antique, linen tablecloth Old Nanny's parents had brought from Scotland. And on the polished coffee table, there were always dishes of sweet wavy ribbon candy and thin-grooved Merry Mint Patties.

My leaking mattress is now flat to the sour carpet. I look over at the folding bathroom door. Both panels are off the overhead track. It hangs connected by one top-end hinge. The glow of a forty-watt bulb hanging over the toilet gives a just-out-of-sight eeriness. With my nostrils overcome by vile smells of urine, alcohol, and cigarettes, I drift into sleep thinking about shiny lights and Christmas candy.

It is 4:00 A.M. when Mumma's hand shakes me awake. I swing her legs around and push her knees together, flattening her bare feet to the floor. In this moment, I see her bare feet at the edge of Sebago Lake, lazy waves washing over naked toes I had seen only in its sunny sand.

"Mumma, you have to use all your strength. I am going to pull you to your feet. Hang on." It takes several tries. She is patient. I am frustrated.

In the bathroom, I lower her to the cracked foam-filthy blackness of the toilet seat. Faint from standing up too fast, I sit on the floor next to her. Her stained, stretched-out, white nylon underpants drop to the dirty beige carpet. "Throw them away," she says weakly.

For three days I pull her from corners of the house she is determined to wander and fall into. For three nights I sleep on the rank living room puddles, looking at the bathroom door. Keep her safe. Keep her fed. Keep her clean. I can do it. It's almost over.

Day four, December 29, 2008. It is a Monday morning, also Tommy's fifty-second birthday. The room at Hill House Assisted Living is ready. It's time to leave. The phone rings next to the rocking chair. Tommy is calling from jail. I sit on the stool next to her. His voice is loud with rage.

"What about me, Mom? If you're in a nursin home, who's gonna pay my bills? Huh? Who's gonna do that? Jeepas, Mom, I never thought there'd be a time when you wouldn't take care of me. I was the good one. Your only child, the only one who really loves you. I'm in jail, ya know, and it's my birthday. How come you're leavin on my birthday, huh?"

Mumma's face is flushing. She starts to speak, then takes the phone away from her ear and shakes her head. Tom keeps yelling. "Now Nancy has total control of you. You sold out to the devil, ya know. She owns you. What's in your will, huh? You never showed me your will. I need money to live here in prison, ya know. You always send me money. What about that, huh?"

Mumma's blood pressure is steaming. Red blotches appear on her face. Finally, she speaks. "Tom, you're fifty-two years old. I guess you'd betta figure that out yourself for a change. I can't help you. I can't stay here any longer. I need help now."

"What if you die before I get out, Mom? Where's my money?" His voice lowers as his thoughts go somewhere else. "Remember what we talked about. If I die first, don't bury me next to Dad. Jeepas."

When it's time to leave, Mumma looks out at the water, then at the birds in the feeder. Then with a small bag containing her clean nightgown, a few pairs of underpants, and an old cookie tin with needle and thread, she walks out the front door for the last time.

113

The Plaque

I HAVE WAITED YEARS for this day. Now that Mumma is safe at Hill House, there is something I need to take care of.

There is one car in the church parking lot. I hope it is the minister's. I turn off my car engine. The interior chills fast. My nose is cold and tingling. My fingers are gripped so tightly to the top of the steering wheel, my nails are digging into my palms. My bowels are rumbling. I begin to review what I will say. But there is no need. I have had eleven years to think about the wall in the Methodist church that honors a pedophile, my father.

The icy, snow-packed path squeaks and crunches under my boots. All muscles are soft and shaky as I pull open the church door and step into the entryway. Shame is rattling every molecule of my being. Anger is boiling up my gut and into my throat. I swallow the acid back down, then cough and choke on it.

I am going to do it. I am going to tell the family secrets.

In the entryway, hanging on the wall to my right, is a large wooden plaque. My father's name is embossed in bold letters across the top. IN MEMORY OF AND IN RECOGNITION OF DEDICATION AND SERVICE TO THE UNITED METHODIST CHURCH. Several brass plates line up underneath it, one for each year since his death. Names of parishioners who represent what the church community believes my father epitomized are linked with the morals of a deviant.

All is silent. I hear nothing but my own breath as I study the hook and wire connection to the wall. I think I can easily lift it and leave without anyone seeing me. But instead, I continue down the hallway, looking for the newly appointed minister, who barely knows my family, even though their membership with this church goes back more than one hundred years.

In his office, he stands and welcomes me. I introduce myself. He invites me to sit in a gathering area beyond the desk. He sits in a chair across from me and smiles. "How is your mother feeling? I really should get out to see her."

"She's well. Thank you for asking." I fidget in the seat.

Something has happened to my fear between the car and this chair. Eleven years of pent-up anger at the old minister, his letters, and people I thought would stand in judgment of me has melted like the icicles dripping from the church entry eaves. Tears begin to trail down my face. I am rambling in half sentences, trying to get to the point of why I am here.

"I need to speak to you about . . . well, my father's plaque in the entryway . . . I am upset because . . ."

He is polite and soft-spoken. "Take your time. There is no rush."

My eyes dart around the room. Nothing looks familiar from my childhood. Nothing that comforts, nothing that threatens. My heart races. My back straightens. I look at the minister, and with one forceful breath I push out what I have waited since his death to reveal. "My father was a pedophile. I don't believe that constitutes honor of any type. Despite what he may have done to help the church and community, incest and abuse is criminal."

The minister's hands clasp together between his knees and his head drops forward. He takes in a deep breath and then lets it out slowly. He looks up at me. "I am so sorry to hear that, Nancy. I am so sorry." For a minute neither of us speaks. His caring eyes watch me. He starts to slowly nod his head up and down. I am biting the inside of one cheek.

He speaks first. "Unfortunately, we have dealt with this same issue before. Someone recently came forward to report their relative's abuse, a man from your father's generation, someone we had also honored."

My brain scans faces from years ago and locks on one. I don't know for sure. I don't ask. We talk for a while, then he walks me to the front door. Next to it is a photo history display of the church and a pyramid of white coffee mugs. UNITED METHODIST CHURCH, BATH, MAINE, WHERE CHRIST IS OUR FOUNDATION, it reads across them. The minister picks one up and hands it to me. I say thank you, thinking it is generous and odd at the same time, like a strange consolation prize.

"Nancy," he says gently. "If there is anything we can do as a community to be of help to you and your family, please do not hesitate to contact us."

"Just the plaque," I say. "That's all I need. Take it down. I don't know what you will give for a reason."

"Don't you worry. You just take care of yourself. We will take care of the plaque."

It will be two years from now, the day of Uncle Ike's funeral, when I return to this church entryway. And in the spot on the wall where my father's honorary plaque once hung will be a beautiful photo of spring flowers.

114

Channel Markers

THE HOUSE KEY shakes in my fingers. I flip it to the flat side and slide it into the lock. "Straighten up," I hear myself echo. I close the door, lock it behind me, and stand in the hallway for a long time. There is a stillness, a feeling like the house has just released one long sigh. I can feel the walls and floorboards crying for what it has seen and absorbed into its fibers. It makes me wonder if that kind of emotion will always be here, swirling its energy and replaying its memories for years to come. You can't expect that kind of fever to leave without an everlasting scar.

Mumma will never be back. I will never again smell her spaghetti sauce cooking on the stove or sip tea with her at the kitchen table. I will never again hear her say, "Of all the trees in our yard, the oaks are always the last to drop their leaves." She said it every year. Tommy will never return. He will remain in prison for the next two and a half years, then come back to his own house down the street. This house will now be sold, per my parents' wishes. I am the one left responsible for ending our journey here. I am the last one standing.

Sitting at the kitchen table, I watch the morning sun glisten in diamonds as it rises up over the Kennebec River. Red and green channel markers bob on salty waves and line the route from here to Fort Popham. I think about how Mumma's favorite pastime was to watch the ice go out of the river in the spring. How seagulls rode the tide to the Carlton Bridge on blocks of frozen Kennebec. And in the blackness of night how we fell asleep to the screams of ice chunks snapping and riding up on each other like victims of the storm. It was our normal.

For the next year and a half, more than eighty years of living will unfold before me as I purge what we called home. Mumma calls it all junk and says to throw it out. But I can't. Alone I sift, watching for clues as to what went wrong. Why two respected churchgoing business-people would adopt a girl and a boy and have it end so badly. Alone, I decide what to throw away, give away, deposit at Tommy's house, take to Hill House, and bring back to Epping. I will pick up each physical item, hold it in my hands, and resolve its destiny. One piece of paper, one button, one nail at a time. Three floors, attic, back shed, outer shed, and boathouse. I will not go under the house. Whatever is there is not that important. In the time continuum of this space are ethereal snapshots of my childhood, and sometimes being filled up with what you can remember leaves no room for hashing out what you can't. And that's okay. I am grateful I am beginning to understand that now.

In the attic, boxes hold old glass medicine bottles, skeletons of trapped birds, dead mice, and a 1950s sex manual. Below it in Mumma's bedroom, I lay a plastic grocery bag onto my old bedroom floor and sit down on it. Blue latex gloves snap over my hands. Next to me is the old pot chair, and next to that, on Daddy's side of the bed and down the edge of the mattress, remain the runny dark outlines of feces marking the day he died here.

One by one, items rise from dusty layers. They pull me back in time. A 1940s shallow white enamel pan with a red ring emerges from under Mumma's bed, the throw-up pan that alternated between bedrooms. I drop it into the plastic garbage bag along with old business receipts, years of greeting cards, dozens of church program audiotapes, and smelly skeins of yarn. Mumma's rubber bathing cap is still in the bottom of her beach bag. I hold it to my face and sniff for Coppertone.

There are drawers of starched linen tablecloths and embroidered pillowcases, too good to use. A first tooth in a crinkly envelope with a dime loosely held to the front of it by a yellowed piece of tape, baptism certificates, baby books, and hospital wrist-bands from when Tommy and I had our tonsils out in 1961. In one drawer there is a box of letters written by my father from when he served in the army, and lying next to it, an anniversary card signed, *I love you, Jim.* Their wedding photo lies upside down below it.

My closet is much smaller than I recall. The wall hooks that once seemed so far up are not far up at all. On the pitched-roof shelf are the quilts I hid among. I reach my arm between the weight of them, thinking how tiny I was to fit there. Old fox furs, covered in a yellowed pillowcase, hang down over my head. Their dried-out clawed feet brush against my shoulders. One snaps off and falls into my lap. I reach forward, grasp the porcelain doorknob, and slowly pull it back toward me. Still, it doesn't shut. I sit in the dark closet staring through the crack, across the old green-flowered linoleum that Mumma called shit-brindle. I can hear the threading of the doorknob and my father calling my name, and I can feel the strength in my little dancer legs as I brace them to the doorframe. My gut clenches. I wait for panic to wash over me. But it doesn't. I am not afraid. I smile. Those days are far behind me. I no longer need them, any more than I need my outgrown plaid Easter coat that hangs at the other end. Neither fit the me I have grown into.

In the lower-floor laundry room there are two stuffed chairs piled high with Tommy's clothes. The farther down I dig, the older the clothes get, going all the way back to junior high school. Two pairs of Tommy's bloody sneakers from his bedroom accident sit under a small plastic table balancing last year's United Methodist Church yearbook and underneath that a 1940 newspaper of the German invasion in France. Below the frayed rope clothes-lines that stretch across the room are empty shells of sunflower seeds left behind by river rats, and pots of dry dirt with dead sticks. On a metal bookcase I find Josh and Jason's thirty-year-old coloring books, a 1940s box camera, and my report card from eighth grade. Two Cs, two Ds, and an E. I sort through teacups and treasures, cartons of crap. All house prisoners in my rescue mission of things Nanny loved, I find crammed out of sight and forgotten with nothing Mumma cherished.

Photographs have been jammed into dresser drawers and shoeboxes. Pictures of this house with polished living room floors, bouquets of flowers, tables spread with big plates of sandwiches and sweets in celebration, family, church friends, and my father's fishing trips to Moosehead Lake. Many people I don't recognize and some of them I do. In one old plastic wallet fold-out there are five black-and-whites. Two of them are smiling naked women, their arms and legs spread, with the downtown photo shop stamp on the back. The three other photos are of separate groups of two. Six little girls, under the age of five. Four of them I recognize.

I HAVE left Mumma's old bedroom for last. This will be the toughest part, erasing the final piece of her. Standing at her closet, I open my arms and grab a huge armful of clothes packed and stretching full width of the metal pipe. With my face buried in the scent of stale perfume, old shoes, and dust, I am quickly transported back to the week before Christmas somewhere in the early 1960s. Hiding behind Mumma's hat boxes I found a doll with yellow braids and homemade clothes. I remember how I snuck in and played with that doll every day and tried to act surprised on Christmas morning when I opened it up. I let go of Mumma's clothes and step away. Then turning my back to the closet, I move into it, holding the ends of her dress sleeves and wrapping them tightly to my body for one last hug. I close my eyes. Tears squeeze out the corners and bounce down my cheeks.

It is midmorning when two huge trash trucks beep their way to the front door. Both the downstairs and upstairs hallways are full of protruding green trash bags. Three men work fast without hesitation, slinging the bags to one another and out the front door to the trucks. They never turn back and ask "Are you sure?" But I am sure.

"Someone die?" I hear a woman shout. "She die?" the mail lady yells as she hangs out the window of her idling jeep.

"Don't you have a route to be on?" jokes the trash man. "Can't you see we're workin here? Stop your yappin and get along." They both laugh. The mail lady drives on.

The men wrestle the front bedroom mattress from its frame and slide it down over the wobbly banister. One man's hair is stuck to his forehead. "This must be the original mattress. Jesus, it's heavy. They don't make em like this anymore. No sa."

From the front door, I watch my parents' bed frame be slowly eaten and swallowed up by the massive steel plate of the trash compactor. The loud snap of wood pounds inside my chest, that kind of stinging vibration you feel when the drum passes by you in the Independence Day parade. The old broken-down living room couch is carried out like a dead corpse long overdue for burial. That too is crushed and disappears into the bowels of the vehicle. Several cars drive by with neighbors gawking to see what's going on. They wave at me. Within an hour the first load is swept out the front door, down over the hill, and disappears out of sight.

115

Perception or Fact

Two NEIGHBOR WOMEN are strolling up behind me, but before I can get into Uncle Ike's walkway, the younger of the two rushes up and talks close to my face. "Your poor mother. All that time she drove Tom around and she could just barely see over the steering wheel, but there she was, taking him for cigarettes." She shakes her head and makes a tisking noise with her tongue. "He was always so loud and disrespectful. He wore her right down to the bone, that's for sure."

The older woman coughs into a hankie. I notice she is wearing only one clip-on earring. "Poor thing, your mother, and what a lovely lady she is."

My back teeth are clenched on one side. "Mmmm, lovely."

She sniffles then stuffs the hankie into her jacket pocket. "Your father was the finest man I ever knew. If there was ever a problem, Jimmy was the one who could fix it." She looks down at the ground and chuckles. "You know, he pursued your mother all through high school until she gave in and married him." Then she looks back at me. "It really threw some people for a loop."

The younger woman leans into me again. "Of course she was in love with someone else at that time." I can see my shock reflect in the woman's face. She lays one hand on my arm and speaks softer, like she is telling a deep secret. "You did know that, didn't you?"

"No," I say. "I didn't." Imagining Mumma in love and happy was the most foreign thing I could ever think about her. I feel myself well up inside, wanting to fall to my knees and cry thinking that Mumma might have loved so deeply and then it was lost. Finally, I inch away from them toward Uncle Ike's door and they walk on, calling back well wishes over their shoulders.

When I go inside, Uncle Ike is sitting in his recliner. Sunshine lights up the wall-framed map of the Kennebec River on the wall beside him. "Well, it's the Barefoot Kid," he says, as I lean down and kiss his cheek. "I am so glad you are here to take care of things, dear. Your mother hasn't done very well all these years since your dad died. After that, she didn't seem to want anything to do with Aunt Lilly and me, and now with Aunt Lilly gone, and me moving slow . . ." His words trail off as he picks up the television remote and puts the volume on Mute. "I understand it must be hard for you, dear, to see your mother so upset from all your brother's problems and arrests." He pulls his ninety-year-old body up higher in the chair, then smoothes down the front of his blue oxford shirt. One hand trembles slightly as he does it. "Your father worked so hard to provide. He was a good man." His brow wrinkles. "But I never understood why he treated Tom the way he did. He just seemed to have some kind of hold on him that Tom couldn't break from. Aunt Lilly used to say that something was wrong with Tom and that's why he never grew up."

I can't listen to anyone else tell me how good my father was, not even Uncle Ike. It may be their truth, but it is not mine. I don't want to hurt him, but I am going to say it anyway. "No, actually he wasn't," I say softly, watching Uncle Ike's expression. "The truth is, my father was not a good man."

"Oh?" His forehead creases. "He wasn't? What do you mean? He was so good to you kids. You had everything."

"I mean, he did some very bad things that I would be ashamed to tell you about. That person you saw by day disappeared at night. My father was deceitful and a fraud, and for reasons I can't wrap my head around, my mother chose to look the other way."

We don't say anything for minutes. He watches the river. I watch him. Then he looks long at me. I can feel my heart throbbing in my eyes. Uncle Ike's words are kind and soothing. "Okay, dear, you don't have to tell me what. You are an honest, respectful person, and if you say it is true, I believe you."

When it was time to go, he said if he and Aunt Lilly had had a daughter, they would have wanted her to be just like me. I hugged him tight and said "I love you."

It will be our last visit together. In April of 2011, Uncle Ike will pass away. The day of his funeral, I will go to Hill House to pick up Mumma, and she will say she can't go. I will remind her that at one time they were best friends, neighbors for sixty years. But she will again say no. Her hair wasn't lookin good that day.

116

It Doesn't Change the Truth

I AM IN THE elevator at Hill House. With my little finger I push *G* for ground floor. The doors ding and close. The handles of three plastic shopping bags line up each arm, new underwear and nightgowns from Sears, lavender soap, mini-pads, and White Shoulders cologne from Walgreens. Wheat Thins, a package of Fig Newtons, and a six-pack of Coke from Brackett's Market. A bag of knickknacks I have washed. A bag of clothes I have washed and mended. And a take-out bag from Jimbo's Diner with Mumma's favorite haddock sandwich, still hot. Two five-pound bags of birdseed, double bagged at Brackett's, weight in each hand. The plastic is cutting into my palms as the doors ding and open. Mumma's church friend stands waiting to go up.

"I just saw your mother," she says with her eyebrows lifted. "Took her some books and the *Times Record*. She's in a mood today. When the nurse came in to take her blood pressure and asked how she was, your mother said, 'Not good. My daughter dumped me here, ya know.'"

"Nice," I say. The woman moves back and I step out with the bags hanging heavy at my knees.

In Mumma's room I drop the birdseed in front of the kitchenette and sit down in the rocker. Six plastic bags peel off my arms. Mumma is sitting in her upholstered wing chair. Get Well and Thinking of You cards line the windowsill next to her. An open box of chocolates sits on top of the low dresser. She reaches over, takes one out of the box with two fingers, then with the other elbow on the arm-rest, waves that hand in the air.

"Look at this, Nance," she says. "Did you ever see me with red fingernails? That little blond nurse painted them. Kinda foolish, isn't it?" She laughs, takes a bite of the chocolate, then looks at the inside center. She watches me unload the bags. "Aren't you tired of comin down here every week for days at a time and stayin at that B and B? Michael needs you home with him. Who fixes his suppa when you're not there?"

I reach to the dresser between us and study the activities calendar. "Michael did just fine for forty-five years before he married me. I'm pretty sure he can heat up leftovers."

"Yeah well, I don't know what the hell you're doin up to the house all this time. I think you betta get home."

I stand up with the fish sandwich and put it onto the kitchenette table. Mumma moves with me, half rolling and half carrying her walker. I sit down with her and pick up a white envelope with Tommy's hand scrawling across the front. The return address says Maine Correctional Center. I lay the letter back down and cut Mumma's sandwich in half as she Velcros a large terry-cloth bib around her neck. I am not sure which upsets me more, the fact that my brother is writing wacky letters from prison or that my mother now needs a bib.

"Is Tommy still mailing you several letters a week?" I pick it back up and pull it out of the envelope. Again, today, it is thirteen pages of scary face emotion circles and large juvenile block letters of rage and delusion.

Mumma taps one foot midair and watches birds land in the feeder outside. "Oh yeah. He's drivin me crazy."

"You don't have to accept them, Mumma."

She bites into the fish. Tartar sauce drips out one corner of her mouth. "Well, of course I do. I'm his mother. He's got nobody else that gives a crap about him." She pushes the fried fish back into the bun and licks her fingers.

I bite at the inside of my lip so hard, it tingles up into my nose. I read silently.

Dear Mom,

How are your birds doing? I hope Nancy that bitch is still bringing bird seed. Poor little things. I am going to sue Nancy for telling my mother not to love me. She took you away from me Mom and paid off the doctor to commit you. Nancy is the devil and she has put you in a prison and now you are homeless. She has given you a death warrant and your days are numbered. Send me your will and tell me what I will get when you die. Don't lie to me, Mom. How could you sign your life away to Nancy? I hate her and she will pay for taking you away from me. She manipulated you into thinking that I was a worthless drunk and would never amount to a damn thing. She is trying to make you feel guilty for not stopping the abuse and that it's all your fault. Why can't we live like before she told what Dad said before he died? Now she has wrecked everything. You could have made me co-everything, but Nancy talked you into believing that I deserve nothing. It's all Nancy's fault. Mom, why did you do this to me? When I get out of prison, I am going to have your estate changed and have all legal authority over you. Yes, Mom, that's right, I am going to get legal custody of you. I want to be with you again 24/7 like it was before. I want you to die at my house with dignity. I won an ice cream sandwich for Jeopardy. I hope you like this Certificate of Excellence I have enclosed. I hate Nancy and I will get that bitch when I get out.

It goes on and on, repeating the same things, and with each page the block letters get larger and thicker. "I'm crying as I'm writing this," he writes at the end. "I hope you are crying too. Write back and tell me you love me Mom. Love your only child. The only one who really loves you. Tom S."

Week after week the letters have gotten worse, pages and pages of threats and suffering. After Mumma reads them she vomits, wets her pants, and refuses to come out of her room. When Tommy telephones on Sundays the nurses can hear him screaming at Mumma, demanding money, raving at her for abandoning him. When Mumma can't take any more, she tells Tommy she is having trouble with her hearing aid and hangs up.

After Mumma has finished her fish, she goes back to the chair by the window and stuffs the letter in the top dresser drawer with all the others. Then she makes a disgusted snort. "I don't know what the hell's the matter with Tom. His birth parents must have been drinkers."

I follow her back to the rocker and sit down. "Come on, Mumma. Do you really think that was Tommy's problem?"

"No, I guess not, but I don't know what it was." She looks away from me and lets out a long, exasperated sigh.

My words are slow and precise. "Yes, you do."

She snaps fast. "Look, Nancy, I don't think that happened to Tom, do you?"

"Of course, absolutely. What happened to me happened to him, and right there, somewhere before he even got into his teens, he stopped growing mentally and emotionally. He's still stuck in a time warp of trauma."

She looks at the floor and talks down into it. "Well, he never said anything."

I lean toward her, my hands gripped to the arms of the rocker. "Of course he did. He's been screaming it for fifty years"

Her voice is raspy and nervous. "I never knew what was going on, ya know. I never knew it."

"Can you live and die with that, Mumma?"

"Yes," she says firmly. Her hollow eyes look past me.

I am in a vacuum. I think I am yelling. I'm not sure. "When a child screams for help and a mother turns a deaf ear, what do you think that does to a child? That child lives in shame. That is her normal. Why do you think Tommy and I kept asking, Mumma, do you love me? Mumma, are you mad at me? We were waiting to be saved by you. But it was never about protecting Tommy and me, was it, Mumma? It was about protecting yourself. Bitterness has been your defense. Denial your anesthetic. If you knew nothing, nothing could be expected of you."

Her body is rigid. Mine has gone completely weak, but I don't stop. "I never believed that you loved me, Mumma. I wanted to. But I never did. Whether you say you did or didn't know about the abuse doesn't change the truth. You listened to your children scream for help and did nothing. Why didn't you save us?"

Her brow is pinched. "Because eventually you'd stopped scream-ing." She picks mindlessly at a pulled thread on her slacks. "I guess I am pretty ashamed of myself," she says.

I fall back into the rocker and lay both hands to the top of my chest. My throat is raw. "You should be. Why didn't you just leave? Did you ever think about that?"

She is mechanical, like she has told herself the story a thousand times. "No, I was being taken care of. I never liked sex, so I figured if your father was out with other women, then he wouldn't be botherin me." Small, disconnected pieces of truth glean through unexpectedly.

"I don't deserve to be here, people waitin on me, draggin me off on bus trips, talkin me into all these foolish activities. Where the hell's all this money comin from, anyway?"

"You fought me the whole way, Mumma—doctor, lawyer, bank, insurance. In their offices you were sweet as pie, told them you under-stood it all, but when it was just us, you criticized and shamed me for getting into your business. All you wanted was to check out and leave it all behind. All the leg work I have done to get your life pulled to-gether so you would be safe and taken care of. You were never grateful for any of it."

"No, I wasn't. You should have left me at home to die in peace."

In the hallway, a short, stout woman pushes her elderly mother in a wheelchair. They stop at Mumma's open doorway. The younger woman calls out hello. Mumma calls back at her. "That's too old to live for God sake. Too bad someone can't just give her a shot and put her to sleep." Then, aiming at the old lady, she scrunches up her shoulders and makes a shot motion with one hand. The younger woman cringes and moves on.

"Mumma. Why do you have to be so mean? That was rude."

She glares at me. "Well, I see all these people here worse off than me in wheelchairs and stuck in bed, and I am so sick of this damn walker. I can't move out of a chair without someone tellin me to hang on to the stupid thing." She lets out another disgusted sigh and leans back into the wing chair. "It's a miserable life I'm leadin here, ya know."

"Well, Jesus, Mumma. Would you rather be in a wheelchair?"

Her voice explodes into the room. "No, I wouldn't rather be in a wheelchair. I'd rather be dead." She drops her head into one hand, shaking it back and forth. "I hope to hell I'm dead before Tom gets out of jail. Too bad he couldn't just go to sleep. God knows he's no good to anyone. He's messed up his whole life. What a waste."

My voice is stuck somewhere in my throat. My eyes begin to sting. I shut them tight and wish her words away.

117

Fire and Ashes

TODAY IS MAY 26, 2010, my fifty-fifth birthday. I am standing outside the front door at Mumma's house. In my hand is a large blue box of kosher salt. I open the spout and allow it to pour to the ground as I walk the perimeter of the building. "Love and light, love and light," I chant as a white line trails behind me, back to where I started. Two miles into town, there is a young family preparing to walk through this front door and begin a new life. A father, mother, daughter, and son.

Inside the house, there are a few things left. Two clear crystals, a small sage bundle, matches, and my father's tweed cap. Today is the day I have chosen to symbolically end my family's sixty-five-year history with this house and land. I have spent the last year and a half purging its contents, reliving its pain, and moving into an understanding of who I am beyond it.

With the crystals in one hand and the lit sage stick in the other, I enter every room of our house, unblocking stuck energy with intention of loving vibrations and that all held memories drift out the open windows to where they can be healed. In each corner and closet, I watch smoke hesitantly snake, then finally rise and disappear.

On the living room side of the bathroom door, which is now detached from its single top-end hinge, I fold the hardware spine and press the two wooden panels against each other. Then, wrapping my arms around the top half, I pull it onto its side. It falls heavy against my chest, exhausted from being pushed back and forth thousands of times over fifty years. Swinging wildly, mostly off its track, it has been thrown against the wall of the living room, then slammed back to the bathroom sink on the other side without ever a handle or safe station. Inches at a time, I drag it toward the kitchen. It makes gouges in the wood floor, now stripped of its disgusting carpet. The warped metal slider screen resists as I rock it wide enough to pull the old folding door through and onto the outside kitchen porch. With my fingers pressed to its dark, sticky grime, I lay the bathroom door down against the railing and look to the yard three stories below. The river watches me, waving at the shore in wait.

On the porch floor next to me is a king-sized black Sharpie, the box of matches, a quart saucepan of water, and an eight-by-ten color print of a 1985 family photo, the only photo ever taken of the four of us, Mumma, Daddy, Tommy, and me. The smell of permanent marker fills my sinuses. The marker squeaks as it presses down the door panel, spelling out three lines in huge, black, bold letters. I AM FREE. Then, with a match in one hand and the photo in the other, I touch the bottom left corner to the flame. I am strong, the strongest I have ever been.

I rotate the photo, watching as fire consumes and separates us from one another. Ashes begin to fall down over the door. Tall orange and black streaks reach high above my hand. I hold the final piece of us until the fire is so close to my fingers I release it to the pan. The fire dies. Smoke clears around one small circle of paper, the only piece that has survived the flames. One face smiles up at me. Mine.

I pour the contents of the pan down over the front of the door, then lifting the bottom end, I slide it up to the railing. It teeters like an unbalanced seesaw for a moment, but I am ready to let go. My childhood world is long past. Across the street, the fields I ran through have grown in and the old farm foundation is underneath new homes. Wooded paths and trees that gave me refuge have been cleared for biking trails. The dock has warped and splintered in cresting tides. Our boat is gone. The ropes finally released their grip. People and places of my youth have long since passed away. And my Nanny, she is not here. Her little home by the shore that was kept like a dollhouse is now overrun with weeds as the front porch rots. I am ready to let go. I push the old bathroom door off the railing. In what feels like slow motion, I watch it open up, turn itself around, and float down into the grass, revealing my message to the river.

Now, with one last piece to my ritual, I am standing on the dock with Daddy's tweed cap in hand. I fill my lungs with salt air and yell out across the Kennebec. "I am done now. Do you hear me? I am done allowing myself to just exist. From now on, I am going to really live life and be happy. I so deserve that." Then like a Frisbee, I fling the hat far out into the water, and watch it float away with the tide.

In the lower backyard, for one last time, I lie on the slant of the land and look up through the weathered branches of the oak trees. I watch them slow dance with the wind. Warm morning sun filters down through the new green leaves in shadow forms. Waves rhythmically lap the mud-covered rocks beneath the dock. I close my eyes and slide my fingers out into the cool grass. I can feel tree bark on the bottoms of my bare feet, pine pitch glued between my fingers. I see the neighborhood kids racing down over the hill on homemade go-karts and hear the sound of our laughter. I see our backyard iced up crusty with Tommy and me breaking holes in it with our fists to keep from sliding down into the river. I feel the snow burn where my mittens have ridden up on my wrists. I can smell hot coconut squares coming from Nanny's kitchen and hear Mumma's clothesline track its way from the laundry room window to the elm at the river-bank. My mother calls out, "Cup a tea, Nance?"

Inside the house there will be no sign of what happened in our family, just a large stain on the wood floor in front of where the couch sat. I stand on it and look into the bathroom. Then one last time I walk the house and say good-bye to each room. Finally, at the front door, I step out onto the tar. Holding tightly to the doorknob, I call out into the emptiness. "I love you." Then, for the last time, I pull the door shut.

118

Saved

At Hill House, Mumma sits slumped down into her wing chair. She looks old. I watch her from the doorway for a minute, then walk over and kiss her forehead.

She pulls herself up straighter in the chair. "Oh, Nance. Here you are." She reaches up and hugs me. "Do you hear that music? That same song has been playin over and over every day since I got here. It used to be louder, but now it's gettin weak and fadin out. I think because it's been played so much. I don't know."

I sit in the rocker across from her. She looks down at a notepad where she has made a list and taps one finger over it. "Now look, Tom called and he needs a cord of wood delivered to his house, and I want you to take me down there so I can get things straightened up. He says he needs the refrigerator cleaned out." She fiddles with his letter on top of the dresser, then stuffs it into the drawer with the others.

"Mumma, you are eighty-nine years old with a walker. You can't go down there. It's not safe. There is no place to walk. I have packed his house full of your furniture and things, and it's filthy. He has left bags of garbage and a frying pan with bacon grease that mice have made tracks through, and after a year and a half with no electricity, I can't imagine what the inside of the refrigerator is like."

She lets out a long sigh and lays her head to the back of the chair. "Well, if I don't do it, who will? He says he's takin me out of here and makin me live in that dump."

"No, he is not taking you anywhere. When Tommy gets out of jail, he will clean up his own house, or he won't. It's not your job, Mumma, and it's not mine."

"Great," she drawls out, her chin pitting and lips pursing together. One foot picks up speed as it taps midair.

"Mumma, I have worked really hard. I have surrounded you with people who care about you. I have emptied the house, and now there is a family excited to begin a new life there on the river. I did everything I could to make you happy." She leans forward, her lips still pursed. "You didn't save me, Mumma, but maybe I tried to save you. That was my choice. Something about it made me feel happy. As hard as it was, I looked forward to taking care of things each week. Weird, huh?"

She stops tapping and looks confused. "Why did you do it? I wondered that."

"Why do you think I did it, Mumma?"

Her voice is meek. "Because you are a good person, Nancy."

"Yes, Mumma, I am. I turned something really horrible into something good. But I didn't do it just for you, I did it for me. I did it to heal myself. I had a choice to stay in the fear or move out of it. Either way, it was work and it was painful. As long as I kept the focus on the anger and abuse, I would never be free. As long as I lived in shame, I was the child. Now I choose love over fear, compassion over hatred. And the person that was most influential, the person that taught me the most, do you know who that was, Mumma?"

Her brow pinches. Both feet go flat to the floor. "No, who was it?"

"It was you. You are the most fearful woman I have ever known, and you were also my greatest teacher. When I saw you give up, it made me work harder. When you spoke cutting, shameful words to me, I softened mine with others. Your lack of compassion made mine greater. And just because you didn't save me doesn't mean I wasn't worth saving. And, Mumma, I don't care if you are mad. It is of no concern to me now. I forgive you."

Maybe I said those three words just to see if I could, and even though I had told myself it was unnecessary, somehow in my heart it felt right.

She stays intent on my words. "It's not about me forgiving you for not saving me or not loving me, Mumma. Because you know what? I

364

think you did love me all along. It's about me forgiving me for not loving myself. But that has changed."

I stand up to leave. She pulls herself to the edge of the chair and stands with me. She takes my face in her hands and smiles. She looks straight into my eyes and I look straight into hers. "I didn't treat you very well, did I, Nancy? I wasn't much of a mother. I'm ashamed. You've taken care of everything. I don't know what I would have done without you."

I start to cry. I don't mean to, it just pours out. "You missed all the good things, Mumma. You have been so addicted to Tommy's drama and so fearful that you had no control of your own life, you missed it all. You had choices, but you weren't able to see them, because you were living as a victim with no survival skills other than to lock yourself up in the dark stench of drama. As of now, I am breaking our trauma bond. Living a lie is not living at all. It's only existing. That may be your life choice, but it is no longer mine."

She sits back in the chair and hangs her head to her chest. "I'm sorry, Nancy. I never should have had kids."

I catch my breath, holding my chest to keep the sobbing in. "Josh and Jason are grown men now, Mumma. They disconnected from all this years ago because they want no part of the drama. They were grown up way before I was. Josh is married and a father. You saw his daughter only once and never asked again. I didn't bring her here to see you, because I was afraid you would be your bitter self. I won't expose her to that." She firms up her chin, closes her eyes, and shakes her head side to side. "Josh is an amazing dad, Mumma. He is teaching me that fathers can love their daughters, and she adores him."

I lean in close to her. With both her eyes she looks at one of mine, then the other. "You've done a good job with those boys, honey. You should be proud. I am so sorry they had to see their mother go through what you did." It was like a tiny window in her heart had been slid open for just a bit, just long enough for me to see that inside she had been the same as me, a scared girl, wanting to be loved, feeling undeserving of it.

"Before I leave, Mumma, I have one last question. Why did you adopt us?"

"I shouldn't have," she says quickly. "I never wanted kids. I just wanted to work. But other women were having children, so I figured that's what was expected of me. And, well, your father . . ." Her voice trails off.

I move to the kitchen sink and pick up the dry-erase board. On it I write the names and telephone numbers for the doctor, the lawyer, the bank, and Brackett's Market. "Here is everyone who can help you, Mumma. Brackett's will deliver your birdseed from now on. Anything you want, Hill House staff will get it for you. That includes fish sandwiches." I lay down the marker and smile. I pick up my purse and start for the door.

She puts both hands on one arm of the chair and turns toward me. "Where are you going?"

"I'm going home. It's time for me now. If something happens and I am needed, I will be here. You can call and talk to me, but I will not listen to Tommy drama. It doesn't mean I don't love you and Tommy. I just can't allow this to consume my life anymore."

Her voice is panicked and sharp. "What's gonna happen when he gets out of jail? How's he supposed to get the house runnin and hooked up again if I don't do it?"

"Mumma, if he can figure out how to get drugs and alcohol, I am pretty sure he's capable of calling the utilities."

She lies back into the chair. One foot begins tapping. She stares out at the birds. "Well, hopefully I'll be dead by then."

"Bye, Mumma. I love you."

I could feel my cheeks radiating heat as I ran up the stairs and hurried out the Hill House entrance. I sat in the car and shook all over. I blew my nose. Tears dripped off my chin. I blew my nose again and looked in the rearview mirror, watching it all sink in. It made me look different. It made my head ache to think of all I had gone through to get to this day. But most of all, it made me mad that I loved her so much.

119

To End Is to Begin

THE DAY WE closed on the sale of Mumma's house it was in June 2010, exactly a year and a half from when she went to live at Hill House. I wore a green-and-blue-figured dress that day, with a light short-sleeve green sweater I had bought just an hour prior to the appointment at a boutique across the street from the bank. In the bank conference room, we all sat around a big polished table, the real estate agents at either end and the new owners across from me. I watched one of the agents flip papers from a stack of neatly-gathered documents. I answered all questions with yes and no, sitting dancer tall and trying not to look over at the young couple who resembled my parents, her with an Ivory-clean complexion and glasses, him with receding hairline and crooked front tooth.

When we had finished, we all stood up, and as I shook the gentleman's hand, my rehearsed best wishes and "I hope you will enjoy," turned into a shortened version of that with one huge sob that I inhaled so deeply, it locked up in my chest and I could not say anything else. There was so much I wanted to say. I forgot to tell you the family dog is buried under the shed. My Morse High School class ring is in the mud flats under the dock. If you find any naked pictures between the walls, try not to look and throw them away. But by then my nose was filled with mucus and no words would come out of my mouth. So I nodded my head, smiled with my eyes, and left.

I walked back across the street, hoping I would not run into anyone I knew, and got into my car. Then I remembered the locket. I never found the locket that Elizabeth gave me. The last time I saw it, it was around the neck of the redheaded doll in the attic. But I guess it really doesn't matter. This is a new beginning.

OVER the next eleven months I made only four trips back to Bath. A meeting with Hill House staff, a doctor's appointment, the bank, the lawyer, and a few trips for fish sandwiches. I missed her so much, sometimes it felt like everything inside me had stopped. Part of me wanted to get into the car, go to Bath, and sit with her. But I knew where that would emotionally lead. Sometimes I called the staff for updates. Sometimes Mumma called me. And sometimes I didn't answer the phone. Each time I did, it began and ended the same. "My life is misery, Tom needs money, when are you gonna take me to clean out his house?" After her receiver slammed in my ear, I sat at my desk writing our conversation word for word. Then I cried and screamed swears at the ceiling. I wondered if she was eating. I wondered if she went outside. I wondered how it would all end.

When Christmas came, I stayed home. Two wrapped gifts I had bought for her hung in a bag on my coatrack. They would never make it out the door. In February when she celebrated her ninetieth birthday at Hill House, I didn't go. It felt hypocritical. I would not see her again until April, the day of Uncle Ike's funeral.

Slowly, I am learning to release myself from what I thought was my parents' emotional grasp of me. It never was. It was my attachment to our family's drama and the hope that I would be loved by them. When I finally realized I deserved to manifest happiness beyond the shaming and blaming of our old paradigm, that was when I stopped being the abused child.

Tommy has remained trapped like the birds in the attic, circling and repeating the same pattern, never finding a way out. It is now April 2011, he has been released from jail, and today is his third visit to Hill House. The staff has asked that Mumma's door be left open so they can monitor Tommy's visit, but Tommy has shut the door. When the head nurse pushes it open, Tommy's six-foot body, now seventy pounds heavier than when he left for jail two and a half years ago, is stretched out on Mumma's bed. His pants are in a heap on the floor beside him. Mumma is angry and embarrassed as she sits in the wing chair facing the blaring television. Tommy is asked to leave.

In two weeks, my brother will be arrested for public drunkenness and taken back to jail for breaking probation. He will serve another six months. The crazy letters will begin again. Mumma will read them all, throw up, and pray to die before he gets out.

120

Strength

THE SCREEN OF my laptop is glowing. I lean closer to the picture and study every detail. In both hands the woman holds a delicate bouquet of purple flowers against her white wedding dress. Wispy brunette hair frames her soft smile, and in it I look for a reflection of me. Michael is leaning over my shoulder.

"Honey, tell me if you think she looks like me." He adjusts his glasses and stares into her face. "It's my sister, Nancy. I just know it."

He straightens back up. "Where did you find that?"

"People Search, her grandson's birth announcement, Facebook. Amazing, huh? In minutes you can know so much about a person. I just started searching by last name, and here is where I ended up, her husband's Facebook page."

"Are you sure?" Michael asks. "Are you sure you are ready for what it may bring?"

I lay my fingers on the keyboard. "It's been thirty years since Elizabeth told me about my sisters. Yes, now I am sure. It's time."

"Okay, honey." His tone is questioning. "Just remember, knock lightly on the door. Don't bust it down."

I tap out a brief note that I am looking for the family of George Levesque, click on Add Friend, and send. After four days with no response, I address an envelope to what I have found on the internet and type out a letter.

April 28, 2011

Dear Nancy,

My name is Nancy Shappell and I am looking for members of my birth family. My father's name was George Levesque, and I believe we could be sisters.

I have known about his family for thirty years, but wasn't sure if anyone would be open to meeting me. With today's technology, it was very easy to find you, based on the information I already had. I am hoping that you indeed are the sister I am looking for and would be willing to get in touch with me. I would so appreciate an opportunity to meet you and gather some history if you would be open to that.

Although I was told that your mother was aware of my birth, I am not sure if that, in fact, is the truth, but here is my story.

I was born May 26, 1955, put up for adoption, and raised in Bath, Maine. I have two amazing sons, a wonderful second husband I married almost thirteen years ago, and a beautiful granddaughter.

In 1981, when I was twenty-six years old, I found my birth mother, who lives in Auburn, Maine. At that time she told me she had a relationship with George Levesque, who was married with two daughters and a son. Not long after finding her, I was able to find where George lived, nearby in Tupper's Trailer Park. Although I did go there one night in search, I decided not to make myself known. For ten years I tucked that information away until George's death in 1991.

My birth mother and I were at George's funeral, which was a very surreal experience for me, knowing this was the only time in my life I would be in the same place with both my parents. I believe it was you who stood next to me at the back of the rotunda. I so wanted to reach out to you, but again, I didn't make myself known because it just didn't feel right. I watched you and your sister, Ann, leave under the cover of umbrellas. So, I have waited all these years in hopes that someday I would know you.

From what I found on-line, it looks like you are both actually younger than I am, which makes me wonder if my birth mother continued to keep in touch with our father after I was born. She had told me that your parents came to her and asked to adopt me, but it was too late. She also said that George was a drinker and urged me to stay away.

In a few weeks, I will turn fifty-six years old. I would be so grateful for the opportunity to meet you. Please believe that I reach to you with the most respectful of intentions. I never had a sister, and how ironic that we were both given the same name.

If you decide that a meeting is not what feels best for you, I totally understand.

Most sincerely,
Nancy

Another two days go by, and just as Michael and I are leaving the house for a Saturday dinner out, I hear my Facebook page ding. Nancy's husband has accepted my friend request, and there is a note attached. "I am the sister you were looking for. So many emotions. Happy to hear from you. "

On the telephone that night, I ask if her life was good. "It is now," she said. It stopped my heart when I heard it, because I knew exactly what that meant. And then I told her it happened to me too. "Oh, Nance." she cried. "I'm so sorry. You'd like to think when a child is adopted they are safe, but I guess that isn't always the case." The next night I talk to Ann. "The bastard." she said fiercely. "There is nothing lower in life than a human being who hurts a child." We made plans to meet in two days.

TODAY is May 2, 2011, the day before my sister, Nancy's, fiftieth birthday and twenty years to the day of our father's death. I am sitting in a booth in the back of Old Country Buffet in South Portland, Maine. My sister, Nancy, is at my side. Across from us sits our sister Ann. She leans her bosom against the table and smoothes a piece of blond hair down over her face, then tucks it back behind one ear. Her hands fold in front of her as she looks at me over her glasses. "You must have a lot of questions. What is it you want to know?"

The corners of my smile are shaking. I can feel tears start to well in my eyes. Nancy reaches for my hand under the table and smiles sweetly. She hums and makes a tender pout with her lips, like she understands how uncomfortable this may be for me, for us.

"I have no expectations," I say. "Just to see you and tell you I have always thought about you. Your faces have been in my mind all these years, and even if I had never found you, or if I never see you again, to me, you will always be my sisters, and I love you." Ann takes in a quick breath. It catches in her throat. I feel her energy relax. Her beautiful rounded cheeks flush a light pink.

Nancy wraps both hands around one of mine. "Oh my goodness, I just can't believe how much we look alike. We even have the same inflections in our voice. Oh, Nance, I am so happy you found us. This is the best birthday present ever. I never dreamed you would be so sweet." She glances at Ann, then back at me, and continues. "Our mother told us about you. She saw you and Elizabeth at the funeral. After that, she told us Dad had an affair with, well, he called her Liz, and she said you had been born."

I can feel my eyes get wide. "I think it's so interesting we were given the same name. My birth name was Deborah."

"Actually, my birth name was Jane," she says. "Our father changed it when I was five."

Ann looks down at the table, shakes her head back and forth, then looks back up at me. "Our father was not a good man, and after our brother, Raymond, died of leukemia at age fifteen, Dad got worse. He never ever held a job for long. Our mother was a nurse and made good money, but Dad spent it all on whiskey, beer, and cigarettes. Our family is saturated with dysfunction, abuse of every kind, alcoholism, and sociopathic behavior. Dad was abusive to us. His father was abusive to him. It goes way back." She makes a sarcastic laugh. "We are at the lowest end of the gene pool. Our father couldn't keep it in his pants." She pauses for a moment with her eyes still on me. "You know, if someone came up to me and said, 'I am your sibling,' I would say, 'Yes, you probably are, but if you are dysfunctional, I want nothing to do with you.' I have worked too hard sorting through my own stuff."

Ann reaches across the table for my hand. "I have to tell you, I am a very private person and don't let many people in. But I felt an instant connection with you. It's very strange." She starts to tear up, lets go of my hand, and takes a sip of Diet Pepsi. "Now I have a story to share. When our father died, Nancy didn't want to be at the funeral. I felt horrible that I left her alone to stand at the back of the rotunda because I wanted to move to the front with the casket. It has bothered me all these years. But now I realize she wasn't alone after all. You were standing next to her. Even though we didn't know you as our sister, when I couldn't be there for her, you were." She wipes her eyes with a paper napkin. "I so admire your bravery to come to that funeral. I have to say, I'm shocked I am so comfortable talking to you, because I don't share with anyone. I guess I didn't expect to love you, but I do."

Nancy's voice is soft and respectful. "It's probably a good thing we didn't find each other until now. It was a bad time when Dad died. He died in that same trailer you went to. He lived there by himself. By then, Mom had finally divorced him. I went there shortly before the end. I told him I forgave him and he needed to forgive himself for everything that happened. I don't actually remember much of the abuse, but Ann does."

"What was it?" I ask. "Cancer?"

Ann rolls her eyes. "Oh, he had emphysema pretty bad, but that wasn't what killed him. He put a gun under his chin and blew his face off. Serves him right, the prick."

Nancy's lips smile politely. Her eyes are sad. "You wouldn't have been any better off if you had been with us, Nance. Us three girls, we had the same life."

That day in the back booth of the Old Country Buffet, my sisters and I didn't talk about the gruesome details of our childhoods. We knew they were all the same. Different places, different faces, but the same story. We talked about how blessed we were with children and loved ones, people we had built a healthy life with away from the trauma drama of the past. We talked about how grateful we were for a chance to know one another as grown women, celebrating our strength and how everything and everybody along our way had brought us to that place.

Healing. It was by choice. It had grown three terrified little girls into strong, grateful women. And loving them, I love myself even more.

121

Fibers of Being

THREE WEEKS HAVE passed since finding my sisters.

Today is my birthday. On the kitchen island, party treats have spilled out of a box mailed to me by a best friend in Arizona. I put the hat on my head, tape the happy birthday banner across the wall, and mix up the package of cupcakes.

For the rest of the day I sit on the back porch, drinking coffee and crying in a great gulping sobbing snotty melt-down. It might have been because I felt mentally and physically exhausted from the last three years of sifting through my past. It might have been because the little girl inside me didn't hear either of her mothers say, "Have a good birthday."

But most of all, I think it was because the wind had shifted and my antenna was up. Something had changed with Mumma. I could feel it in every fiber of my being.

THE next day was Friday, my weekly dance day with Harper. At noontime after her class ended, my four-year-old grand-baby girl and I slid into a booth at Uberblast in North Conway and ordered pizza. When we had finished, Harper ran to the inflatable bouncy house and, as I sat down on a bench to watch her, my cell phone rang. Hill House, it read across the screen. It's Mumma, I think. She is calling a day late to wish me happy birthday. I keep my eyes on Harper and let it go to voice mail. I wait ten minutes before I ask the mother of Harper's dance mate to watch her while I step outside with my phone.

You have one new message, my voice mail says. I wait. It is the head nurse. "Nancy, this is Betty at Hill House. Mum had a fall. I am going to send her out to the hospital. I have an ambulance on the way. She is on the floor and can't move her legs. Please give me a call as soon as you get this."

I feel a rope lasso my organs and pull knot tight.

122

History

THE ONLY TIME Mumma was ever sick in the hospital was when she had pneumonia on her twenty-fifth wedding anniversary. That night, Daddy took Tommy and me bowling, and at the concession bar, I slid my hot dog and chips right off the counter and onto the floor, then Tommy laughed and Daddy bought me another. That's what I am thinking as I step through the front doors of Brunswick Hospital emergency room. My cell phone reads 4:30 P.M.

In the curtained cubic, a Hill House nurse stands next to the gurney. "Oh, good," she says, looking at me, then bends down over Mumma. "Look who's here, Doris." She steps back.

Mumma lifts her head off the pillow, lets out a long sigh, and lays her head back down, like she is melting into it.

I am chuckling as I say it. "Well, this is one heck of a field trip." I lean down and kiss her forehead.

Her eyes are frightened. "It's one hell of a nightmare, that's what it is." She closes her eyes and shivers.

I pick up a water glass and put the straw to her lips. She takes a long drink, staring at a place above my head.

The Hill House nurse is standing next to me, one hand pulling hair up out of her eyes, the other gripping just above my wrist. "Your mother was in her chair reading one of Tom's letters, got coughing, and wet her pants. She got up for clean slacks in the closet and, of course, you know how she hates that walker."

Mumma rolls her eyes. "Hate the damn thing, but yup, I guess you're right, shoulda had it with me."

"Well, anyway," the nurse continues, looking down at Mumma, "she reached up for the slacks and fell sideways. We all thought you had bones of steel, Doris, for all the times you've fallen, but I guess not this time."

"Is it broken?" I ask.

The nurse nods yes. "I'm going along now," she says, pulling me into the hall with her. She speaks quietly, close to my face. "When your mother saw you, she let go of my hand and relaxed for the first time this afternoon. It was you that she wanted to see. I know you and Doris have a history, but you need to know how important it is to her that you are here. She won't say it, but she's happy you are." I am looking at a freckle on her cheek. "Shut the hell up," I am thinking. She continues, fingers still to my arm. "We all have stuff, Nancy. Let go of it."

Mumma's chin is pitted-up determined. "Isn't it time you went home? Michael's wonderin where you are and who's gonna fix his suppa."

"Mumma, I just drove two hours to get here, and I am staying until they take you up to your room."

She stares lost out the window. "Yeah well. I think you betta get home."

THE next afternoon when Michael and I get to the hospital, Mumma is already in the surgery prep room. I reach across the gurney and lay my hand on top of hers.

"Well, this is one hell of a mess I've gotten myself into," she spits.

"Grace and dignity, Mumma, grace and dignity. Be grateful."

"Grateful? What the hell do I have to be grateful for?"

The anesthesiologist is waiting on a stool next to us. I glance at him, then back at Mumma. "In ninety years of living you have nothing to be grateful for?"

Her words are cutting and fast. "No, I don't, not a damn thing. What did anyone ever do for me?"

The surgeon moves his lips to one side of his face and bites at his lip. "Mumma, these doctors are trying to help you. A broken hip is fixable. Be grateful for that."

Her cheeks are flushing red. "Well, they're takin their own sweet time aren't they? Let's get this over with for God sake."

The surgeon passes me a clipboard. I sign my name to it. His eyes shift between Mumma and me. "There is no guarantee she will come through the surgery. Do you want her to be resuscitated if her heart stops?"

"That's her call," I say, looking back at her. "Mumma, if your heart stops, do you want to be resuscitated? You have a Do Not Resuscitate order on file here at the hospital."

She answers immediately. "Well, of course I do for God sake, why wouldn't I? I mean don't pound on me for hours. God." Her chin is quivering.

I turn back to the doctor. "Yes."

"Mumma, calm down. You can't go into surgery all worked up like this. Think of something happy as you're going under, like how much you enjoyed the boys when they were little."

With her head still anger wobbling, she makes a stiff smile. "Yup. They were some cute, weren't they? All that curly hair."

I kiss her lips, hoping she will put her arms up and hug me, but she doesn't. "I love you," I say, as she is wheeled out of the room. I listen, waiting for her to say it back. But there is only the sound of the gurney wheels.

123

Get Me out of Here

Michael and I are sitting in the lobby when the surgeon comes out still in his scrubs. "She's done," he says, fingering a small blue plastic box in both hands. "Her hip went beautifully. We put three pins in it. But she's got some bad tooth issues. Her mouth is disgusting." I wait for him to talk. "When we pulled the intubation tube out of her throat, all her front teeth were gone. They must have fallen down her throat. We may have to go into her lungs. She may have inhaled them. We looked everywhere and found only two on the floor. Four more are missing." He hands me the box and scratches at his head. "They were black. Roots all rotted. I don't understand how she could eat. Weird," he says. "We are going to have to get someone in here and take the rest out before she leaves the hospital. It's amazing what people ignore. They had to have been like that for years, just hanging on by a thread." He is still talking as he walks away.

I peel back the cover of the blue tub. Two dark brown teeth stare up at me.

Mumma's hospital room is empty except for a night table and two chairs. It is 7:00 P.M. when they bring her back from recovery. Blood is dried to the place above her lip. A nurse reaches under her and pulls at a sheet. Mumma groans and winces her face.

"Stop it," I yell at the nurse.

Her eyes go wide. "I need to get this sheet from underneath her," she says, pulling a second time. Mumma groans louder.

"Don't touch her. You're hurting her." Michael nudges at my arm. The nurse steps back.

Mumma's lips are dry and cracked. I can hear her tongue making a sticking noise as she opens and closes her mouth. "When did she have water last?" I ask the nurse. One side of her face lifts like she is thinking and does not answer. "I need you to get me a glass of water, a straw, a washcloth, and a Chap Stick. Can you do that, please?"

"For Christ sake, what is the matter with her?" Mumma shouts. "These stupid people. I am in one hell of a mess, that's for damn sure. When am I gettin out of here?"

After several minutes go by and the nurse has not returned, I see a wall cabinet with a key stuck in the lock. Inside I find washclothes, towels, and some glycerin sticks to moisten her mouth and out in the hallway I find a water fountain. With a wet washcloth I wipe around Mumma's mouth, and chip dried blood off her chin. I hold the straw to her lips and ask her to drink.

"Get me the hell out of here," she shouts. "Nancy, I want you to go find the stupid doctor that talked me into this and tell him I want to get out of here."

It is now 11:00 P.M. For four hours I have sat next to her, wiping moistening swabs around her lips, telling her to calm down, listening to her scream ungrateful comments to everyone who has come in to check on her. Finally, Michael stands up and puts his hand on my shoulder. "Honey, it's time to go. Maybe she'll sleep if you aren't here. I know you're trying to calm her down, but she is not listening to you and she doesn't want to."

I stand up next to the bed. "I'm going now, Mumma."

"What do you mean you're goin? What about me? You're not gonna leave me here, are you?"

I kiss her cheek and say "I love you." Her body is shaking angry. Michael walks me closer to the door. I look back at her. "Mumma, you have to calm down. Your body won't heal if you don't. Everyone is trying to help you."

"To hell they are. Get me out of here. Nancy, get back here. You're not gonna just leave me here, are you? Don't leave me."

"Please, Mumma, just try. I love you."

As we walk out the door and start down the hallway, I can hear Mumma calling out for me. "Nancy, help me. Don't leave me alone. No one will listen to me. Get me out of here."

They are the last words I will ever hear my mother say.

124

Passing

MY BEDSIDE CLOCK glows 11:11 P.M. A tingle runs up my spine. "My phone, where is it?" Michael is half asleep next to me in bed. He jumps as I shout it. "Oh my God, it's Mumma." I rush down the stairs, through the house and out to the studio. I grab my cell phone off the desk.

You have one new message, it says. "Ms. Shappell, this is Dr. Heath at Brunswick Hospital. I have been attending to your mother for the last forty-five minutes. It is urgent that I speak with you. It is 11:10 P.M., Monday the thirtieth. Again, it is urgent that I speak with you immediately."

Dial, dial. My fingers are clumsy to the keys.

"Your mother has been unresponsive for the last forty minutes," the doctor tells me.

"Is this it? You mean . . . " I swallow hard. One hand grips the front of my bathrobe. "I am two hours away. Can I get there in time?"

"I am sorry, Ms. Shappell. Your mother is taking her last breaths. I don't think it is possible that she will last two hours, but you can try."

"Can you get the phone to her? I need her to hear my voice." I curl into my desk chair. My shoulders begin to shake. I can feel the collar of my robe on my free ear. There is a hold silence on the other end.

Within two minutes the doctor comes back on the line. "Okay, I am going to put the phone up to your mother. Take as long as you like."

Long, graveled moans come loud in my ear. I grip tighter to the chest of my bathrobe. "Mumma? It's Nancy." Her groan rises in octave as I speak. "Mumma, I know you can hear me and I know you are scared. It's okay, Mumma. You are getting ready to pass. Someone is coming for you, and it is going to be so beautiful. Soon there will be no pain and no fear, I promise. I will be there in two hours. If you need to go before I get there, go. I love you, Mumma. I am on my way."

THE midnight road is mostly empty. Only a few lonely cars pass us. I wonder where they are going. I wonder if anyone else wonders that. They could be peacefully listening to music on their way home, or they could be fear-gripped to the wheel on their way to say good-bye to a loved one. I am calm, calmer than I should be. The exit lamp post lights up the side of Michael's face and make streaks of yellow across it. He says it's going to be okay, but I am not sure. He watches me, glancing from the smooth blackness of the highway, then reaches for my hand. "How are you doing, sweetie?

"Rolling with it," I say, looking straight ahead.

"I know you are," he says softly. "You have done such a good job taking care of everything. I'm proud of you."

I am folded up in the passenger seat, listening to my steady breath as we get closer. We ride by darkened homes and deserted streets where people I know are asleep, unaware that I am riding past on the way to say a final good-bye to Mumma.

125

Moments

In the hospital corridors, the lights are bright and no one is around. "It's time," I say to Michael. "All the times I have asked you, 'How will it end?' and now it is time."

I reach for Mumma's door. Michael lets go of my hand. I hear his low voice speak toward the nurse's station. "Doris Steen's daughter is here." I don't wait for them.

Mumma's room is still. I let the door close behind me. My eyes blink and adjust to the dim lamp glowing from the headboard of her bed. A wide red cloth has been spread across the foot of the blankets. Two nurses sit in silence on either side of Mumma. They watch me walk to the red cloth. They say nothing. My eyes are on her motionless body.

"I am her daughter," I say.

They leave. I stand at her right side. She lies on her back, head propped, hair swept up, an oxygen tube split at her nostrils. Her glasses are lying on the nightstand, her round face looking long and smoother without them. I pull the blankets farther up her chest, and I kiss her forehead. "I'm here, Mumma. Michael and I are both here." She groans, her eyes fluttering, not able to open. I take a white blanket off the chair and lay it over her on top of the others. I sit down and take her hand in both of mine. It is cold. Dark blotches of blood pool beneath thinning skin. "Can you move your fingers in my hand, Mumma?" I know she can't.

I pull a full breath into my lungs and let it out slowly with my words. "Well, you got your wish, Mumma. You're going to die." She groans long, a death-rattle wheeze fighting out her throat. I begin to laugh. "Yup, I can hear you. It's about time for God sake. That's what you're saying, isn't it, Mumma?" I fold her fingers around mine. They lay dead in my palm. "All the times I asked 'How will it end?' All the times you wished it, but we never saw it like this, did we?"

Her voice is strangled, air going in and out, vibrating and strained. "Ahhhhh. Ahhhhh." Like anger stuck and unformed torturously trying to escape. Then an exasperated "Hmmmmfff" flutters over her parched lips.

"I know you can hear me, Mumma. How ironic, my voice is all you have now. You can't ignore me or shame me, and I am no longer afraid of making you mad. But you are mad, aren't you, Mumma? You lived in fear and you are dying in fear, still in that vibe right to the very end." Tears run hot and fast down my face. "Thank you, Mumma. Thank you for teaching me not to be afraid like you."

She groans long. "Ahhhhh."

"There are things I want to talk about, and then I am going to help you be at peace. I won't leave until you have left your body. I promise."

I am not sure how long Michael is at the nurses' desk. I think it is only minutes before he comes back in and moves a chair to the end of the bed. He watches my mother and me breathe in and out, like ocean waves for the next three hours, the small muscles of her mouth quivering in response to my words.

"What were your favorite things in life? You collected shoes, a pair each week before you were married. I remember you told me that. And the winter, the way seagulls rode thick blocks of frozen Kennebec toward the bridge when the ice went out of the river. You loved that too. And the way the snow crunched under your boots when you winter walked. That was the most beautiful thing I ever heard you say."

I hold a small white stick in my hand, a tiny pink sponge at the end. I dip it into a glass of water, run it over her lips, then lay it to her tongue. Her mouth clamps to it and sucks the water in. We do it again.

"And how could a woman with all that fear twisted up inside her have such perfect penmanship? Or be able to sing so sweetly in church? Before you were my mother, who were you? I never really knew that. I never saw you with a hobby, although I once saw you crochet an afghan. Green-and-cream-colored, wasn't it? It must have got tossed out with the couch. And ice cream. Before you went to bed you put pin curls in the side of your hair and ate a dish of vanilla ice cream. You always used your finger to push food onto your fork, and you never liked a ketchup or milk bottle on the table. You said it wasn't good manners." Her eyes roll, lashes flutter. She sucks hard on the sponge.

"We are part of each other, Mumma. We always will be. Christmas, Disney, cups of tea, all the times we argued with each other, and all the times we laughed with Josh and Jason. Please watch over them if you can, their wives and babies too." I start to cry.

"Ahhhhh hmmmmfff."

"All right, I know the dress you want to wear. The one you wore when Michael and I had our second wedding reception. That was a good day, three months after the wedding. I am so happy you and Tommy were there. I hope you understand why I couldn't have you on the mountain with us. You would have bitched and moaned and wrecked my day, you know you would have." I laugh. She moans and sucks on the sponge.

"And the pearl earrings and necklace, the ones with the gold leaves, your favorite. And I guess that's it. You won't need stockings or shoes."

"Ahhhhh ahhhhh hmmmmfff."

"I hear you. Underwear, slip, stockings, and shoes. You hate bare feet. I know, sorry. And your hair and lipstick, I will make sure they are perfect."

It is 4:45 A.M. when her breathing changes. I stand up, still locked to her hand, and shout for Michael to go find a Bible. I don't even know why I say it. It just seems like the right thing to do. When he comes back, I have no clue where to read, so I start on the first page, but quickly close the book and start singing random verses of old church hymns.

Then, realizing the sun is coming up, I ask Michael to put up the shade, and when he does, brightness pours into the room.

"It's morning now, Mumma. The sun is up. You picked a beautiful day for your journey. You're going home soon."

I get up on my knees in the chair, one arm around her pillow, one hand still connected to hers. "Breathe in, Mumma. Now out. That's right, nice and smooth. It won't be long. Breathe in. Now out. Take the hand that reaches for you. Breathe in. Now out. Don't be afraid. There will be no more fear. Only love." Her breath is dry and strained.

For ten minutes, we work as a team, birthing from here to there. Her body relaxes in my arms. Every breath we take, we take together. It is our greatest lesson.

"One more breath, Mumma. You're almost there. Do you see the light? Step to the other side. They are waiting for you."

Her chin pits up determined, lips pressed together. "One more. You can do it. This is it. I am so proud of you." And then, very gently, with a final sigh, the last bit of her slips out of her Earth suit and rises with the morning sun.

"Mumma, Mumma." I strain to hear her, but all is silent. I climb up onto the bed, one knee in the chair, one at her side. My tears drip into her hair and disappear between the silky strands. A long moan rolls from my gut and fills the room. I kiss her face over and over. I cry and cling to her.

A nurse comes in with a stethoscope. I put both knees back on the chair. I hold my breath and wait. She shakes her head no. I put my head on Mumma's chest and cry, unable to control the sobbing. I don't look up at the second nurse who stands next to her. "I concur," she says. "Mrs. Steen has expired."

Then it is Dr. Heath in their place on the other side of the bed, with his hand on mine wrapped to the top of Mumma's head.

"No, don't take her away. I'm not ready yet."

"Take your time," he comforts, watching and smiling softly. "You obviously had a very special love for each other, I can tell."

"Maybe we did." How odd those words sound after all we've been through.

For two and a half hours I hold her hand as it grows colder in mine. The fingers of my left hand again and again, combing her white hair, always stiff with hair spray, now silky and soft.

It is 7:35 A.M. when the undertaker comes for her. His wife hugs me and says she's sorry. "Your mother was so beautiful. I always loved her."

"Mmmm." I sigh.

I wait in the hallway until I see them wheel her out of the room, zipped in a red bag. They stop when they see me, him looking professional with both hands folded in front, her with mauve lips, sadly smiling.

Michael wraps one arm around my shoulders and walks me back through the corridors and out to the parking lot. His fingers dig into my flesh like the indents of them will stay and always remind me of this moment.

The cool morning air of a new day feels good on my cheeks. At the car, Michael holds the door for me, but I don't get in right away. I look up at the hospital window and wonder where she is. Michael's voice is breathy as he pulls my head to his chest and hugs me tight.

"You did good, honey. What I saw was the way you held on to her and came to terms with the fact that she was never going to say 'I love you,' the way you wanted her to. You did your best, and I know it is hard for you to understand, but she also did her best. In those final moments, you two made peace with each other."

"Strange, isn't it?" I muse. "In the final moments, we had peace. Not months, or years. Moments. Sometimes I think Mumma and I had a life that was never lived, but then again, maybe it was."

126

Tar and Roses

THE MINISTER STANDING next to me in the entry of Desmond Funeral Home looks like Jesus. His brown robe comes all the way to his sandals, and there is a woman on the other side of me asking what he has on underneath, and snickering. Michael is trying not to laugh. The minister is chuckling, one hand smoothing down his full beard. The Methodist minister is not here. Mumma said no way did she want him or the Baptist clergy to do her funeral service, they weren't real pastors. She said she'd known some good ones when she was young, then laughed when I told her that plan didn't seem doable. Three days ago I found Jesus from the Congregational church. Even Mumma should be okay with that.

"Amazing Grace" is softly playing in the background as people begin to arrive, faces from my youth grown older in the twenty-three years since I moved out of Bath, yet still the same, all held timeless in the hearts of Morse High School alumni who wait for their classmate's return like a ship gone out to sea.

Jason steps closer to me with one hand on my back and talks quietly in my ear. "Tommy is coming up the front walk, Mom. Looks like a deputy sheriff with him. I'm surprised they let him out of jail for the afternoon." Joshua and Michael seal in around me.

I don't recognize the man who struggles up the steps and through the door of the funeral home. The skeletal frame I knew from two years ago, which could have been blown down with a river gust and a shot of whiskey, is now seventy pounds heavier. His arms hang long and rounded on the sides of his six-foot body, puffed and poisoned like lethal-raising bread dough ready to pop and spew fifty years of pain across a row full of sweet church ladies. His once sunken cheeks are fat with prison starch and still pitted red with anger. His eyes are sunken and ghostly, with no sign of him inside. They don't focus until I step toward him, two wobbly window panes, glassy and medicated. I put out my arms. I can feel the boys and Michael take a breath behind me, waiting to jump to my rescue.

Tommy stares at me with his open mouth. His body is tree-trunk solid in my arms as I hug him. The deputy steps up to my brother's elbow. Neither of Tommy's arms move from his sides. "I'm glad you are here," I say, then step back.

His beaten eyes blink and both eyebrows twitch. "Nancy," he says deeply, nodding his heavy head, then steps up to the casket. His long gray hair hangs in front of his neck as he bends and kisses Mumma's cheek. "Jeepas." He shakes his head, then sits in the front row across from the minister's podium. The folding chair disappears under his toxic body.

Joshua guides me to the wall on the opposite side of the room. "Mom, you're going to sit on the other end of the row now. Michael will sit between you and Tommy, Jason and I will sit behind you."

The deputy is next to Tommy with her hands planted on her waist belt. Tommy leans over his knees and looks down at the floor. His denim pant leg rides up a white sock. A black ankle monitor is strapped above a scuffed brown shoe.

The funeral director squats next to me with one hand on the back of my chair. She smells like soap and breath mints. "If you are uncomfortable and can't stand at the podium when it's time for the eulogy, I can bring the microphone to you. Just give me a wave."

"The Old Rugged Cross" plays down out of the ceiling, and a woman behind me sings over everyone else, "The emblem of suffering and shame." The minister talks about the river and how Mumma loved the city of Bath and her grandsons. He reads the Serenity Prayer, and a few people proudly recite every word.

When it is time for me to stand at the podium, I can't do it. Not in front of Tommy. It feels disrespectful. In the funeral director's hand, the microphone squeals all the way across the room. Still sitting in my chair, I hold it away from my mouth, take a breath, let my shoulders drop, and with one finger, pull Michael's knee against mine. My voice sounds calm as I begin.

"'To know her is to love her. Doris is one of the sweetest girls in Morse.' That's what it says in the 1940 yearbook beside her photo."

I talk about how she enjoyed serving desserts at the church suppers, and that she loved to watch a once-in-a-while eagle perch in the oak trees over our boathouse. I hear a woman sobbing behind me. I don't turn around to see who it is.

"I believe we all arrive in each other's lives at just the right time, whether we appreciate it or not. We are all here to teach and to learn. However, life circumstances, and the way we connect or disconnect from them, have a way of wearing us down. We are all pulled with the tide of life, sinking to our deepest places, then with great fortune, rise back up to try again. We do our best, we do our worst. We learn lessons, or we don't. My mother and I lived fifty-six years of anger together. Fear, no matter how you look at it, no matter what the label is, is a waste of precious days."

After I pass the microphone back to the funeral director, I reach behind me to the boys. They both take my hand and hold it until "Arms of the Angel" has finished playing.

As the service ends, Joshua and Jason move to the entry with the other pallbearers and shake hands with people they don't remember, who call them by name. Michael stands with me at the front row. He keeps one hand on my back, rubbing it gently between greeters.

One woman takes my hand in both of hers. "You are so brave. We came here thinking we would comfort you, but you comforted us." You never know how truth will touch people. Two women behind her have their heads together. "You would think Nancy could have put better earrings on Doris," one of them says. They leave without stopping in front of me.

When everyone has walked down the front steps to get into the cemetery car procession, I move over to the casket and study every detail of Mumma. Her hair is styled perfectly and her mouth is lined with her favorite lipstick. "Doesn't she look good?" I say to Michael. With my hand on the shoulder of her dress, I lean over and kiss her forehead. She is cold and hard like a frozen package of chicken.

"I shouldn't have loved her." Michael's arms are snug around me. "It didn't make sense. She abandoned me in the worst possible way a mother could. She gave me up as a sacrifice to save herself. Part of me is ashamed that I loved her."

"I know," he says.

"But more ashamed that I wasted all these years not loving myself."

"Honey, if you hadn't loved her, she wouldn't have been able to hurt you so deeply. Elizabeth might have given birth to you. But Doris was your mother."

"You can only have one mother," I say quietly. "A long lifetime ago, someone told me that."

"I know it's hard to believe, honey, but your mother did love you. You and she were the same. Two abused women who never felt safe or loved. You just did different things with your experiences. You fought to understand it. She fought to keep it hidden." Tears drip off my face and onto Mumma's cold body.

With both hands, Michael turns me toward him. "Honey, she was supposed to take care of you and in the end you took care of her, but remember, she was also the one who told you to leave Bath. Don't you think somewhere inside she thought you and the boys would be safer somewhere beyond here?" He takes a tissue from the podium and wipes my eyes.

"But I was always going backward, Michael. I was sick and drugged and hospitalized. Look what I did to Bobby and the boys and you. Some days I still feel like I could spin backward."

His eyes are soft under hair still thick, now streaked with gray. "I see you healing, then you level off for a while, then you heal. But no, I don't see you going backward, honey. Every bad day for you is another day of learning and attempting to understand how these people could allow this to happen. He was very ill. There is no question about that, and I believe she was also victimized when she was young, but shut down to it." I can see Joshua motioning me to hurry. My eyes flash between him and Michael.

"Honey, I am just telling you what I see as an outsider. I don't know why it happened. It's not in the realm of my understanding, and I have no point of reference, but I can listen to you and love you and you don't have to go through this alone." He hugs me tight. I can smell Banana Republic cologne on his shirt collar. "But I truly can't feel what you are feeling. Only someone who has been through it can understand to that extreme. I don't think I have ever known anyone who has been abused other than you."

"Yes you have." I take a step away from the casket. "They walk past you every day. They smile when you go through their checkout line at the grocery store. They wait on you at the bank. They flip your burgers and do our taxes. They are the homeless, the drug-addicted, the lawyers, the doctors, maybe even the mechanics you work with. They are beautiful men, women, and children who are called crazy and swallow drugs that can never cure or answer the question every one of us has asked while contemplating a bottle of whiskey or a gun to our head. Why didn't anyone love me?"

It was the kind of June day that people wait for in Maine, the first Saturday after Memorial Day and the start of the summer season. The cemetery crew had mowed the lawns the day prior and it had rained over night. Clumps of grass sat next to grave-stones. Small ruts in the narrow road in front of Mumma's lot were half full of water. Cars lined up and some people got out. Others waited, watching us climb the embankment to where Mumma's casket sat suspended over a freshly dug hole.

Five folding chairs sit on the family lot, where Daddy and Old Nanny's remains wait for Mumma. Four to the right, one to the left. Joshua hurries ahead to level out the legs into the ground. Jason and Michael are at my side, their arms supporting mine, my black high heels sinking into the ground with each step. Sitting in the chairs, we stare over a spray of pink roses covering Mumma's sealed casket. Tommy sits alone on the other side, his mouth a zombie slash of red, unaware he is resting on top of his own plot. He looks haunted, caught between two worlds.

I don't hear anything the minister says as he stands at the foot of my mother's dead body. I watch my brother's face drop into his hands, and when he picks it up he isn't crying. None of us are.

I can't imagine Tommy's life without Mumma, no longer the child. I wonder if he thinks his final death will soon follow hers. But in truth, they have been dead for years. How could Tommy and I have had the same experience and turn out so differently, with different interpretations of what happened? Same setting, same characters, but living like we had been in two different shows, our father still alive in the blood-drunk veins of my brother.

Before he was a prisoner at the Maine Correctional Center, Tommy was a strong teenage football player and a boy who loved dachshunds and swimming. And before that he was a precious child, my baby brother. The people who grew up with him know that. But to others he is the scary old drunk man who lives in the shack at the end of Washington Street. They say it is the alcohol that ruined him. But it was Daddy and Mumma. The alcohol came later. And every time he puked it up, a bit of those dark memories came with it, but never all. It is not possible for a chosen child to be that empty and still be breathing.

We choose to live, we choose to die based on the belief system we hook into about what remains inside us. We are the chosen children with secret, fragmented memories encoded in every cell of our bodies. Choices. That's what makes us or breaks us.

When the minister is finished speaking, we all take a rose off the top of the casket and watch it being lowered into the hole. One at a time, we each drop full pink rose blossoms to Mumma. Tommy kneels down on one knee, and when he gets up, there is grass stuck to his pants. He glares at me across the open grave with his angry glassy eyes. Before my brother hated me, he loved me. He is the child I loved, the man I didn't know, the boy who chose to be unconscious so he wouldn't feel the pain, lost in the circle of the sting.

On the narrow road in front of Mumma's lot, Tommy stands with one foot in a puddle. The deputy watches us closely as I stand in front of my brother. "I know you don't believe it, Tommy, but I always loved you, and I am so sorry your life has been difficult."

Both fists are tight at his legs. He looks like he will explode. His teeth are clenched as he speaks. "Okay, Nancy." The deputy opens the door, guides him into the backseat, then gets into the front and starts the engine. I see Tommy mouth words at me through the window, a membrane between us. I watch them drive away over a pile of loose tar, left for mourners' tires to pack. It gravels up and pings at the back fender.

In my hand is a small velvet burgundy bag, passed to me by the funeral director. I pull open the cinching and poke down inside it. Mumma's amethyst ring slides up to the knuckle of my right ring finger. It spins around and disappears into the center of my hand. A shiver goes down my arms as I close my fingers around it and look back at the open grave. Two men stand next to it, waiting with shovels.

"Good-bye, Mumma," I call back softly. "I'm leaving now. I am going to live the rest of my life in truth, grateful to be wide awake and conscious to who we were, and who I am because of it. I am dumping out the fear and letting it die right here in this cemetery. I am going home to heal. I so deserve that."

TODAY is a good day for truth. The tide can rip your life away and it can bring it back. Sometimes holding your breath under its thundering waves can save your life, and just when you think you can't stand the pain for one more second, you find yourself rising to the top and being dragged back to shore. And the only thing that saved you was the voice in your head saying, "A little longer. You can do it. I believe in you."

When memories and people float away like driftwood, and the farther out you wade to reach them, the farther away they drift, that voice is all you will have in the deafening silence of the tide. And sometimes you have to throw things to the tide and let go of what never was, listening to the winds that ripple its surface, and come to an understanding that it is ever changing.

When I was young, the river was the only path I knew to somewhere else. It was on those waves I learned when you are in the tide the only true voice that can save you is your own. Roll on, river, ocean that I love. I will always return to you, your salt is in my soul, but for now I have a journey to take without you. And I trust the me I have grown into to know the way.

And the day came when the risk it took to remain tight
    inside the bud
was more painful than the risk it took to bloom.

—*Anais Nin*

With Love and Gratitude

THANK YOU, WITH my whole heart, to the beautiful beings who have been guiding lights along my path. Thank you for sharing myriad adventures, on our life journey together, all of which have brought me in the most profound ways, to where I am today: Eva, Bud, Betty, Gail, Maria, Susan, Becky, Kathy, Bobby, Fay, David, Alex, Darrin, Lisa, Deni, Glenn, Peg, AnnElissa, and Nancy.

Many heartfelt thanks to my early readers who gave their candid feedback throughout the first few drafts: Debbie, Barbara, Carol, Lisa, Susie, Amanda, Bridget, Hannah, Linda, Eileen, and Samantha. And a very special thank you to my early editor, Dayle Dawes, who's many hours of work, is appreciated far beyond words.

To my spiritual mentors, Lucrecia and Diana. Thank you for wisdom that will always remain in my soul and for being a genuine combination of mother, sister, and friend. Libby Barnett, my Reiki Master Teacher, thank you for your guidance and boundless radiant energy. Sherry Anshara, founder and director of QuantumPathic Center of Consciousness, thank you from every cell of my being for your truth, knowledge, and passion for conscious healing.

To Suzanne Kingsbury, my development editor and writing shaman: You are off-the-chart amazing in every creative way. Thank you for four years of encouragement, literary magic, and running beside me with your toolbox. To Dede Cummings, literary guru, thank you for your mentorship and wisdom extraordinaire. To my copy-editors, Michael Fleming and Margaret Wimberger, thank you for your talents and polish.

To Susan Richardson, your dear friendship, devotion, and luminescent spirit always raise my happiness factor to a place beyond fear, time, and troubles. Laughing with you, my best friend, has been my favorite healing modality of all. I love you, Sista.

To my final draft readers:

Trish Faucher, thank you for your friendship, your love, your honesty, your interest in my story, and our extra special hair salon time. I treasure you.

Tina Titzer, my gypsy sister, you are the exemplary teacher of what a cherished relationship consists of. I have learned so much from the way you listen with your heart and dance with your soul. Knowing you has made me a stronger woman. Thank you for everything.

Linda Foote, the happiest person I have ever known. Everyone should have a best friend like you, someone who will break out in spontaneous song and dance, wear funny hats, communicate in rhyme, and travel across the whole country in a beat up car, picnicking on pie and garlic, and loving each adventurous moment in that no-time place. You have been my constant writing muse, mentor, and head cheerleader. Thank you for dancing through my studio door in 2005 and changing my life with your friendship.

Rose Mulligan, my treasured childhood sister-friend. When my door closed at the end of the day, it was your laughter that remained in my heart and kept my dearest childhood memories alive all these years. Thank you for loving me always, even when we lost touch for almost thirty years. And a very special thank you for the brilliant final copy-edit / proofread, fifty years in the making. I love you forever.

To my family:

Nanny, my beautiful grandmother, I can still feel your arms around me and hear you say, "Nancy, dear, you can do anything you put your mind to." Thank you, Nanny, for loving me "a bushel and a peck, a hug around the neck, and a kiss in the bargain."

To my precious husband, Michael, there are no words sweet enough, no colors vibrant enough, no songs with an octave high enough, that could begin to describe the kind of love you have taught me. In your quiet, patient way, you have nurtured my children, calmed every storm, and danced lead and follow with me throughout our marriage. Thank you, honey, for guiding me to love myself.

To my sons Joshua and Jason, thank you for believing in me and encouraging me to birth our story into the hands of others. Thank you for being my number one fans and never doubting the importance of healing our truth so that our example could serve as a healing tool for others. I am so proud of the men you have grown to be, men of integrity and compassion for the world around you. Yet, as boys, you also possessed these qualities. I am inspired every day by your creativity, intelligence, and passion for your future. I cherish all of our family moments, especially as I watch you loving your own beautiful children. It is the greatest love of all.

And to my granddaughters Harper and Josslyn. My wish for you is that you listen to your own voice when the water is racing and the tide pulls at your feet. Remember that you are strong, that you are loved, and that you have everything you need already inside you to become the women you were meant to be. And that forever and ever, Granmamma' loves you oceans.

CPSIA information can be obtained at www.ICGtesting.com
Printed in the USA
LVOW07s1610240216

476537LV00007B/697/P